The
Brain
Bible

The
Brain
Bible

How to Stay Vital, Productive, and Happy for a Lifetime

JOHN ARDEN, PhD

New York Chicago San Francisco Athens London Madrid
Mexico City Milan New Delhi Singapore Sydney Toronto

1 2 3 4 5 6 7 8 9 0   DOC/DOC   1 0 9 8 7 6 5 4 3

ISBN   978-0-07-182654-9
MHID 0-07-182654-8

e-ISBN   978-0-07-182657-0
e-MHID 0-07-182657-2

Library of Congress Cataloging-in-Publication Data
Arden, John Boghosian.
   The brain bible : how to stay vital, productive, and happy for a lifetime /
John Arden.
      pages cm.
   Includes bibliographical references.
   ISBN 978-0-07-182654-9 (alk. paper) — ISBN 0-07-182654-8
(alk. paper) 1. Brain—Popular works. 2. Mental health—Popular
works. 3. Cognition—Popular works. 4. Self-care, Health. I. Title.
   QP376.A695 2014
   612.8'2—dc23   2013036523

McGraw-Hill Education books are available at special quantity dis-
counts to use as premiums and sales promotions or for use in corporate
training programs. To contact a representative, please visit the Contact
Us pages at www.mhprofessional.com.

Contents

PART THREE

Putting It All Together

Acknowledgments

A book owes much to its many contributors. This book is no exception. Singling out the many people who helped this one along the way to its final form would blur the paramount contribution of two people. Without their efforts there would be no *Brain Bible*.

Tom Miller, my editor at McGraw-Hill, took this book with him to his new company, as it was about to suffer the fate of books that are orphaned when a publishing house closes down a division while books are still in the pipeline for production. He had a vision for this book, and he helped craft all aspects of it from the macro level to the micro level, making it far, far better along the way.

Roger Williams, my literary agent, has been a friend, teacher, and astute navigator through the many complexities of the publishing industry. His wisdom and counsel not only provided constant advocacy for this book but also gave me a great education on the changing landscape of the commerce of the written word. I thank him for promoting healthcare by ushering this book into being.

Preface

This book emerged out my concern for the scores of patients who have told me about their confusion and frustration with the often conflicting news stories and misinformation on ways to keep the brain healthy. One week they read that pomegranate juice is a magic potion, and the next week they read that keeping the mind quiet preserves the brain for later challenges. Next they read that crossword puzzles are the ticket, only to read the following week that there is limited benefit. What are reasonable people to believe?

There are far too many products sold with great promise, many of them snake oil. The truth is that there is no one thing alone, no miraculous pill or computer-based program, that will ensure a long and happy life for your brain. There are instead a variety of brain-healthy factors that you should know about and practice.

Perhaps you, like many people, don't want to sift through the maze of data to establish a clear road map and regimen for keeping your brain sharp. This book is in part an effort to pull all the loose ends together and provide a path. Instead of offering you myriad facts about the brain or pieces of information without cohesion, I have tried to organize the information about what you can do to maintain a sharp brain around five central factors. These well-researched factors can be considered a formula of behaviors and practices that will help protect and nurture your brain.

Having spent roughly 40 years helping people enhance their mental health, I have seen many theories arrive with great fanfare and fade away with a shrug of the shoulders. Frustrated with the tendency of psychology to feature the flavor of the week, I looked to neuroscience to weave it all together. To this end, in the mid-1980s I retrained in neuropsychology to focus the help that I provide on a brain-based approach.

As the director of one of the largest mental health training programs in the United States I am tasked with ensuring that our over 100 postdoctoral residents and interns receive training in practices that are steeped in science and are evidence-based. In other words, part of my job is to distill science and theory to central factors that enable our graduates to receive the best that science and healthcare offer. These training programs take place in 22 medical centers that offer integrative medical care, meaning that all healthcare providers collaborate for comprehensive, state-of-art healthcare. Integrative healthcare is our mission. An integrative approach to personal healthcare is the focus of this book.

In my non–Kaiser Permanente life I have taught practical neuroscience with mental health professionals throughout the United States and abroad. I have led 30 seminars on an annual basis for the last several years. I have been fortunate to meet thousands of mental health professionals over the years who are eager to learn about practical neuroscience, not only to help their clients but also for themselves.

This book is meant for all of us who care about and want to nurture a healthy brain.

PART ONE

The Good News About Your Brain

CHAPTER 1

Brain Bible Basics

What can we mature adults do to sharpen our brains? This book aims to answer that question with a deceptively simple formula. The differences between a sharp and a dull brain can depend on whether you establish and maintain the factors that I will cover in this book. A large body of research has shown that without these factors the brain dulls, resulting in major health problems, including dementia. By applying them to your daily life you can cultivate a healthy brain capable of thinking clearly and feel positive through the rest of your life.

I have cast the net wide to include the main factors that have been consistently associated with longevity and brain health. In no other period in history have so many fields of scientific inquiry converged to offer a comprehensive understanding of the factors that contribute to a healthy brain. Fields such as cognitive neuroscience, behavioral neurology, gerontology, developmental psychology, and neuropsychology all shed light on the factors that have been shown to contribute to longevity.

Each of the factors described in this book has been discovered by researchers who have followed people on a longitudinal basis through most of their lives. Some subjects in the studies aged well, and others did not. Some developed dementia, whereas others were sharp through the end of their lives. The researchers conducting the studies have identified the common characteristics of those who age successfully and those factors which have led to premature death or dementia.

Though there is no quick fix that can keep your brain healthy, there are plenty of vendors retailing products on the Internet and in health food stores that they claim provide a magic tonic for the brain. The research behind them is extremely weak at best and more regularly fraudulent. The brain, as I will explain in this book, changes with practice. You cannot do just one thing, one time, and rewire your brain for health.

Instead of a gimmicky quick fix, this book offers a formula of the five main factors that have been shown to contribute to brain health. The Brain Bible formula represents the important healthy brain factors that you need to plant now and cultivate for the rest of your life. The research behind each factor in the formula is rich with new developments from neuroscience that have overthrown many of preconceived beliefs about longevity and indeed about the brain. That formula is introduced in Chapter 2, and the remaining chapters describe the factors in detail. Here is a brief description of the chapters that follow.

Chapter 2
Brain Research Breakthroughs

This chapter begins by describing how the mature brain is going through a major transition, ripe with opportunity as well as laced with potential risks. Research shows that the health of middle-aged people diverges greatly at this pivotal period as a result of lifestyle and habits. What can mature adults do to take advantage of the opportunities and avoid the pitfalls? The chapter presents the Brain

Bible formula that describes five categories of actions mature adults can take to promote healthy, sharp brains through the middle years and into old age. You will learn how brains develop new connections between neurons.

Chapter 3
The Education Factor

New learning is critical for the mature adult brain. People who are more highly educated and use their brains to learn new things throughout their lives are more resistant to the symptoms of dementia. The concept of cognitive reserve describes the relationship between learning and the number of synaptic connections between neurons in the brain. The more brain connections that exist, the greater your brain's longevity. A brain that is intellectually challenged demonstrates the positive side of the old adage "Use it or lose it." You'll read several suggestions about learning in order to achieve maximize brain-boosting benefit. Since one of the main complaints by mature adults concerns their spotty memories, the chapter includes suggestions to improve one's memory.

Chapter 4
The Diet Factor

Diet dramatically affects the way the brain functions. By learning how to maximize a healthy diet you can enhance brain performance. A wide spectrum of amino acids, precursors to the cornucopia of neurotransmitters and neurohormones, are critical to healthy brain chemistry. Avoiding unhealthy fats and consuming healthy fats can help form the actual structure of the brain cells. Also, avoiding simple carbohydrates, including sugar, is critical for a healthy brain. You'll read suggestions about an optimum diet for a healthy brain.

Chapter 5
The Exercise Factor

Exercise has been shown to boost the longevity of the brain. Mature adults must engage in exercise to thrive in their later years. During aerobic exercise a substance sometimes called Miracle-Gro but technically called brain-derived neurotrophic factor is released. It is a kind of tonic for the brain that promotes neuroplasticity and neurogenesis (the birth of new neurons). Exercise promotes a healthy brain in many other ways too, all of which are described in this chapter. You'll read several suggestions for including regular exercise in your daily routine, including many unconventional ones that are not ordinarily considered exercise.

Chapter 6
The Social Factor

This chapter presents new research on the "social brain" and the importance of healthy relationships to a sharp brain. The brain thrives on compassionate communication with others and is starved without it. From the first few days of life to our last, relationships have a dramatic effect on our mental health. The social factor, in short, expands our longevity and boosts the brain's vitality. I describe the discovery of mirror neurons and spindle cells and suggest how to activate these neural systems to build relationships and shared empathy. Whereas negative relationships are toxic to the brain, many studies have shown that people who maintain positive social relationships live longer and develop the symptoms of dementia later.

Chapter 7
The Sleep Factor

Most people do not know how important sleep is to the brain. Because sleep accounts for roughly one-third of our lives, a healthy sleep cycle can enhance memory and clarity of thought. But when the brain is deprived of sleep, it can fail to take advantage of those critical cognitive abilities. Researchers have shown that not only sleep deprivation but shallow sleep can impair the brain, especially the hippocampus (the part of the brain critical for memory) by increasing stress hormones such as cortisol. Sleep cycles change for mature adults who find it harder to fall asleep and stay asleep. You'll read many suggestions for achieving a healthy night's sleep.

Chapter 8
Moderating Your Stress

This chapter addresses the importance of focusing attention on the present moment while combining all the factors of the Brain Bible formula. Attention to the here and now better allows you to apply the factors and simultaneously decrease stress. A present focus is an antidote to the passive and superficial lack of focus endemic in contemporary society, which increases stress. The practice of moderating stress is critical for a sharp brain. Since there are always bumps on the road of life, flexible attention to the present moment increases your resiliency and allows you to embrace the rich complexity of life that is critical for sharpening the brain.

Chapter 9
The Brain Bible Seven-Day Jump Start

Since many people wonder where to start, I offer some ideas about how you may want to structure in a seven-day jump start. By making incremental and progressively intensified steps to keep cultivating a healthy brain, you can live better longer!

CHAPTER 2

Brain Research Breakthroughs

When I first met Beth, she appeared glum as she said, "I think I'm all used up." She went on to describe how she had built an identity around being a mother and a social worker. After I got to know her, it became evident that she was not just good but great in both roles. Her two sons had happy families of their own, and they came to visit her often because she was so warm and loving. In her capacity as a social worker she had risen through the ranks to become a director at Child Protective Services. Despite constant budget cuts to her department, she managed to stretch the shrinking resources while working hard to keep the morale of the staff high.

Beth, however, stated, "I guess being the glue for everyone means that it all came at a cost, with my glue cracking." She looked at me with tired eyes. "Have I done irreparable damage to my brain?"

We talked about the many things she could do to rekindle her vitality and boost the health of her brain for many years to come. Her face blossomed in a beautiful smile. "I was so afraid that I had hastened my own demise."

I told her, "It looks like you have been a fantastic caregiver for your family and your employees. It's time to reap some of the benefits of your caregiving yourself." I went on to describe how recent developments in psychology and neuroscience have made it clear that there is much a person can do to keep her brain healthy throughout life. Not only can she protect her brain from needless and preventable insult, she can engage in behaviors that have consistently been shown to be brain-healthy. Indeed, she can take good care of her brain while she ages and simultaneously enjoy a rich and satisfying life.

Building a Healthy Brain

There is good news and bad news for mature adults. The good news, which was particularly reassuring to Beth, is that the brain reaches its peak in middle adulthood and that people can continue to sharpen their brains and even grow new brain cells. The bad news is that these enhancements do not happen automatically. You must do certain things to optimize your brain's longevity. In fact, failing to engage in brain-healthy behaviors can make you more vulnerable to developing dementia. By your late middle years your brain is indeed at a crossroads. Recent studies indicate that this period is pivotal for the long-term health of the brain.

Though you can't roll back the clock and transform your mature brain into a 20-year-old brain, you can keep it healthy. You can slow down the aging process and take a brain-healthy turn at the crossroads to sharpen your brain instead of letting it grow dull. A strict "brain age" is a fiction, as no two brains are the same. We all vary in our experiences. Some people cultivate healthier brains than others by engaging in regular physical and mental exercise, maintaining a healthy diet, and establishing robust social networks. Others are hard on their brains with very poor diets, no exercise (mental or physical), poor sleep habits, and social isolation. Apart from genetic vulnerabilities, the second group will most likely be more depressed or easily stressed and show signs of dementia earlier in their lives.

This book offers a broad-based formula that includes the key factors to keep your brain healthy as you age. Your brain has the potential to build on the gains of your earlier life and rewire brain areas that were neglected. Now is the time to revitalize your brain to continue to live a vibrant life.

The Good News about Mature Brains

Mature brains are dramatically different from younger brains. Though their reaction time is significantly lessened, there are several cognitive abilities that allow mature adults to outperform younger adults. For example, older adults do better on tests that include complex problem solving, vocabulary, spatial organization, and verbal memory.[1] Think of it this way: your brain is more experienced. You have built up a library of knowledge from which to base judgments and decisions. Mature brains tend to be far denser in the number of connections between neurons, which means they are capable of greater complexity of thought. Instead of being like a young tree with a few branches, they have complex interlocking branches that make the accumulated knowledge possible.

Drawing on your library of knowledge allows you to outthink younger adults; you are better able to put all the information you have gathered than you were when you were younger. In contrast to adapting to new situations, in which younger adults have a significant edge, when you are faced with information that you already know, your brain can discern patterns and form logical conclusions much more efficiently than is possible for a young adult.

Younger adults use one hemisphere disproportionally more than they use both together. In contrast, bright older adults use the left and the right hemispheres together efficiently.[2] Mature brains show a higher degree of what has been referred to as *bilateralization*. This is the tendency to use both sides of the brain together, providing you with the ability to analyze situations and see the larger context more efficiently. Bilateralization allows you to better understand the interdependence of the various aspects of a situation than you could when you were 20.

Let's take a closer look at what you gain from the enhanced coordination of the two hemispheres. Both hemispheres have different talents that can add up to greater brain efficiency when used together. The right hemisphere processes visual and spatial information, enabling you to grasp the big picture. It pays more attention to the context or the gist of a situation. The left hemisphere, in contrast, is adept at details, categories, and linearly arranged information such as language. Since the two hemispheres of mature brains work better together, one hemisphere does not dominate the other. This enables you to synthesize the talents of both hemispheres. Thus, you can more easily keep the big picture in mind (a right hemisphere talent) while resolving complicated detailed problems (a left hemisphere talent).

Another change occurring to the mature brain involves the enhanced ability to control emotions. On average, mature adults are less bothered if someone looks at them with a frown or scowl and take things in stride. They don't consider as many situations to be potential threats as they did when they were younger. This is the case partly because the amygdala, a structure deep within the temporal lobes (right above the ears), which is a principal part of your homeland security system, is much less reactive than it was when you were young.

There is also a change in neurochemistry that contributes to the general mellowing of older adults. A study performed by Dilip Jeste at the University of California looked at brain scans from 3,000 people and found that older people are less dependent on the neurotransmitter dopamine, making them less impulsive and controlled by emotion. In contrast to younger adults, who possess a significant edge in attention skills, mature adults respond less thoughtlessly to negative emotional stimuli and are more rational and wise in finding solutions to problems than are younger people.

The edge that mature adults possess in the control and balance of their emotions over younger adults makes them focus less on negative aspects of life, perhaps because they have already learned about potential dangers in the world. Mature adults, because they have learned many lessons about the world, have a wider reference and more wisdom. They tend to become less anxious, more focused, and in better control of their emotions as they age.

Another major change occurring to mature brains involves the so-called white matter, of which myelin is a part. Myelin coats the axons, the long extensions of neurons that send information out to other neurons in the same way that plastic covers the wires in an electrical cord to prevent it from shorting out. When axons are covered with myelin, the neurons fire more efficiently and thousands of times more quickly. Myelin is so critical to brain health that demyelinating diseases such as multiple sclerosis can devastate a person's brain.

It was once thought that adolescence marked the peak and end of myelination, but it is now known that myelination peaks at around age 50 and in some cases at 60 in two critical areas of the brain: the frontal lobes (responsible for decision making and controlling the emotions) and the temporal lobes (involved in language and memory). After the peak in myelination older adults incur differing degrees of impairments in myelin as a result of a variety of genetic and self-care practices.

Healthy myelin depends on a number of factors, especially diet. Essential fatty acids and high-density cholesterol (HDL) account for a significant amount of the composition of myelin. Eating foods that promote healthy myelin is critical for the brain. Also, it is important to avoid foods that degrade myelin such as saturated fat, trans fatty acids, and simple carbohydrates such as sugar. In fact, consuming large amounts of simple carbohydrates can lead not only to type 2 diabetes but also to premature aging.

The Truth About the Aging Brain

A variety of factors have been associated with aging. For example, aging is associated with the gradual shortening of telomeres, the protective caps at the ends of chromosomes that prevent cell senescence from the loss of replenishment. Telomere shortening is similar to the aglets at the end of shoelaces, which shorten with wear and tear over time. Telomere length is regulated by a cellular enzyme called telomerase. The actions of telomerase decrease under repeated exposure to antigenic stimuli and approaching cellular senescence.

Telomere length measured during midlife has been used to predict mortality related to a number of diseases, including heart disease, diabetes, vascular dementia, and Alzheimer's disease.[3] A number of factors can influence telomere length, including social support, education, and exercise.

There are, in fact, a variety of theories of aging, including the programmed theories, which include descriptions of how certain genes are programmed to be switched on and off over time, the way changes in hormones control aging, and the way immunological systems decline over time, leaving people more susceptible to diseases.

There are also so-called error theories, which include descriptions of how cells and tissues simply wear out as proteins can become cross-linked and accumulate, slowing down body processes; there are descriptions of free radicals causing damage to cells, which eventually impair functions; and there are descriptions of DNA damage with genetic mutations causing cells to malfunction.

The truth about aging is that it results from a combination of these factors. There are things you can do to either slow down or speed up these processes. This book is about what you can do to slow them down.

In fact, when you consider the process of aging, never before in history have the parameters of aging extended so far. Though the overall structure of the brain has not changed in thousands of years, people are living much longer than ever before. In 1950 the life expectancy of an American was 68.2 years, by 2002 it had risen to 77.3 years, and it is expected to rise to 82.6 years by 2050. There are greater societal and cognitive demands on our brains than ever before, with aging brains experiencing multiple challenges. In just one day we may meet as many people as our ancestors met in a year.

In meeting these challenges, the aging brain has limitations and vulnerabilities. Toward the end of the middle years there are a variety of ways in which the aging brain differs from younger brains, including the following:

- Neurotransmitters and other aspects of the neurochemistry of the brain begin to work differently.
- There is an increase in mutations in the mitochondria (the cellular power plant) that make them spew out free radicals, which damage neurons.
- The neurons shrink.
- There is a loss of myelin.
- There is a loss of synapses.
- Instead of making new synapses, there is broadening of the existing synapses, making people more prone to be set in their ways
- There are age-related neurogenerative changes, including senile plaques and neurofibrillary tangles (not only Alzheimer's disease patients have plaques and tangles).

However, not all mature brains are the same. Indeed, researchers at Wayne State University examined brain changes in mature adults and found significant variation among individuals as they age.[4] Since mature brains are going through such a pivotal period, what you do now will determine whether your brain will be sharper, more capable of wisdom, and filled with positive emotions for the rest of your life.

There are many lifestyle factors that can accelerate these neurodegenerative processes. Not only can you avoid those destructive
behaviors, you can practice healthy behaviors to slow down and even
reverse these hazards. Consider the differences between two clients
who came to see me recently.

Stella and Carol

Stella and Carol had similar presenting problems but could not have
been more different. Both were warm and caring people who came
to see me because they were experiencing stress related to placing their mothers in assisted living programs. Both were 60 years
old, but Stella seemed older and was taking a different turn at the
crossroads, as if saying "I've run out of gas." Carol, in contrast, was
filling up the tank for a healthy tomorrow while functioning quite
well in the present.

Stella had already begun to flirt with type 2 diabetes. She was
overweight and joked about "having a sugar tooth." When I asked
her if she had structured exercise into her daily life, she laughed and
said, "Good idea, if I had the energy for it!" She went on to complain
about difficulty concentrating at work: "My mind is dead by the time
I get to lunch, or should I say brunch? The rest of the day is so hard.
When I get home, all I want to do is tune out. Then I fall asleep in
front of the TV, and then my husband prods me to go to bed. Then
I toss and turn all night long trying to get back to sleep." She had
isolated herself from friends as soon as the demands of placing her
mother became overwhelming: "They wouldn't understand anyway."
She avoided her husband, too: "Maybe I shouldn't be married. It
takes too much work." If she stayed on this path, her future would
be as dull as she anticipated.

Carol not only had fewer symptoms of stress than Stella but also
built a robust foundation of health-sustaining factors to help her
bounce back after her mother was settled. She had a wide group of

friends she looked to for support; in fact, a few of them were in her walking group. In contrast to Stella, she was quite fit. When I asked her about her diet, her eyes lit up, pleased that someone found it important enough to evaluate. Not even her primary care physician had asked her about it. She was also an avid reader, especially in subject areas she knew nothing about initially: "I love to learn new things. It also shifts me away from what is stressing me." Her only complaint was that she had trouble falling asleep. She also had a difficult time "turning my mind off."

Carol told me that she made the appointment to see me only to please her doctor and asked, "Do you really think I need to see you again?" After I gave her a few suggestions about how to deal with insomnia, we agreed that she could call later if she needed me. She later did call to thank me and report that she had used the suggestions and was enjoying good quality sleep.

Stella, by contrast, was not only unknowingly making her current situation more difficult but also setting herself up for a duller brain later in life. We worked together over the next few months, making significant changes to her self-care and the way she engaged with the world. Two years later she checked in with me, and I was delighted to see her eyes beam with vitality as she told me that her life transformation had been made possible because she had been practicing all the life skills that I had discussed. She had lost 20 pounds. Her brain was sharper, and she was proud to announce, "I am taking classes at the university. I am the oldest in there, but my brain is the youngest!"

The initial difference between Carol and Stella illustrates the way a variety of factors can insulate a person from stress and bolster resiliency. More important, several factors can work together to sharpen the brain as people age. A 1994 study conducted in Japan compared 60 people with Alzheimer's disease with 120 people without it. Five lifestyle factors significantly increased the risk of Alzheimer's disease: (1) low education, (2) social inactivity,

(3) physical inactivity, (4) head injury, and (5) loss of teeth. If a person had all five risk factors, he was 943.5 times more likely to develop Alzheimer's than was someone who had none of them. In a study of centenarians in Okinawa three factors were identified as common among them: (1) a calorie-limited diet, (2) regular exercise, and (3) strong social bonds in the community. Similarly, the Harvard Grant Study found that education, regular exercise, a stable marriage, and a healthy weight as well as avoiding drinking alcohol and smoking are critical for healthy aging.[5] On the basis of these and other studies we can identify a set of factors that contribute to a healthy aging brain.

In their book *Successful Aging,* John Rowe and Robert Kahn point out that there is a widening range of cognitive abilities among people as they age. Some people show no cognitive decline, whereas others show a significant decline. This demonstrates, they argue, that there is not an obligatory cognitive decline associated with aging and that "senility is a myth." Various types of dementias occur in some people during aging, but others are spared. This may account for the dramatic lack of cognitive decline for some and significant decline for others. Thus, cognitive decline is not inevitable. Alzheimer's disease accounts for approximately 50 percent of dementias, and the percentage of people who develop it increases with age. By age 65, only about 10 percent of the population is afflicted with one of the dementias, yet by age 85, 35 to 45 percent of people have some degree of dementia.[6] The incidence of developing Alzheimer's disease is partially dependent on healthy or unhealthy habits during a person's young adult and middle years.

Overall, the studies on successful aging have indicated that a variety of factors are associated with brain health. Though one factor alone cannot insulate you from unhealthy behaviors, you can apply the healthy factors together for a greater likelihood of brain health. The factors that research has consistently shown to be brain-healthy are as follows:

- A robust social support system
- Aerobic exercise
- Lifelong cognitive challenges and education early in life through late life
- A balanced diet
- Minimizing sleep deprivation and maximizing healthy sleep

The Five Factors of the Brain Bible Program

The formula for building a healthy brain includes five main factors that are based on the points noted above. These are the important healthy brain skills that you need to plant now and cultivate throughout the rest of your life.

The first factor is education. Engaging in learning activities on a regular basis boosts the brain's longevity. It has been shown that people with higher levels of education manifest symptoms of dementia much later than do people with less education. When applied to the brain, the maxim "use it or lose it" means that the less you use your brain for learning, the less it will be available to make learning possible. Alternatively, the more you use your brain for learning, the more cognitive reserve you will have for use later in life. Cognitive reserve represents structural changes to the brain, which will promote greater longevity.

Consider that you have roughly 100 billion neurons in your brain. Each neuron maintains about 10,000 connections with other neurons. The more you learn, the more you build and maintain new connections. If, however, you learn nothing new and turn off your brain by watching the same television shows each evening, you will maintain fewer connections and more connections between neurons will pruned away. Overall you can boost the number of connections and the health of your brain by challenging yourself intellectually. Chapter 3 describes the education factor in detail.

The second factor is diet. What you eat can determine whether your brain is capable of learning and producing positive emotions. A balanced diet forms the foundation for generating the cornucopia of neurotransmitters. This foundation allows you to enjoy positive moods, be calm, and have a sharper focus. Chapter 4 describes the diet factor in detail.

The third factor is exercise. Exercise changes the brain's chemistry and boosts its longevity. One way it does this is by stimulating the production and release of a magic tonic for the brain called brain-derived neurotrophic factor (BDNF). BDNF serves as a sort of Miracle-Gro for the brain and the birth of new neurons, which is called neurogenesis.

Aerobic exercise also serves as a powerful antidepressant and anti-anxiety agent, not to mention an energy booster. For example, it has been shown that 10 minutes of fast walking will boost the levels of various brain chemicals called neurotransmitters, such as dopamine, norepinephrine, and serotonin. Those 10 minutes of exercise will result in 90 minutes of more energy, greater focus, more positive moods, and overall calmness. Chapter 5 describes the exercise factor in detail.

The fourth factor is the social factor. Fifty years of psychological research has shown that people with a strong social support system live longer, are happier, and are more cognitively astute. In contrast, people who are cut off from social contact are emotionally starved, are ill more often, and are more depressed. They also may be more vulnerable to certain types of dementia. New developments in neuroscience have identified parts of the brain often referred to as the social brain that thrive on healthy relationships. Chapter 6 describes the social factor in detail.

The fifth factor is sleep. Most people don't know that the amount and quality of sleep has a major effect on how the brain functions over the long term. For example, getting poor quality sleep or missing a few hours of sleep increases your stress hormones, including cortisol. Higher levels of cortisol affect the prefrontal cortex; you are less able to focus, make clear decisions, and remember what you are attempting to learn. Also, higher levels of cortisol are corrosive to your brain and are associated with atrophy in the hippocampus, the area critical for laying down new memories. Chapter 7 describes the sleep factor in detail.

The greatest benefit to your brain will come by combining the Brain Bible factors, utilizing the social, education, exercise, diet, and sleep factors, not just one or two at a time, but together. An example of this combination could be a walking book club right after dinner. Because you and your friends will be getting together for a brisk walk to talk about the book you are all reading, the social, educational, and exercise factors will be combined. Also, the exercise three to six hours before bedtime will promote a better night's sleep. If you go on that walk after a nutritious dinner, the diet factor will help you cover all the factors.

Sylvia's Story

Sylvia came to see me because she had begun to worry that her mind was not as sharp as it had been in her thirties. At age 65, she found herself juggling the end of a career, empty nest issues after the kids left, and increasing demands by her aging parents. She found that her energy level had been dropping and along with it her sense of enjoyment in life. As she sat down in my office, one of the first things out of her mouth was, "Maybe this is early dementia."

She described how her sleep was restless and how she often woke up about three hours into her sleep cycle "as if the lights go on and will not go off." She tossed and turned the next hour or two worrying about not being able to hold things together. Each morning she dragged herself to work only to find it difficult to generate the energy to deal with the multiple demands of her job. Often after work she had little energy for her parents. Routinely, she plopped down in front of the television to "chill out."

Living in the Wine Country area of northern California gave her access to many premier wineries. For her, chilling out always included two glasses of great wine. She consumed one while cooking dinner and the other in front of the TV set. When I asked her about her diet, she told me that she started the day at the local McBucks Coffee Drive-Through. She typically ordered a tall skinny latte with a chocolate croissant. Lunch, when she had it, amounted to some tortilla chips and occasionally an energy bar. Dinner was "sketchy" because she was "trying to lose weight." She noted that she "grazed" while cooking dinner but often found herself too tired to sit down with her husband to eat.

When I asked about exercise, she said, "Are you joking? I'm beat!"

Sylvia told me that her friends had drifted away: "They have their own lives. Besides, who has time for friends?"

Though she wasn't clinically depressed and did not have signs of dementia as she feared, her sleep and energy were compromised, in part because of her poor diet and lack of exercise. Also, her impoverished cognitive activity essentially was dulling her mind, especially as she sat in front of the television.

She was irritated when I suggested that she try building a healthy foundation by making some lifestyle changes. She simply wanted medication.

"How about using a broad-based plan first, before we consider medication," I said as I introduced the Brain Bible formula.

She was missing all the factors in the Brain Bible formula. I started with the social factor, as she was socially starved. She responded by asking, "What do you want me to do, go pretend that I want to be with people and put on a happy face?!"

"Actually, yes. Sounds weird, doesn't it?" I explained that not only does your brain send information to your face, but changing your facial expression sends information back to your brain. If your face is contracted into a frown, you will feel sad. If your face puts on a smile, you will feel pleased and happy. A full smile activates the left prefrontal cortex and positive emotions. In contrast, a frown activates the right prefrontal cortex and negative feelings. "So yes, put on a happy face," I told her. I went on to describe how important the left prefrontal cortex is to taking action. In contrast, the right prefrontal cortex is involved in withdrawal behaviors such as retreating from activities. In other words, withdrawing from friends activates negative feelings. Also, a number of areas in the brain are associated with the social brain networks that are starved in the absence of social contact. Since we are perhaps the most social of all species, these social brain networks need to be continually activated for mental health and brain longevity.

Next I told her that exercise is the best medication and has good rather than bad side effects. I also told her about brain-derived neurotrophic factor and its role as Miracle-Gro in neurogenesis: the birth of new neurons. Since she was concerned about the possibility of early dementia, I emphasized that exercise is the best way to increase the brain's functioning at a higher level and increase its longevity.

"I don't have the energy for exercise," she said.

I told her that just 10 minutes of exercise will give her 90 minutes of energy. This is the case because of the resulting increases in the neurotransmitters such as serotonin, norepinephrine, and dopamine. "Think of what you can do with 30 minutes of exercise. Plus, if you exercise three to six hours before you go to sleep, you will increase the chances of sleeping through the night restfully."

Next we moved to education. She immediately responded by protesting, "Oh, no! On top of the rest of it you are telling me to go off and get a degree or something?"

I described several things she could do to get the brain-boosting effects of education. To begin with, she should look at the time and energy she was wasting watching brainless television shows. I suggested watching PBS or other stations with shows that can be both entertaining and informative.

"But I want to turn off my brain at night so that I can have enough mental energy for the next day!"

"Think of the maxim 'Use it or lose it,'" I told her. "It has great truth to it. By turning off your brain all the time, as you put it, you are not building a dense network of connections between your neurons that can serve you later when you need mental ability. As a result of the mental inactivity, your brain is less able to deal with the complexity of the world." I also told her about the phenomenon of cognitive reserve, which enables people to have fewer symptoms of dementia later in life.

We then discussed diet. "Since you are interested in medication, you ought to know that an imbalanced diet will undermine the effects of medication and that diet is more critical to the brain chemistry than medication," I explained. "Here's how it works: a balanced diet provides the essential amino acids that are the precursors to the neurotransmitters that many medications affect. The body synthesizes these amino acids and creates the neurotransmitters and the cornucopia of brain chemicals that give you energy, lift your mood, and keep you focused. You wouldn't drive around in a car with an empty gas tank. Why do such a thing to your brain? By the way, skipping dinner also makes it difficult to sleep at night.

"Your two glasses of wine each evening cost you in a number of areas. Waking up in the middle of the night and not being able to get back to sleep is often associated with drinking alcohol in the evening."

"But it relaxes me!"

"Actually, it accomplishes that only for the first two hours. Then it wears off in the middle of the night when you want to be asleep." I explained that this happens because of the temporary dampening of one of the activating neurotransmitters called Glutamate in your brain and for a short time helps you relax. Alcohol fools your brain into behaving as if there is plenty of a neurotransmitter called GABA, which when present promotes calmness, and when the alcohol wears off you don't have GABA available to calm you down while there is a surge of Glutamate. "GABA and other neurotransmitters will be depleted up to two months after your last drink, making you more anxious, easily stressed, and depressed than you would have been had you not been drinking each night."

Finally, we moved to solve her complaint about sleep. I recommended that in addition to cutting out the alcohol in the evening, she should avoid spending time in the late evening at the computer. "When do you expect me to send my e-mail? And what's wrong with using the computer? "

"Think of it this way: the light of the computer screen is taken in by your retina, which sends that light information directly to your pineal gland. Essentially, this tells your brain, 'It's daytime; do not secrete the sleeping hormone melatonin.' And there you have computer-induced insomnia."

I went on to suggest that she take a walk three to six hours before bedtime to promote a good drop in body temperature, which is critical for a good night's sleep. "You want your coolest body temperature to occur in the middle of your sleep cycle. Keep your bedroom cool at night to help accomplish this. Also, make sure that your dinner contains an ample amount of complex carbohydrates, not simple carbohydrates."

Sylvia agreed that she would give the Brain Bible method a serious try before we talked again about the feasibility of medication. She checked in with me every other week to monitor her progress and gradually began to feel more alive and energized. Instead of feeling like her life was winding down, she began to feel that there was a kind of Renaissance occurring. She began to think more wisely and feel that her moods were more balanced. In contrast to overreacting to stress and the demands of life, she began to take things in stride. She was pleasantly surprised that at the beginning of her senior years, she became more focused, engaged, and satisfied with her life. To reap the benefits of this period and build on them, she had to break old habits and firmly establish brain-sharpening habits.

You, like Sylvia, can reap the benefits of using all the Brain Bible factors together. Planting them now and continuing to cultivate them throughout your life will contribute to a sharper brain not only now but throughout your senior years.

Rewiring the Mature Brain

As Sylvia discovered, the brain is not fixed and hardwired or doomed to wither away. It is actually quite plastic and has been constantly rewired by your experiences throughout your life. Under certain conditions new brain cells can be born even as you age. You may have heard the popular hype about genes determining behaviors and be worried that you cannot change. The reality is that genes only lay out potentials and vulnerabilities. Genes do not dictate your thoughts, your feelings, or your behavior. You can actually turn genes on or off by changing your behavior and environment. And when you change your behavior and environment, your brain changes.

The old nature versus nurture debate has been replaced by the new model: nurtured nature. Just as the concepts of nature and nurture unreasonably represent separate processes, the mind and the brain also had been thought to be separate. They are actually two sides of the same coin. As you change your mind, your brain changes. As you change your brain, your mind changes.

You can nurture your brain by maximizing your potentials and minimizing your vulnerabilities. In other words, you can change your biology by what you do and how you think within the potentials limited by the biology of our species. You can't live until age 200 or fly like a bird, but you can potentially live beyond the average human life span by optimizing your health throughout your life. More important, you can keep your brain sharp well into old age.

You can extend the health and life of your brain by following our suggestions about the Brain Bible factors.

To explain how to rewire your brain, let's start with the big picture. Your brain has a hundred billion nerve cells called *neurons* (the gray matter) and about 10 times as many glial cells (the white matter). Each neuron is capable of establishing and maintaining connections with about 10,000 other neurons.

Communication between neurons occurs across a gap called a *synapse* (Figure 2.1). Specialized brain chemicals called neurotransmitters are released by one neuron and float across the synapse to reach a receptor on the other neuron and can cause it to "fire." There are approximately 100 different neurotransmitters and related neurochemicals in the brain. Your diet has a major effect on the structure of your brain, the supply of neurotransmitters, and the health of your neurotransmitters.

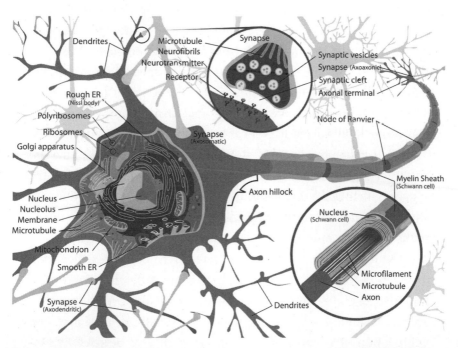

Figure 2.1 Neurons and Their Synapses   *Courtesy Wikimedia*

Your synapses are not hardwired to make you think or behave in predetermined ways. You could say that they are softwired. Like a computer, you have hardware and software. Synapses change as you learn new skills, such as speaking a new language, text messaging, and skiing. Synapses are therefore quite plastic. This is what is meant by the terms *neuroplasticity* and *synaptic plasticity*.

Learning something new rewires your brain, making and strengthening synaptic connections. For example, when you orchestrate your thoughts on a beautiful image, such as a village in the Cinque Terre in Italy, you begin to construct new synaptic connections between groups of neurons that encode that image into memory. Every time you recall the image of that village, you strengthen the synaptic connections that code the memory. Every time you recall that image, you make the recall stronger later.

The popular phrase "cells that fire together wire together" describes how the brain rewires when a person learns something new. The more you practice speaking Spanish, for example, the more neurons fire together and wire together as you improve your vocabulary and enunciation. The more you practice speaking Spanish, the more likely it is that those neurons will fire together in the future. The bottom line: the more you do something, the more likely it is that you will do it again without as much effort as you made initially.

What happens when you stop practicing Spanish? The maxim "use it or lose it" not only describes how practicing strengthens the synapses that make that skill possible but indicates that when you stop practicing, those synaptic connections weaken. This is similar to the way your muscles atrophy after you stop exercising.

The learning curve is always greater in the beginning. Learning a new skill (e.g., speaking Spanish) is more difficult in the beginning because, pardon the pun, you are in totally foreign territory. As you become more familiar with the intonations, grammar, and conjugation of verbs, you build an infrastructure of synaptic networks to support that knowledge. For these reasons I often tell people that learning a new skill requires that they "do what they don't feel like doing." Otherwise what you will do is what you always have done. Remember years ago when you played a record on a turntable but found that the record was scratched? You had to get up from the couch to "bump the needle" to get the record to play past that scratched point. Learning a new skill is like creating a new groove or like traveling on a snowy road in the tracks of another car that ran off the road. To establish your own new tracks and stay on the road you must jerk the wheel to make new tracks. The next time you drive that road, it will be easier to stay in the new tracks. This is how rewiring works: get out of the old tracks or habits and forge a different and positive path. The more times you take the new path, the easier it will be to find it.

When your neurons fire together often, they fire together at a quicker rate. This increased efficiency allows more precision in the number of neurons that are required to perform a particular skill. For example, when you learn to ski, you use more muscles and neurons at first. As you learn to ski more efficiently, less muscular effort and fewer neurons are required to ski with greater skill.

One of the most famous examples of how neuroplasticity affects the brain involved research done on London cab drivers. To acquire a license to drive a cab in London you must go through a long training called the Knowledge and pass a number of tests. All the training and test taking requires learning the layout of London streets in great detail. Not long ago after I spoke at a seminar on the new developments in neuroscience for the British Psychological Society in London, a few of the attendees, my wife, and I jumped in a cab. We asked the cabbie about his experience with the Knowledge. He said, "It took me four years and 17 tests to get my license. But my friend got through in three years!"

Researchers from University College London scanned the brains of a sizable group of these cabbies and found that their posterior right hippocampal areas (responsible for laying down new spatial memories) were much larger than those of noncabbies. In other words, the cabbies had strengthened this area of their brains through neuroplasticity much more than you or I (unless, of course, you are a London cabbie).

Specifically, the researchers scanned the brains of 16 London taxi drivers and compared them with the scans of 50 non–taxi drivers.[7] They found that the taxi drivers had a larger right posterior hippocampus. The hippocampus is critical for learning and memory. It's as if they developed a GPS and map of London in their brains. The greater the number of years on they had the job, the larger the hippocampi were in the individual drivers. This finding was apparent despite the age of the driver, which is quite significant because with age there is a gradual atrophy of the hippocampus. Thus, use trumps aging. In other words, not only can use-based neuroplasticity halt the age-related atrophy, it can reverse it. Instead of losing it, we gain.

Acquisition of a wide variety of other skills has also been shown to change the brain through neuroplasticity. For example, researchers at the Wellcome Department of Imaging Neuroscience at the Institute of Neurology in London examined the brain scans of bilingual people and compared them with those of monolingual people. An area called the left angular gyrus, part of the cortex at the junction of the parietal, temporal, and occipital lobes, is among the most important areas corresponding to understanding language and its complexity. The angular gyrus was found to contain more gray matter, and the underlying white matter was denser in bilingual people.[8]

Musicians using specific fingers to play their instruments showed enlarged areas of the somatosensory strips associated with those fingers.[9] An area in the temporal lobe called Heschl's gyrus that is critical for processing acoustic stimuli has been found to be twice as large in professional musicians as in musically untrained people. In fact, just as with the London cabbies, there was a positive relationship between years on the job and size of the corresponding area of the brain that made the skill possible, in this case Heschl's gyrus.[10]

Blind Braille readers showed enlarged cortical areas associated with the reading finger compared with blind non-Braille readers and sighted people.[11] Adults who juggled three balls for three months increased gray matter in the midtemporal area and left posterior intraparietal sulcus, the areas that are associated with making the movements to juggle. After months of little or no juggling, the gray matter decreased and approached baseline values.[12] Again, just like muscles that atrophy because of lack of use, brain networks revert to the condition they were in before use.

These studies represent only a clue to the importance of the education factor, the focus of Chapter 3. Education provides robust development of synaptic connections that have been called cognitive reserve, which is critical to brain longevity. The greater the cognitive reserve is (brain development), the more you can lose without looking like you have lost it. This is one of the principal reasons more highly educated people are less likely to develop symptoms of dementia than are less educated people.

You can't just say to yourself, "Well, I've got a few college degrees, so I've got all the cognitive reserve I need." No, you need to keep learning to keep your cognitive reserve available in reserve. Remember the jugglers? Or to use another analogy, a garden needs continual cultivation through working the soil, pulling the weeds, and adequately watering it or it will go fallow—it will turn into a dry weed patch.

Earlier in this chapter I hinted at another new discovery in neuroscience that is relevant to the health of the brain that involves the potential for the birth of new neurons. Not long ago it was thought that we are born with as many neurons as we will ever possess. As recently as the 1980s, when I was studying neuropsychology, that was the orthodox belief. The truth is that neurons can be born, but only in a few very important parts of the brain. *Neurogenesis,* as it is called, can occur in the hippocampus, olfactory bulbs (in pregnant women), and prefrontal cortex.

Both neurogenesis and neuroplasticity are facilitated by an amazing substance called *brain-derived neurotrophic factor*. Since BDNF helps give birth to neurons, it has been referred to as Miracle-Gro. BDNF enhances learning and the process called long-term potentiation (LTP), which is fundamental to neuroplasticity and means that the long-term potential for neurons to fire together and wire together increases as you learn something new. LTP and BDNF promote each other, as illustrated by researchers who have shown that stimulating LTP increases BDNF levels. When researchers deprived brains of BDNF, those brains lost their capacity for LTP—new learning.

BDNF prevents cells from dying at the same time that it boosts their growth and vitality. It does this by working within cells to activate the genes that increase the production of proteins, serotonin, and even more BDNF. It also binds to the receptors at the synapse, triggering a flow of ions that increases the voltage, which in turn strengthens the connectivity between the neurons.

Rewiring your brain, technically called neuroplasticity, and the potential birth of new neurons, technically called neurogenesis, are possible throughout your life by making an effort:

- Neuroplasticity and learning are two sides of the same coin.
- Neuroplasticity works with a moderate degree of discomfort—getting out of your comfort zone.
- New neurons in the hippocampus and prefrontal cortex can be produced throughout life.
- Aerobic exercise is one of the best ways to boost brain-derived neurotrophic factor.

Your mind/brain has an executive officer that decides what to learn and how to direct your energy. Sharpening your brain to promote its long-term health requires that you apply the skills of this CEO. It provides you with the capacity for the sustained attention, willpower, and mood stability that you need to maintain your motivation to sharpen your brain.

Activating Your Brain's Brain

Humans are ruled far less by instincts than are other species because of our much larger frontal lobes. The frontal lobes represent the most recent evolutionary advance of the brains of any species and make up about 20 percent of the human brain. To put things in perspective, the frontal lobes of cats and dogs occupy about 3.5 percent of their brains. Cats or dogs don't ask questions about how to sharpen their brains. Humans do. The frontal lobes made such questions possible as well as the search for answers.

The most advanced part of the frontal lobes is called the *prefrontal cortex* (PFC), which is positioned at the forefront of the frontal lobes. It is often called the executive brain or the brain's brain because it directs the resources of the rest of the brain and attention and decides what to do, how to stay positive, and how to appreciate the larger picture of life. Your PFC allows you to direct your attention to what is important in your life, such as your long-term health. To accomplish this it orchestrates complex cognitive and emotional skills that provide you with the capacity to behave with purpose.

Two parts of the PFC that are essential to effectively manage your life are the *dorsolateral prefrontal cortex* (DLPFC) and the *orbital frontal cortex* (OFC). The DLPFC is so named because of the way it is positioned, with *dorsal* meaning "upper" or "top" and *lateral* meaning "side." Your OFC is so named because it lies just behind the orbs of your eyes, as is illustrated in Figure 2.2.

The DLPFC is the last part of the brain to fully develop and the earliest to falter during the later years of life. Many researchers suggest that the DLPFC is not fully developed until age 25 in women and 30 in men. Though many of us hate to admit it, men are a little

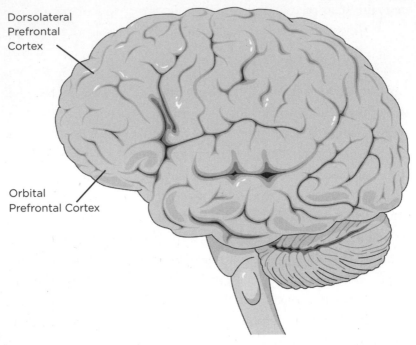

Dorsolateral
Prefrontal
Cortex

Orbital
Prefrontal Cortex

Courtesy Wikimedia

Figure 2.2 The prefrontal cortex

slower in development. To put the late maturity of the DLPFC in perspective, consider that we send young adults to war not only because they are relatively more physically fit but also because, like adolescents, they tend to disregard danger. Their sergeant may command them to "storm that hill over there!" and the young troops may compete with one another on who gets there first. Older individuals (those with fully developed DLPFCs) may say, "Now wait a minute! There's a bunch of soldiers up there with machine guns. That's suicide if we rush it!"

When I was 22 years old, I circled the globe for one year. This was during the Vietnam War and the war of attrition in the Middle East. I explored the Golden Triangle where the borders of Laos, Burma, and Thailand meet and also the Golan Heights at the border of Israel and Syria. Both were not very safe places to go. Now that my DLPFC is relatively mature, I would not go to such places!

Unfortunately, what is the last to mature is also the first to falter as we age. This follows an evolutionary law that the last to evolve is the slowest to develop and the first to go in old age. Nevertheless, you can exercise your DLPFC and through neuroplasticity keep it relatively healthy.

The DLPFC is deeply involved in complex thinking, attention, and what is referred to as working memory because it processes what your mind is working on at any one time. When you walk into a room and forget what you intended to do there, it's your DLPFC that is skipping a beat. You can usually keep something you're working on in your mind for 20 to 30 seconds. Then you need to renew it again with your attention. Your DLPFC is also involved with complex problem solving, and since attention is the gateway to memory, it maintains strong connections with the hippocampus, which is involved in laying down long-term explicit memory. This partnership helps you form memories.

We especially pay attention to and remember novelty. When we experience something novel, such as meeting a new person who is attractive and/or interesting, key brain systems activate to code in the memory of that meeting. Then the prefrontal cortex activates and tells the hippocampus to "remember this person." To ensure that the memory gets coded, the ventral tegmental area in the midbrain and the substantia nigra (both within the brainstem) get involved by releasing the neurotransmitter dopamine, which adds to the attention to and anticipation of the experience. All this further activates the hippocampus to code the experience into memory. With some acetyl-choline added in, the brain gets tuned in, sharpening the memories.

In contrast to the DLPFC, the orbital frontal cortex develops earlier in life and does not falter in old age. It appears to have a close relationship with the amygdala, a part of the brain that processes emotions. Because it helps regulate emotions, the OFC is closely associated with other parts of the brain that allow a person to possess social skills. If your OFC were seriously damaged, you could be like the most famous neurology patient in history, Phineas Gage, who lost his social skills. Gage suffered a near-death accident at work when a steel rod skewered his OFC but left everything else in his brain intact. It was 1848 when Gage was setting up blasting caps in preparation for laying rail. Then it happened: a tamping iron one inch thick and three feet long shot through his skull like a missile, entering below his left eye and exiting at the top of his head. Amazingly, he lived for another 20 years. Gage had previously worked as a supervisor and was widely respected for being even-tempered and thoughtful. After the accident he became unstable, erratic, and rude. Though he retained many of his cognitive abilities, he lost the ability to emotionally inhibit impulses and urges. When he was in the presence of a woman he wanted, he just grabbed her. He said whatever he felt like saying. After a stint as circus freak with the fateful iron rod on display, he died penniless in San Francisco.

In addition to being a major convergence center of highly processed emotional, visceral, and sensory information, the OFC interprets the emotional significance of the experience through its extensive connections to the amygdala.[13] It also plays a significant role in controlling behavior during conflict when the situation needs to be reversed.[14] It helps you control your temper in favor of reaching an equitable compromise.

Together, your OFC and DLPFC make up part of your prefrontal cortex and function as your brain's brain, which decides what is important and what should be remembered. Your hippocampus takes direction from your DLPFC, which holds on to information in working memory, and then your OFC gives it emotional interpretation though its connection to the amygdala and relates back to previous experience and sends all that information to the hippocampus, analyzes it, puts the information in a sequence, and combines it, allowing you take advantage of opportunities and avoid dangerous situations.

When working effectively, your executive brain (PFC) is essential to sharpen your brain. It is the conductor of the orchestrator that helps you anticipate and predict what may occur in the future on the basis of what has occurred in the past and what may logically result from what is occurring in the present. All the while you maintain flexibility to adapt to changing conditions and switch to an appropriate frame of mind that is based on the current situation, inhibiting immediate emotional urges and distractions in favor of reaching long-range goals.

All these skills help you engage effectively in the world. Without them you could live in an endless sea of daydreaming and rumination. Sharpening your brain requires that you continually cultivate the skills of your executive brain. It's the engagement in the here and now that allows you to be an active participant in the world.

The executive brain, your prefrontal cortex, is your brain's brain. Through its various parts, such as the orbital frontal cortex and the dorsolateral prefrontal cortex, it helps you do the following:

- Control your emotions
- Maintain social graces
- Stay focused
- Follow through on goal-directed behavior
- Think about thinking (insight)

Adjusting Your Brain's Set Points

It's a rare person who can be totally present each moment of the day. Most of us periodically spend time on autopilot, marginally engaged with the world around us while drifting off into fantasy, daydreaming, and rumination. Take driving, for example. Five miles can go by while you are in a state of "highway hypnosis," lost in ruminations and daydreaming, especially if you are driving in familiar territory.

When your executive brain is at rest, the other parts of your brain are actually quite active. Let's say another car swerves into your lane, activating your attention to induce you to drive defensively. After you pass the car and find a safe niche in the flow of traffic, you slip back into daydreaming. While your mind wanders again, your brain uses about 20 times as much energy resting as it used when you paid attention to the car swerving into your lane. In other words, your brain is not really resting when you are daydreaming.

Indeed, recent neuroimaging research has shown that contrary to the old belief that the brain is hardly active while at rest, the activity in your brain required to read this sentence uses a minimal increment of energy over that which is already being consumed. In other words, there is a highly active default baseline state operating in the background where we spend a huge amount of time each day.

This baseline activity in your brain that occurs during the time you do not focus on activities or demands such as a car drifting to your lane has been referred to as the default mode network (DMN). The DMN is associated with self-referential daydreaming and rumination. The DMN involves dispersed areas of the brain that continue chattering away yet are synchronized in a readiness mode, set to be used in conscious activity such as directing your attention to the car.

These brain areas include the medial parietal area (which includes the posterior cingulate cortex and the adjacent precuneus) and the medial prefrontal cortex (which includes the ventral anterior cingulate cortex). The medial parietal area is involved in reflecting on memories of personal events in your life. The medial prefrontal cortex is involved in imagining what other people are thinking as well as reflecting on aspects of your emotional state. Both areas experience decreased activity from their baseline resting state when you attend to a task or pay attention to a stimulus such as the car drifting into your lane.

The DMN is believed to behave like a self-referential orchestra conductor directing the timing signals to coordinate activity among different areas of the brain. The DMN ensures that these areas of the brain are ready to react in concert to stimuli from the environment such as trying to discern if the driver of the car is drunk and that it may be a good idea to call the highway patrol.

Your dorsolateral prefrontal cortex helps you focus on the here and now. Since it is one of the first areas of the brain to atrophy, some people have a growing tendency to fade off into the DMN so that there is an increase in daydreaming when the situation demands that they stay focused. Some also gravitate to a new baseline anxious or depressed mood when they fade into daydreaming. If you find that these tendencies have been increasing, you can work to alleviate depression and/or anxiety by strengthening your attention skills, for example, by resisting the temptation to avoid situations that make you anxious and the tendency to withdraw from others, as is described in more detail in my book *Rewire Your Brain*.

Novel cognitive activities awaken your brain out of the DMN, activating your attention to the present moment. Let's say on the way home you chose to drive through areas you had never visited; the experience is novel. Or better yet, you drive on your usual routes, attempting to spot houses, buildings, and trees you have never noticed before. I am fortunate to drive through the rolling hills of northern California with vineyards and farmland but still must remind myself to stay in the present, all along exercising my attention skills. Whenever you are staying in the present, you are less likely to drift into your DMN.

Nevertheless, there is a constant and natural interplay between maintaining focused attention on what is going on in your environment and reverie or daydreaming. The activities of the DMN must give way to the demands of the outside world when the experience is novel or meaningful. This may occur because of an unexpected sensation or a novel situation or because you suddenly remember to stop at the grocery store to pick up food for dinner on the drive home from work.

Problems arise if the DMN takes over when you need to maintain focused attention. Let's say that after remembering to stop at the store you fade back off into daydreaming again. You find yourself at home without food for dinner. Your dorsolateral prefrontal cortex was not doing its job of keeping you in the present. What if this happens all the time? In depression, for example, a person can frequently slip into the DMN when goal-directed tasks demand otherwise. The DMN in a depressed person may possess weak links between motivation and reward-seeking behavioral and attention networks in the brain. The excessive activity between the DMN circuits may account for the lack of concentration and increased ruminations so common with depression.

The DMN is not inherently bad or good. We all have a tendency throughout the day to fade out into daydreaming, reverie, or rumination. The DMN can be useful in the following situations:

- It becomes a source of creativity.
- You can focus on the here and now.
- You reflect on novel thoughts and images and make connections with the present moment.

Another area of research that may account for a default baseline of particular mood is called the emotional set point. Consider that most people fantasize about winning the lottery, thinking that their lives would totally change forever and that their problems would evaporate. But several studies have revealed that roughly one year after collecting their millions lottery winners revert back to their previous baseline emotional state. If they were slightly depressed before becoming millionaires, they fall back to that depressed baseline state. Money does not serve as an antidepressant; it does not buy them long-term happiness. Similarly, many people who become paraplegic after a devastating injury revert back to their baseline emotional set point a year or so after the accident. If they were generally optimistic and made the most out of adversity, they manage to work their way back to their original baseline emotional set point.

The concept of an emotional set point has received strong empirical support from Richard Davidson, the director of the Laboratory for Affective Neuroscience at the University of Wisconsin. Using functional magnetic resonance imaging (fMRI) technology and electroencephalographic (EEG) analysis, he has identified an index for the brain's emotional set points. He discovered that people who tend to have positive moods and are enthusiastic, upbeat about life, and energized have heightened activity in the left prefrontal cortex (L-PFC). In contrast, people who tend to have negative moods and be depressed and/or anxious have heightened activity in the right prefrontal cortex (R-PFC). Their R-PFC seems to be activated along with the amygdala (the brain's panic button) when they are stressed and feeling anxiety. It is the L-PFC that can inhibit the overactivity of the amygdala and the anxiety associated with its overactivity.

Davidson's method of indexing a person's emotional set point involves reading the baseline levels of the R-PFC and L-PFC areas. If that ratio tilts toward the left, the person tends to be more enthusiastic and happy. If that ratio tilts toward the right, the person tends to be unhappy and often distressed. He took readings from hundreds of people and established a bell curve. Those in the middle of the curve have a mix of positive and negative moods.

You can change your emotional set point through focused attention and continuous practice that rewires the brain to make it gradually easier to stay focused and positive. To demonstrate how people can change their emotional set point, Davidson teamed with Jon Kabat-Zinn, founder of the Mindfulness-Based Stress Reduction Clinic at the University of Massachusetts Medical School. That clinic teaches mindfulness meditation practices to patients with chronic illnesses, including chronic pain. The study explored the effects of teaching mindfulness for three hours per week over the course of two months to employees in a high-pressure biotech business.

Before the mindfulness training, the workers were on average tilted to the right side in the ratio for the emotional set point. Indeed, they complained of being stressed out and suffered from negative moods. After the training, the ratio shifted to the left and they reported positive moods and less anxiety and felt more engaged in their work. The here-and-now focus of mindfulness helped them be more purposeful and observe their moods instead of stewing in them. The mindfulness training taught the workers to focus attention or simply observe and accept what occurs each moment. Maintaining focus on each moment allowed them to detach from their rumination and negative moods. This shift in attention also contributed to left side activation and better inhibition of the amygdala, which tends to stir up anxiety when it is overactivated. The workers rewired their set points, resulting in more positive moods and more easygoing attitudes.

An added bonus for the workers was bolstered immune systems. When exposed to the flu virus, those who received the mindfulness training had less severe flu symptoms. The greater the shift to the left in the emotional set point, the larger the increase in immune response. In other words, the more positive moods, the stronger the immune system.

By balancing the ratio of activity in each hemisphere to adjust your set point, you may do the following:

- Turn on your prefrontal cortex by a be here now focus.
- Act with purpose, kindling your left prefrontal cortex.

The baseline activity of both the emotional set point and the DMN represents a baseline mode of functioning that can be rewired, as the study above illustrated. The baseline mode occurs automatically as your brain does what it is accustomed to doing when the cells that fire together wire together. Your task is to bump your baseline to moderate the amount of time you spend on autopilot by enlisting your executive brain (especially your DLPFC). It goes online when you get focused on the here and now and allows you to make executive decisions about whether to apply your efforts to a particular goal. When your executive brain goes online, your DMN goes offline. There is a kind of a push and pull going on throughout the day. What Davidson and Kabat-Zinn showed in the experiment described above is that by training yourself to be more present and observant, you can bump your default baseline (emotional set point) to the left side, which can help you feel more positive and involved in the world around you.

Beginning during your middle years, you spend more time in your DMN than you did during your young adult years. It therefore is important to cultivate a DMN and emotional set point that generates better moods and health. Cultivating these healthy networks involves utilizing your capacity for neuroplasticity and the here-and-now approach of mindfulness. A method of rewiring the brain that I teach combines a calm attentive observance of the present moment with purposeful engagement with the world.

The next several chapters will describe ways you can rewire your baseline and sharpen your brain. If you incorporate the factors represented in the Brain Bible formula together, your brain can grow healthier as you age.

Sara's New Brain Baseline

Sara came to me complaining that she was too often falling into daydreaming at staff meetings. She was particularly convinced that she was "over the hill" and that the staff members in their twenties and thirties seemed to be "on top of everything," while she, at age 65, was "ready to go out to pasture." She had to work another year before she could retire and wondered if she could hang in there that long.

She had actually been juggling several challenges at once. Her daughter had just gone through a divorce and Sara helped her with her teenage kids, added to that challenge her aging parents were failing in health, and her husband seemed to be more focused on his career than on being a full participant in running the household. Just 10 years earlier she had felt on top of all the demands of being a full-time employee, mother, and wife. She made it through menopause without much difficulty. In fact, about a year afterward she felt increased energy. But when her parents began to lose their health and mobility, they became more dependent on her.

Her first goal was to ask her two sisters to share in the increasing demands from their parents. It was difficult for her to move out of the caretaker role, but with considerable encouragement she managed to do so. Though her sisters began to help with the care of their parents, Sara continued to have difficulty focusing at work. She had grown to expect that it was next to impossible to compete with the younger staff members. Worrying about her inadequacies much more than acknowledging her talents, she increasingly faded off into her DMN, musing about how she had been sharper in the past. She wondered if her peers thought she was dead weight and should be let go for the sake of the company.

Her emotional set point had an anxious and slightly depressed tone. I explained that this pattern represented a right PFC shift and that she needed to activate her left PFC to generate a positive mood. This meant that she had to be more purposeful and goal-directed in her daily life instead of passive and avoidant.

"But isn't that how my brain was wired? Isn't it all genetics?" she asked.

"Genes lay down potentials and limitations," I told her. "You have the potential to rewire your brain to enjoy positive moods and to be more focused and engaged in the world around you. Let's consider your relatively underactive left prefrontal cortex. You can jump-start it by using its talents that are called approach behaviors, meaning taking action to do something. Your right prefrontal cortex is involved in the opposite—withdrawal behaviors. Withdrawing from people and the world around you activates your right prefrontal cortex and leads to more feelings of being overwhelmed. Since you are a good caretaker of others but not of yourself, it's time to invest your energies in taking care of yourself. You're not going to feel like it initially."

I went on to tell her about how old habits are hard to break and that neuroplasticity necessitates making an effort to do what you don't feel like doing. If you continue to do only what you feel like doing, you will do what you always have done. The brain does what comes easy unless you make an extra effort to establish new connections. She could revitalize her brain through neuroplasticity and neurogenesis by challenging herself even though she did not feel ready. She chose to take an art class at the local junior college and take brisk walks five times a week.

After a few weeks of classes and walking she said that she was beginning to feel a slight boost in energy, as if she were stirring from a long slumber. I suggested that she include an intellectually stimulating exercise. She chose to read about art history with the intent of eventually taking a class on the topic the next semester, after the painting class was over. During each session she commented on a growing sense of enthusiasm for cultivating her creativity. She found it particularly surprising that she actually had more energy while at work although she was busier than ever with her new activities.

During the course in art history she found herself particularly fascinated by the Renaissance period with its emphasis on perspective in painting and more realistic depiction of the subject matter. What particularly struck her was the symbolic meaning of the Renaissance itself. She stated that just as the Renaissance period meant a revival from a dark period in history, she too was experiencing a revival from a dark period. She felt that her revival brought with it a renewed sense of vitality and hunger for new experiences. No longer did she feel that she was over the hill. Rather she felt "that there were many hills to explore."

Just like Sara, you can use the processes of neuroplasticity and neurogenesis to rewire and revitalize your brain. This is especially important during this pivotal period of your life. Rewiring your brain by following the Brain Bible factors will promote the greatest longevity.

PART TWO

The Brain Bible Program

CHAPTER 3

The Education Factor

Christine was a 65-year-old former court reporter who came to me because she thought she was developing dementia. A year before retiring she reassigned herself to a clerical job because she had a "tired mind," but in the clerical position she continued to complain about feeling mentally dull. She assumed that she had dementia after watching an evening television magazine program about people whose memory had failed during their last year of employment. Initially, I employed a memory test and other measures, and it appeared that she did not have dementia. She remembered having problems with attention after menopause and thought she had to "rest my mind so that it would clear up . . . but it never did." Now, 12 years after menopause, she said, "I still have the problem no matter how much I rest."

Her belief that she "wore out" her brain reflected a misconception about how the brain works. The truth is that the brain operates with a use it or lose it process, not a use it and wear it down process. She told me that she rested her mind by watching television. In fact, as she talked more about her life, it became clear that television formed the context in which she described most aspects of her life.

"So how much time do you spend watching TV?" I asked.

She laughed, "I flick it on as I walk into my house after work and turn off my bedroom set after I turn out the light on my nightstand. Sometimes I fall asleep with it on. And of course I watch the morning shows when I eat breakfast."

"Do you set aside time to read or do anything else with your mind?"

She laughed again, "Are you joking? Do you know what I did for a living? As a court reporter I had to be superfocused on every word uttered by anyone in the courtroom. No, when I'm home, it's time to turn my mind off. I need to rest my brain for the next day."

Christine suffered from the very common misconception that mental inactivity is good for the brain. Her belief that she needed to rest her brain to store up enough energy to pay attention the next day was the opposite of the truth. I needed to come up with a metaphor that made sense to her by describing how her mind/brain could atrophy from lack of use.

Interestingly, 100 years ago rest was a popular treatment for women. It was prescribed for women who were having trouble with stress and making adjustments in life. In contrast, during the same period, men were prescribed a trip out West to rejuvenate themselves. Teddy Roosevelt and Walt Whitman complied with the "go west treatment" and returned stronger. Unfortunately, the sexist rest treatment for women was far less rejuvenating.

"The way to sharpen your brain is to challenge it. You are doing the opposite at home," I told her. I explained how neuroplasticity and neurogenesis sharpen the brain through mental challenges. By cultivating her intellectual skills, she could boost what is called *cognitive reserve*; that means that the more synaptic connections she made, the greater the overall longevity of her brain would be. I asked her if she had ever heard of the concept of use it or lose it and explained that nonuse of the brain leads to a loss of capacity. In response she quipped, "Hey, you don't understand. I've already lost it. Now I don't think it's anywhere to be found." I reassured her that her intellectual skills were not lost; rather, they could be built up.

"Oh, great," she responded. "Are you trying to say that I've got to use my brain to build this reserve power you're talking about?"

"Yes!"

"But I'm too old to enroll at some university to get a degree."

"You're not too old for a degree, but getting one is not necessary. Just taking a class in something of interest would be a good way to engage your brain."

Eventually, despite her protest that "her flame to learn had burned out," she agreed to take a class. She decided the subject would be art history, an area of interest from her past.

Though she was very resistant to turning off her constant companion the television, I encouraged her to watch it selectively. "How about thinking of TV as one of the many areas of entertainment? Select one or at most two programs each evening and don't cheapen them by adding more brain-numbing TV watching." The phrase *brain numbing* seemed to strike a chord with her.

"You think my brain is numb?"

"No, but brain-numbing activities have dulled its ability to think clearly and quickly. And what you do now for your brain will determine its health for years to come."

She had a great fear of developing dementia in later life. That fear was part of her rationalization that she needed to rest her mind, as if she were storing up mental energy to use later. When she found out that she had to use mental energy now to sharpen her brain, there was a marked shift in her perspective. She became far less resistant to my suggestions. Over the course of the next several months she engaged in a variety of mentally challenging activities and became less surprised that her mind/brain was capable of vigorous change. I was very pleased that she looked and sounded so much healthier and in fact exuded a wonderful sense of enthusiasm for learning. At our last session she said with a laugh, "I can't believe I am saying this, but there is simply not enough time to learn about all the things I want to know!"

Education Factor Questionnaire

Yes No

☐ ☐ Do you think that having earned a college degree insulates you from the need for continued learning?

☐ ☐ If you have a stressful job or life experiences, do you think it best to stay away from taxing your brain?

☐ ☐ When you engage in learning experiences, do you generally stay with the subject matter with which you are familiar?

☐ ☐ Do you regard passive learning such as watching an educational show on television as valuable as active learning that requires a sustained effort?

☐ ☐ Do you shy away from nonfiction books because they are too dry?

☐ ☐ Do you regard games such as chess as far too complicated and intimidating?

☐ ☐ Do you regarding thinking as cognitive exercise?

☐ ☐ Are structured learning experiences such as classes and seminars too much of a bother?

☐ ☐ When you travel, do you go to areas you already have visited many times?

☐ ☐ Do you know as much as you need to know already?

If you answered yes to any of these questions, you are unnecessarily limiting your brain's ability to thrive and build cognitive reserve.

Richard's Education Lift

As a retired physician, Richard had a comfortable pension. He had achieved many of his goals, even rising to the position of physician in chief of the medical center where we both worked. He was surprised that he didn't feel positive and sharp, but he did not. He spent a good deal of time on the golf course with a tight group of friends. His diet and sleep were within normal health limits. What was missing? he wondered. Through his extensive contacts at the hospital, he had a complete medical work-up. Nothing stood out that could explain his mental dulling and weakened memory.

He came to see me because of my integrative approach and knew that I would not look for psychological causes without considering all health-related factors. At our first session he said, "I've got everything going for me and nothing dragging me down, at least psychologically. With your neuropsychological background I thought you might shed some light on what might be going on. I don't want to go to one of our neurologists; I need a fine-grain assessment. I haven't had a stroke or have Alzheimer's disease; at least I hope not."

Richard and I had collaborated in the past a few times with patients whose diagnoses were muddy at best, and we had been able to tease out a clear picture of the problem.

I gave him a few neuropsychological screening tests and factored in his educational level—this is referred to as the premorbid level of functioning—and the results were unremarkable. What was remarkable was that before his retirement he had managed to deal well with a fairly high level of cognitive challenge. Now he was essentially doing very little cognitively.

"True," he said, as if to say "So what?"

"Think of it as if you once were an athlete and now you haven't even been to the gym in a year. Wouldn't your muscles atrophy?'

"The brain is not a muscle," he retorted.

"Speaking metaphorically, it still does operate in a use it or lose it manner."

"Look, I'm tired. I did my bit. What are you suggesting that I do?"

"Cognitive exercise would keep your brain in shape and keep it sharp."

He sighed. "I've never been one to read books. You know what they do to you in med school and in premed undergrad for that matter; they narrow the frame and kill the excitement for learning."

"Maybe it's time to get excited."

"That's for you PhDs."

"Richard, if you had only a GED, we would be talking about your brain. You don't need only to earn a high degree for cognitive reserve; you still need to keep on learning." I went on to describe the concept of cognitive reserve and brought up the Nun Study to drive home the point that lifelong education is one of the pillars of brain health. "You get the greatest boost by learning things you previously knew nothing about, say, a language, and chart into areas that are a little unsettling."

"I guess you're saying that though I may be out on the golf course, I need not be out to pasture."

"There you go."

Increasing Cognitive Longevity

Higher education levels are associated with longevity and brain health. According to the Study of Adult Development, among people in the general population who reach age 60, only one-third will live past 80. In contrast, over two-thirds (70 percent) of college-educated people alive at age 60 will live past age 80.

It is generally the case that people who are more highly educated are more likely to take care of themselves in terms of diet and exercise and have better access to healthcare. It also is reasonable to say that the more highly educated are more aware of what lifestyle practices are important to stay healthy.

A study funded by the MacArthur Foundation Network on successful aging found that education was the most powerful predictor of cognitive vigor in old age. The longest-running longitudinal study on aging, the Harvard Grant Study, found that education was one of the principal factors in successful aging: living longer not only with fewer physical problems but with fewer mental deficits.[1]

A variety of other factors are associated with longevity and education. As was noted in Chapter 2, shorter telomere length is associated with accelerated aging. A study of 450 civil servants age 53 to 76 that was performed by researchers at University College London found that telomere length was correlated with level of education. In other words, lower educational attainment was found to be associated with shorter telomere length.[2]

Robert Katzman of Albert Einstein College of Medicine was one of the first to show that educated people are less likely to succumb to the effects of dementia.[3] Education provides protective effects against the symptoms of dementia. Several studies suggest that more highly educated or intellectually developed individuals have 35 to 40 percent less risk of manifesting dementia, including Alzheimer's disease.[4] Among those with Alzheimer's disease the brain pathology will still occur, but the symptoms will not be as evident. When the brains of highly educated individuals are examined at autopsy, evidence of plaques and tangles is found. What is astounding is that up to 20 percent of the people who did not present with any significant problems in their daily lives had full-blown Alzheimer's pathology in their brains. Those individuals functioned in later life at a high capacity because of the brain-protective effects of education.

A study reported in the *New England Journal of Medicine* that examined the leisure activities of seniors over a 20-year period found that those who engaged in more mental activities were less likely to develop the symptoms of dementia. Those who engaged in one mental activity a week reduced the risk of dementia by 7 percent. The reduction in risk for dementia shot up to 63 percent for those who participated in more mental activities frequently. Thus, people who engage in higher numbers of cognitively stimulating activities lower their risk of developing Alzheimer's disease symptoms. For each additional type of cognitive activity the risks are lowered by 8 to 38 percent.[5] Approximately 10 percent of brains examined in autopsy will show evidence of Alzheimer's disease, including the characteristic plaques and tangles. In contrast, those examined who had higher levels of academic achievement are less likely to demonstrate cognitive decline even with Alzheimer's pathology evident in the brain.[6]

What is it about education that extends the life of the brain? There is a critically important factor that makes education a factor in extending life of the brain. Just as Christine discovered that education provides a powerful antidote to feeling mentally dull, neuroscience has shown that it is a critical factor in brain health. Education sharpens the mind/brain in a use it or lose it way. Learning over a period of time builds the brain like a muscle mass. Muscles that are not used will atrophy, and the brain must be exercised to strengthen it.

Education boosts your wealth of synaptic connections. The more synaptic connections you have developed, the more you can lose without also losing cognitive competency because of the abundance of connections in reserve. That is what is meant by the term *cognitive reserve*, your insurance policy for brain longevity. Think of it this way: cognitive exercise spurs neuroplasticity and increases synaptic connections, giving you greater brain reserve to withstand any neurological loss. To use a sports analogy, you have a bigger bench to draw from if players on the field are injured so that your team can continue playing without apparent loss. From a bottom line perspective, the more you have, the more you can lose without functioning at a deficit.

Building cognitive reserve requires neuroplasticity and neurogenesis. Each of your 100 billion neurons maintains on average 10,000 synaptic connections with other neurons. As was described in Chapter 2, neuroplasticity involves making, strengthening, and establishing new synaptic connections. Cognitive reserve therefore involves establishing dense and elaborate systems of synaptic connections that grow and strengthen as a result of your efforts to expand your mind. Cognitive reserve gives your brain the power to stay sharp as you age. You are not born with cognitive reserve. You must build it by engaging in cognitive exercise. A wide variety of international studies have demonstrated that people can be trained to build brain reserve through cognitive exercise.

The great benefits of exercising your brain by learning to maintain its strength are most evident if you sustain a brain injury, a stroke, or even dementia. Neurological rehabilitation at medical centers such as the one where I work involves various types of cognitive rehabilitation, which can include attention training and speech therapy. Though you don't grow back damaged cells, you can build new circuits of synaptic connections through compensatory neuroplasticity. For example, Fred had a stroke in his left hemisphere and had a great deal of difficulty moving his limbs on the right side of his body; this occurred because the brain's motor movement functions control the opposite side of the body. Because language is generally controlled by the left hemisphere, Fred will probably have aphasia (inability to find words to express—called Broca's aphasia— or understand what is being said—called Wernicke's aphasia). He will also have difficulty moving the right side of his body. If he is a right-hander, he may now favor his left hand and give up the use of his right hand. His rehabilitation will include speech therapy so that he can develop compensatory neuroplasticity to rewire his language skills. Also, his now good hand (the left) will be tied down in limb restraint therapy so that he will be forced to use his right hand and rewire the movement circuits. Despite being extraordinarily clumsy initially, he will eventually rewire his movement circuits.

Beyond injury or stroke, you can use the same neuroplasticity and neurogenesis processes to build greater cognitive reserve. You will have more brain power in reserve to keep you sharper than you would be if you had not built up the cognitive reserve. In other words, building cognitive reserve promotes brain longevity and cushions your brain from the wear and tear of injury and disease.

Cognitive reserve research has been conducted for half a century. Initially done with animals, principally rats, these studies, referred to as *enrichment* studies, demonstrated that animals that have been treated to stimulating environments enhance their brains. They boost the production of new brain cells, both the gray matter (the neurons) and the white matter (the glial cells). The new neurons show up especially in the hippocampus and the occipital lobes. There is also production of new blood cell vessels and brain-derived neurotrophic factor (Miracle-Gro) as well as specific neurotransmitters such as serotonin and acetylcholine.[7]

Lifelong learning is neuroprotective as a result of the power of neuroplasticity and the cognitive reserve that is gained. Studies that show enrichment to the adult human brain have focused on a wide variety of cognitive activities. For example, Ian Robertson, a neuroscientist from Trinity College Dublin, reported that among approximately 3,000 people ages 65 to 94, those given 10 hours of brain training in memory, problem-solving, and decision-making tasks over the course of several weeks showed significant and lasting improvements in their cognitive ability. One year later the participants were given booster sessions that resulted in further improvement in mental functioning that was equivalent to that typically lost to older people over a 7- to 14-year period. As Robertson put it, "The training on average took about a decade off the cognitive age of these volunteers."

The famed Nun Study described a classic example of cognitive reserve. The Sisters of Notre Dame of Mankato, Minnesota, were known for their longevity and remarkable absence of dementia. The nuns regularly engaged in many cognitive exercises, including debating current events, puzzles, and card games.[8] Although as a group they were cognitively ahead of the norm, within the group, health differences corresponded to level of education. Those with college degrees who taught school generally lived longer than did the less educated nuns.

The Nun Study also examined their cognitive abilities over a lifetime. Since the convent records contained autobiographies of the nuns written when they were in their twenties, those writings were examined and rated for their grammatical complexity and conceptual richness. The nuns who had written more complex autobiographies were more likely to retain their cognitive vigor for much longer.

Sister Mary, the star of the Nun Study, lived until age 101 and was bright, well educated, and mentally active. She performed very well on cognitive tests right before her death, yet an autopsy revealed that she had multiple neurofibrillary tangles and plaques, the hallmarks of Alzheimer's disease. She apparently had enough cognitive reserve to avoid showing obvious symptoms of cognitive decline compared with other people with the same level of neurological impairment. Sister Mary provided a vivid example of cognitive reserve. She challenged her brain with intellectual and social stimulation and remained sharp.

As Sister Mary demonstrated, cognitive exercise must not be narrow to obtain robust benefits to the brain. To use a body-building analogy, if you spend all of your weight-lifting effort building your biceps, all your other muscles will atrophy and only your biceps will increase in strength. In the case of your brain, focusing your intellectual efforts on one skill or subject area promotes a narrow focus that will boost your brain's talents on that skill or subject area only. Your ability to remember information about that subject area will improve, but if you broaden your focus, you will achieve a robust brain workout.

Cognitive reserve is boosted by novel and complex experiences. Let's say you are interested in the architecture of the missions in California. A narrow focus on the structure of the roofs would be a limited exercise. But if you explore in depth the historical development of Spanish missions in California, pursuing the historical chain of events and associated architectural styles, you will cognitively stimulate the broad-based associations that build wider networks of synaptic connections in the brain. Your cognitive exercise should be perpetually covering new ground, expanding your knowledge in areas about which you previously knew nothing. In this way, you are building new neural connections, not simply strengthening the old ones by learning more details about the architecture of missions you already know. When you expand that body of knowledge by exploring the historical developments in the world at the same time, you build a vastly more complex network of synaptic connections.

My Personal Experience

I have been fortunate to know firsthand several friends and relatives who personify cognitive reserve. When I was a child, my 80-year-old maternal grandfather came to live with us because of a health issue. Even during his last weeks of life he sat up in bed with a magnifying glass, searching the dictionary in an effort to learn six new words each day. He had already gained fluency in five languages and transcended the traumatic loss of his first wife and child during the Armenian genocide. He considered education the key to success in life, and every significant conversation I had with him centered on the power of education. Although he knew little about the brain, he did know that education was the means by which to transcend whatever he had previously endured.

My father also was a great example of someone who had highly developed cognitive reserve. After he graduated from law school, for the next 60 years he continued to take college classes each year in subjects as diverse as geology, oceanography, and art history. He had earned the equivalent of two more college degrees by the time of his death, at which point he was a graduate student in painting. Every year he would go to Paris for one month, spending one week in the Louvre. He would also go to the Picasso Museum, for which I would often tease him by saying, "Dad, I thought you told me that you don't like Picasso's work."

He would respond by saying, "I don't."

"Then why do you go?"

"Because it's interesting."

The fact that he would go to a museum devoted to an artist whose work he did not enjoy but found interesting demonstrates a critical point about cognitive reserve. If you try to understand, appreciate, and/or explore subjects you are unfamiliar with or perhaps don't even like, you broaden your cognitive reserve. This is the case because by learning to appreciate and understand things that push your attention into a foreign field, you force your brain to build new synaptic connections. Like building new bridges and roads into unexplored areas, your brain builds new networks. Just like traveling into a foreign country, you need to be alert and push yourself out of familiar territory.

Having visited the Picasso Museum with my father twice, I could see that he was not comfortable and appeared to strain to grasp Picasso's later works. He was quite comfortable with Impressionism, especially Renoir, and even Picasso during his Blue Period. By the time Picasso's work entered the Cubist period, my father's comfort level was shattered, just like the broken-up forms in Cubist paintings. But Picasso and Braque had possibly intended that people like my father would be provoked to stand before the paintings and attempt to weave together a sense of order in what appeared to be disorder, providing a means of challenging the brain to move out of its comfort zone to build more complexity—more synaptic connections and therefore more cognitive reserve.

Attending to Attention

Attention and memory skills are essential for building cognitive reserve. Short-term memory is only one of many facets of a range of cognitive skills. In 1956 the imminent psychologist George Miller's landmark article "The Magic of Number Seven, Plus or Minus Two: Some Limits on Our Capacity for Processing Information" contained in the title the central point that there is an inherent limit to the brain's capacity to hold information in mind. He noted that it is no accident that we have Seven Wonders of the World, seven notes on the musical scale, and seven ages of man, not to mention seven digits in telephone numbers.

As you age, one of the areas of your brain that tends to atrophy is the dorsolateral prefrontal cortex, which is involved in attention and working memory. When you walk into a room to get your keys, you are working on a goal. But if you find yourself in the room without any idea why, you have experienced a temporary glitch in working memory. Perhaps on your way to the room someone asks a question and you reply; then, as you walk into the room, your working memory has lost what you were working on because of the distraction. This type of event is actually quite common.

Working memory refers to your ability to remember information for up to 20 to 30 seconds so that you can follow a task to completion. You need to hold and manipulate the immediate details of the task in your mind so that you can work on the task to complete it. Because getting distracted can get you off task, working memory is critical for controlling attention. After reading an earlier draft of this chapter, my wife created and now adheres to a policy she calls "30 seconds." When she is working and someone interrupts her, she will say, "Thirty seconds," indicating that she will not respond for that period of time and thus ensuring the focus needed to remember a multitude of details.

Alan Baddeley, one of the principal researchers on the topic, states, "The term working memory refers to a brain system that provides temporary storage and manipulation of information necessary for such complex cognitive tasks as language comprehension, learning, and reasoning."[9] In contrast to long-term memory, in which synaptic connections are permanently altered with the production of new proteins, working memory is temporary and provides an immediate method of storing information through patterns of electrical activity that can be established in a matter of milliseconds. The more activity and the stronger those connections, the better the working memory. These patterns of activity can also be disrupted when you lose track of what you were working on, for example, when someone engages you in conversation when you are trying to complete a task.

Whereas simple short-term memory merely involves the retention and repetition of information such as a string of numbers, working memory incorporates short-term memory tasks but goes beyond that by requiring manipulation of the information while you are enduring some form of distraction or demands for a degree of simultaneous performance. Working memory can be described as the ability to keep information and its associated neural activity online while you manipulate it for a short period.

For all these reasons working memory has a high correlation with general intelligence and especially what has been called *fluid intelligence*.[10] Fluid intelligence involves processing speed and the ability to manipulate concepts or information in the mind to discover a solution. Doing mathematical problems in the mind, not on paper, taps into fluid intelligence and relies on working memory.

As we age, the speed of processing information and reaction time slow. Simultaneously, sensory input, such as hearing and vision, also tends to slow. Together with some atrophy in the dorsolateral prefrontal cortex, the capacity to stay focused and flexible slows. It takes more effort to tune out distractions and stay focused. Thus, adapting to new environments, problem solving in novel situations, and maintaining dexterity and flexibility while trying to stay focused also becomes more difficult.

As a result of these losses, fluid intelligence tends to decline with age. In contrast, crystallized intelligence does not appear to decline with age. It involves long-term memory of facts and gaining general knowledge. This is why crystallized intelligence grows with age: we accumulate more facts and information the longer we live.

Aging results in an increase in crystallized intelligence during middle age, whereas there is a waning of fluid intelligence, partly because of the simultaneous waning of working memory skills from age 30 with a more pronounced decline after age 60. In fact, the working memory skills of an average 60-year-old are similar to those of the average 12-year-old. Though with aging there is a general retention of crystallized intelligence related to language skills and facts, after around age 80 many people have increasing difficulty understanding long, complex sentences. This problem is partly related to the slowing of processing speed and attention.

With the age-related decline in working memory and related fluid intelligence, it is increasingly difficult to keep from being distracted. Throughout the day we are exposed to a huge amount of stimuli and need a way to filter out the distractions so that we can effectively attend to what is important. This spam filter requires increased activity in the prefrontal cortex and the basal ganglia. People with higher activation in these areas tend to have better working memory. The ability to control your attention is essential as you drive down the highway so that you don't get distracted by the spam of billboards, which threatens to grab your attention and could result in a fatal accident.

Things can get more complicated when the distraction becomes social and emotional. Imagine walking to the grocery store to buy the ingredients for a meal you plan to prepare for a dinner party that evening. As you enter the store, you realize you left the list of ingredients at home. Then you encounter a friend who is not on your guest list who engages you in conversation as you try to reconstruct the list of ingredients and shop and talk at the same time. How likely is it you will forget one or more ingredients as a result of the distraction? Very likely.

Controlled attention and stimulus-driven attention represent two parallel systems of attention. You use controlled attention when you consciously direct your attention to a task such as trying to remember what is on your store list. In contrast, you use stimulus-driven attention when you are involuntarily attracted to an unexpected event in your environment such as meeting your friend as you are trying to remember what to buy at the store.

Most people are able to engage in a conversation with one person at a party and filter out the chatter of the other people. Yet the "cocktail party effect" can occur while you are talking to one person and hear someone else mention your name; then you direct your attention to the gossip and away from the person you had been talking with initially. The degree of potential distractibility represents the dynamic tension between the controlled attention system and the stimulus-driven attention system as you direct your attention back to the person with whom you were talking unless the stimulus-driven attention system takes over. Research has shown that one in three people find themselves distracted by the cocktail party situation. Those people who also have the lowest working memory capacity are especially vulnerable to this situation.[11] Working memory fails when the information load exceeds the working memory capacity and the stimulus-driven system takes over. As a task becomes more demanding, so does the working memory load and the potential for the stimulus-driven system to take over. Thus, a person's ability to multitask is related to the degree of information load on working memory.

Talking on a cell phone while driving is a good example of the working memory load and being in the danger zone. Driving while using a cell phone is comparable to driving with a blood alcohol level above the legal limit. According to the Human Factors and Ergonomic Society, on average 5,600 deaths and 333,000 injuries are caused each year in the United States by drivers speaking on cell phones. In my state of California it is now illegal to talk on a cell phone while driving. Despite this, I still see people doing it all the time, in complete denial and thinking the proverbial "It would never happen to me." Each day as I turn onto the road to the medical center and my office, I notice a cross marking the location at that interaction where a person talking on a cell phone killed a motorcyclist.

Since attention and working memory represent the gateway to long-term memory, distractibility closes the gate to what we remember. Mature adults are more easily distracted than are younger adults. Using fMRI technology, Cheryl Grady, a neuroscientist at the University of Toronto, found that young adults had increased activity in the dorsolateral prefrontal cortex when asked to recall words or pictures they had just been shown, whereas activity in the default mode network associated with daydreaming decreased. Older adults, in contrast, used their dorsolateral prefrontal cortex somewhat less and the default mode network more.

You might ask yourself, Do I spend more time driving along in that state of highway hypnosis than I used to? In other words, do you find yourself driving and daydreaming, perhaps even missing the turn for the road you had intended to take? Are you spending more time "somewhere else," ruminating instead of being in the present moment? If the answer to these questions is yes, you are increasing the time you are spending in your default mode network and decreasing the time you are exercising your prefrontal cortex.

Can working memory improve with practice? To answer that question, Torkel Klingberg at the Aging Research Center at the Karolinska Institute in Stockholm trained young and old individuals to increase their working memory.[12] Observable changes were made in the multimodel "overlap" areas including the PFC and the intraparietalis sulcus, which have been identified as key areas associated with working memory.

In fact, over the last few years there has been an increasing amount of promising research demonstrating that people, including seniors, can be taught to improve their working memory skills. Some of these training programs have used computer programs, and others have emphasized meditation skills.

The recent popularity of a meditation practice called mindfulness represents one instance of focus on working memory. Training yourself to be completely saturated in the present moment exercises your attention skills and your dorsolateral prefrontal cortex, which as I noted earlier tends to atrophy somewhat with age. Mindfulness is an excellent way to teach yourself to be in the present. Most of us too often fade into our default mode network. Rarely are we where we are when we are here. We spend a great deal of time reflecting and even ruminating about the past or being overly concerned and even anxious about the future. Developing a keen talent for being in the present will actually help you code in long-term memories.

Extending Long-Term Memory

You have two broad-based long-term memory systems: implicit and explicit. Implicit memory is often called nondeclarative because it is nonconscious and thus cannot be declared. Procedural memory is one type of implicit memory that you "do" out of habit, like riding a bicycle or typing. Once you acquire the habit or learn how to balance yourself on the bicycle as you peddle or find the correct letter keys with your fingers when typing, you just do it without thinking about it or trying to recall the memories. That is what is meant by the term *implicit*; once it's been learned, it's implicitly there without your thinking about it or consciously declaring that it is there.

Procedural memories, such as how to play the violin or ride a bicycle, do not fade completely away with age. I remember that late in her life my mother picked up my mandolin and played it, having never played the mandolin before. Since it is fretted like a violin, which she did remember how to play, she "remembered" how to play the mandolin. The funny thing about that was that she had not played the violin in 40 years!

Interestingly, once you learn an implicit memory, your prefrontal cortex is no longer necessary for its recollection. In fact, when you also invite your PFC into the activity, the implicit procedural memory becomes impaired. For example, after riding a bicycle for most of your life, you may begin to wobble if you think too much about how to ride. Or when you type, when you try too hard to remember where the *r* or the *t* is on the keyboard, you may increase the chances of typos. Though I never had the audacity to try this, you can use this phenomenon to your advantage if you are losing badly in a game of tennis. You simply ask your opponent, "How is it that you serve so perfectly? Do you jump up six inches? Do you bend your elbow?"

You have invited his PFC into the game, and he will become more self-conscious. When he serves again, his attention is shifted to the details of his serve, which begins to falter, going wide or long or even hitting the net. Soon the score will even out!

Another type of implicit memory is referred to as emotional memory. You develop a particular feeling for being with a particular person or place. You feel that way with that person without remembering why. You can say your implicit memory is unconscious. Emotionally based implicit memory is governed by the amygdala.

The amygdala is essentially a relevance detector that retains the motivational value of events. It aids in the facilitation of attention toward emotionally significant stimuli. It orchestrates a wide range of physiological reactions and can turn on the fight-or-flight response.

Emotionally based implicit memory is at play when you see a person who draws out of you a particular behavior or emotion, an old habit that you learned when you were young or developed over a period when you were around people similar to that person. If one of those people stirred fear in you, the implicit memory can be encoded quite quickly. Whenever you are around that person or someone like her, you may feel anxious and perhaps "forget" why.

In contrast to implicit memory, explicit memory involves what you can consciously remember. Explicit memories are the types of memories you normally think of as memory. You can recall them or declare them, which is why it is also often called declarative memory. These memories include the names of people, places, and events in your life. They are facts, words, descriptions, and sequences of events or how you feel about a particular type of person.

We learned much about explicit memory from a man named Henry Molaison, who lost his explicit memory skills in 1954 after the surgical removal of his right and left hippocampus. Until his death in December 2008 he thought Eisenhower was the President. Every day was a new day for Henry. If you met him on Monday and came back on Tuesday, he thought he was meeting you for the first time.

The surgery was a treatment for seizures that steadily became worse after a traumatic brain injury from a bicycle accident when he was nine years old. By the time he was 27 his parents wanted to find a way to help him get permanent treatment for his seizures. Pioneered by Wilder Penfield, the treatment of the day was to surgically remove the areas of the brain that were seizing. If you find that bizarre, don't forget that lobotomies were still being performed. In fact, Antonio Moniz received the Nobel Prize for his discovery of the lobotomy technique. When Henry's parents took him to a neurosurgeon named William Scoville in Hartford, Connecticut, where they lived, he received the treatment of the day. Scoville, however, admitted later that during the surgery, when he was taking out Henry's left hippocampus, he thought, "I was already in there and thought I might as well take out his right hippocampus to see what would happen."

Scoville was alarmed to find that though Henry's seizures subsided, his explicit memory capacity disappeared. He sought out the opinion of Penfield, who was teaching and practicing in Montreal at the time. Penfield contacted Dr. Brenda Milner, a neuropsychologist, who would subsequently make monthly train trips to Harford to evaluate Henry by using various neuropsychological tests. Every time Henry met Dr. Milner, he thought he was meeting her for the first time. One day she brought another neuropsychologist who had a joke buzzer in his hand so that when they exchanged a handshake, the buzzer elicited a mutual laugh. The next day the two neuropsychologists came back. Henry again exchanged a courteous handshake with Dr. Milner as if meeting her for the first time. When the other neuropsychologist reached out to shake hands, Henry pulled his back. The man asked, "What's the matter? Have we met before?"

"No, I have never met you before in my life," Henry responded. Then he politely changed the subject. Henry had lost his explicit memory but retained his implicit memory. He had a feeling about the man but no knowledge why.

Henry's explicit memory had been fine before his surgery. This occurred because the hippocampi do not store memories. They help code explicit memories by coactivating neurons in the cortex. The more dispersed the activation of neurons in the cortex, the more robust the memories. In other words, the more associations you make for a particular memory, the better the chance you have of remembering it later. When the dispersed clusters of neurons fire together, often the memory is stronger. This is why people studying for exams should begin early and study on a regular basis. Once the memories are strengthened in the cortex, there is less need for hippocampal input unless new memories are made and associated with those already acquired on the subject. The hippocampus is needed temporarily to bind together distributed sites in the neocortex that together represent a whole memory. It is like a librarian, an index to the database of memory.

The hippocampus is also a novelty detector that compares incoming information to stored knowledge; if there is a difference, dopamine levels increase. Its specialty is binding new to old information, and it ceases to play a role in the retention of a specific memory after about two years.

The hippocampus and amygdala often work together to create complex memories with explicit and implicit components. For its part the amygdala is a relevance detector and aids in the facilitation of attention toward emotionally significant stimuli. It generates emotionally driven reactions to relevant events in your life and orchestrates a wide range of physiological responses. Since attention is critical to the coding of new memory, a moderate degree of amygdala activation works best to facilitate neuroplasticity and the new memory. The "inverted U" represents how too little stimulation (e.g., boredom) or too much stimulation (e.g., trauma) conflicts with the coding of new memory. Picture the inverted U as an upside-down U. At the high point in the middle, it illustrates an optimum level of stimulation for brain activity.

Too much stress disrupts the prefrontal cortex, and too little stress (activation) bores you and your prefrontal cortex stays offline. A moderate amount of stress is optimal and turns on the prefrontal cortex.

There is a neurochemistry of the inverted U function. A moderate level of norepinephrine is needed to turn on the prefrontal cortex and consolidate memory. Insufficient norepinephrine will fail to optimally activate the prefrontal cortex, and too much takes the prefrontal cortex offline. This is one of the reasons you remember your vacation and forget about the preceding two months.

When your amygdala and your hippocampus work together, your memories become more lasting. Consider flashbulb memories. It is rare to find a person who does not remember what she was doing on 9/11, but it is extremely common for people to have forgotten what they were doing the preceding two months. In multiple presentations not only in the United States but throughout the world I have asked people to raise their hands if they did not remember what they were doing on that horrible day. In Perth, Australia, for example, not 1 person out of 100 attending my seminar raised his hand. The same result took place in South Africa. In both cases, however, when asked about memories of the two months leading up to 9/11 no one raised his or her hand, indicating that they had forgotten what the audience were doing the preceding two months.

Unless you had personally significant experiences during those preceding two months such as having a grandchild, taking a life-changing vacation, or having a close friend or relative die, your amygdala did not code those months as particularly significant. But 9/11 was different. The alarm rang not only in New York City but all over the world as we all experienced significant amygdala activation and our prefrontal cortexes sharpened their attention on what was going on, exploring the many potential consequences.

Apparently, for most people the preceding months did not mean much to the amygdala and therefore to the hippocampus. But on 9/11 things were different. The hippocampus for its part was activated by the novelty, and increased activation ramped up the amygdala and the corresponding neurochemistry. Our working memory increased through heightened prefrontal cortex activation.

Too much activation impairs memory, as is the case with trauma. Most of the people at ground zero on 9/11 did not forget the horrific events of the day, but their memory of the events may be fragmented and perhaps even disorganized. At times their prefrontal cortexes were focused only on what to do to stay safe, not the details of the many events occurring in New York City at the time that did not relate to their safety.

You certainly do not need a 9/11 to get your amygdala and hippocampus to work together, but you do need to get excited about what you want to learn. For example, long ago, when I took the psychology licensing exam, I knew I had to pass because my wife and I were soon to have a baby. After the birth I would lose all hope of having time to study. During the mid-1980s there was a 26 percent pass rate, so I needed to do something intense to ensure my chances of passing. I needed also to maximize the inverted U. If I'd procrastinated and studied at the last minute, I would have been unprepared for the exam; my prefrontal cortex would have been turned off because I was too overwhelmed with anxiety related to the possibility of not passing. In that case, the sympathetic branch of the autonomic nervous system would have been in hyperdrive and in the fight-or-flight mode, with my brain flooded with stress chemicals such as adrenaline, norepinephrine, and cortisol.

Norepinephrine and epinephrine (adrenaline) play a central role in encoding and consolidating memories by the amygdala. A moderate level of these catecholamines and the inverted U is optimal for full-spectrum memories. Too little activation (e.g., boredom) results in not enough attention and no consolidation of memories. Too much activation of these stress neurochemicals narrows attention to the threat or danger at the expense of attention to the rest of the world.

Because PhD holders are trained to be the scientists, the exam at the time had a heavy emphasis on statistics, research design, and test construction, and so I knew I had to get my amygdala involved and convince myself that I loved statistics instead of considering it what some people have called "sadistics." My attitude shifted to generate thoughts and questions such as, "Have you seen the formula for the standard error of estimate? It is divine!" I would carry pieces of paper with the formulas in my pocket in case I had a moment while standing in a supermarket checkout line to gaze at those exquisite formulas. Through my focused attention, my amygdala helped me bathe in this bliss of the mathematical formulas, and my hippocampus got the boost it needed to code them into memory material. You may wonder if I still remember the formulas. Well, actually I went back to baseline. After acing the exam, I never had to use those formulas again; however, I certainly remember how to code and "recollect" a memory. You strengthen memories when you get your amygdala and hippocampus to team up, making what you want to remember emotionally relevant.

Aging results in mild amygdala atrophies, in fact, between 2 and 20 percent depending on the study. For healthy adults, MRI studies show an average of 7 percent reduction of the size of the amygdala compared with healthy young adults. The reduction is greatest after age 60, which results in a decreasing tendency to overreact in favor of taking life more in stride. For its part the hippocampus is particularly vulnerable to the neurotoxic effects of obesity, diabetes, hypertension, sleep apnea, and high levels of cortisol. Patients with Alzheimer's disease incur a 14 to 60 percent reduction in their hippocampi. Along with the hippocampus and the entorhinal cortex, there are significant plaques and tangles.

As noted in Chapter 2, one of the best ways to stimulate neurogenesis in the hippocampus is aerobic exercise. New neurons can be developed in the dentate gyrus of the hippocampus, spurred on by brain-derived neurotrophic factor, which is released after an episode of aerobic exercise. It is best to engage in cognitive exercise after the physical exercise.

Improving Your Memory Skills

If you are like most people, as you get a little older, the name of a person, a place, or even a movie evades you. The phenomenon known as tip of the tongue (TOT) is well known by people advancing in age. The TOT phenomenon is a problem of retrieval of memories that are dispersed in different parts of the brain, such as the sound of your boss's name, the shape of a letter, and the meaning of a name. As you age, the connections weaken between the areas of the brain where the memories are stored.

The TOT phenomenon occurs not because you lose neurons that encode specific words but because connections representing the associations between words are lost. To remember a word, you may have to resort to circumlocution, which involves using several words to describe the word you are looking for, such as "It's that utensil that I use to eat my cereal" because "spoon" is on the tip of the tongue.

The names of people who you just met may be subject to the TOT phenomenon because names can be quite arbitrary, as they often don't provide associations to other memories. The name of your mechanic, Frank, has little meaning by itself and may be subject to the TOT problem in your attempt to remember it. The more associations you make with his name and his characteristics, the greater the probability is that you will remember his name. For example, you might associate his name with his honest, straightforward, and frank manner when he tells you about needed car repairs.

Memory improvement techniques maximize associations and necessitate neuroplasticity, as cells that fire together wire together to form memories. The more associations that you make to code in a memory, the more robust that memory is. This is true for implicit and explicit memory. The more complex the memory, the greater the chance of recalling it later.

Though physical exercise is very good for brain health and cognition, it generally does not improve memory by itself. For a boost in memory capacity and improved specific cognitive abilities you need physical and mental exercise. To create observable neuroplastic change in the brain, the new learning must include tasks that are of sufficient difficulty and increase in the level of difficulty after one masters the initial level. The learning should intensify in terms of learning sessions per day as well as per week. Think of the analogy of body building. To build muscles you need to lift more weight than you thought possible. You must include three repetitions of lifts at least three times per week and do all this for several weeks before you see any results. Though physical exercise is very good for brain health and cognition, it generally does not improve memory by itself. For a boost in memory, capacity-directed cognitive training—mental exercise—improves not only specific cognitive abilities but also memory.

When you perform a task, say, a particular series of commands on the computer, the more you involve multiple brain systems in performing that task, the greater the chance of a good result. Most important, those brain systems are the very ones you will later use when you perform the computer command on your own. There are a variety of facts that you should keep in mind when you try to improve your memory:

- Meaningful events that are rare are more easily remembered than are repetitive and random events.
- Intentional learning is better than learning from incidental events.
- Your memory recall is better for actions than for thoughts.
- Information that you generate is learned better than if you read or hear it. Therefore, learning a task with guidance serves you better than simply observing someone as she shows you how it's done. This is the concept behind on-the-job training. Memory is better if you perform a task rather than watch someone else do it or read about it. Passively observing barely activates the prefrontal cortex. Motivation is key.

- Actively discovering information that you wish to remember moves the information from out there to inside your brain.
- Pictures and mental images are remembered better than are words. This is the case because as primates we have emphasized sight, in contrast to rodents and dogs, which have emphasized smell.
- Memory improves the second time you learn something. Memory improves when the same information is encountered frequently.
- Concrete information is remembered better than abstract information.
- Positive information is remembered better than negative (Pollyanna effect) except in the case of sudden or negative trauma. Even in the case of frightening memories, what is remembered is the danger, not other aspects of the environment.
- Memory improves for rare and novel information.
- You can't code anything into long-term memory without attention and working memory. Attention is the gateway to memory.
- Emotional engagement improves memory because the amygdala becomes involved with the hypothalamus. Get emotionally involved in what you attempt to learn.
- Novelty snaps you out of autopilot and alerts the prefrontal cortex and hippocampus to a new situation or new idea.
- Associations make connections between one idea and another. The more associations, the more complex and durable the memory.
- Elaborative rehearsal works better than rote memory as you try to memorize something. The more associations and added dimensions to the memory, the more robust the memory.
- Read–recite–review–read again works well because repetition and varied methods of recall help develop neuroplasticity.

Here are a few factoids to entertain people at a party. Chewing gum leads to a 35 percent improvement in memory because it raises the heart rate and increases blood flow to the brain. Doodlers recall 7.5 names and places—29 percent more than the average 5.8 remembered by people who are not doodlers.

Exercise Your Brain

Boosting cognitive reserve is an active, not a passive process. Watching television and other passive activities show no benefits; in fact, passive activities contribute to cognitive loss. I call watching television dead time because unless you are watching an informative program, your mind is barely conscious. There is nothing to do intellectually, no challenge. Watching television is essentially vicarious living. A little is okay, but it should not be a staple part of your life as it was for Christine, whom you met at the beginning of this chapter. Just as ice cream is not part of every meal, a little TV can be a periodic treat. When you choose a program ahead of time and don't just watch whatever is on, television can be a noncorrosive part of your life.

Studies have shown that elders who have engaged in at least one intellectual activity a day will reduce cognitive decline by 7 percent. For those in the top third of intellectual activity, there is a 63 percent diminished risk of cognitive decline.[13]

Some computer-based cognitive training programs have been shown to boost cognitive reserve in the elderly. For example, one study included 10 sessions with 4 booster sessions and was shown to slow age-related decline for over five years.[14] The brains of older individuals who engage in cognitive conditioning show evidence of neuroplasticity on fMRI enhancement.[15]

Researchers from the Netherlands Institute for Brain Research in Amsterdam have proposed that activation of specific brain areas throughout life may prevent or delay degeneration in those parts of the brain.[16] This could occur by working in a specific occupation or engaging in a lifelong hobby. Yet increasing "cognitive fitness" entails using a systemic cognitive exercise program that involves most of the brain. Comprehensive cognitive fitness effort can actually serve to help keep the brain fit.

In a study called the Einstein Aging Study performed by Joe Verghese and colleagues at the Albert Einstein College of Medicine, over 400 senior citizens were observed for an average of five years.[17] The subjects were asked to take a cognitive test and describe their leisure activities, which included board games (chess), golf, dancing, power walking, and a wide range of other activities. The researchers found that chess, reading, playing a musical instrument, and dancing were all associated with later improved cognitive abilities and a lower risk of dementia. These activities had to be done several times a week to achieve cognitive reserve. Intensity and frequency were also important. Engaging in activities just once or twice a week did not result in a positive effect. However, if the subjects engaged in eight or more cognitive activities/mental exercises a week, their risk of developing dementia was cut in half. Chess was the activity with the most significant training effect, tapping into exercise of the working memory. To play chess well you must think several moves ahead. Reading complex material also requires working memory and has a positive cognitive-boosting effect. But the most popular cognitive exercise, crossword puzzles, had a barely statistically significant positive effect. Doing crossword puzzles represents a cognitive activity rather than cognitive exercise.

Cognitive exercise that builds brain reserve requires mental stimulation that involves variety, challenge, and novelty. The best strategy is to experience a cognitive workout circuit, similar to a physical workout in which you exercise as many parts of the body as possible. Cognitive exercise therefore should not be specialized; it should focus on a variety of cognitive skills. Challenge should involve increasing levels of difficulty so that the task never becomes too easy or routine. You need to get out of your routine comfort zone.

Finally, novelty involves trying new things to activate the prefrontal cortex and hippocampus to open the gate for new learning.

Complex mental activities require effort to be fully engaged, whereas cognitive activity that is relatively simple is not a mental exercise because it demands little engagement and effort. If it is rote and passive, such as a hobby that you have practiced for years and now describe by saying, "I've got the hang of this," there is little if any new learning occurring and therefore no brain building.

Mental activity (i.e., just thinking) is not the same as mental exercise. Everyone thinks, but not everyone trains his brain by mental exercise. Brain training/mental exercise involves the structured use of cognitive exercises or techniques. Mental activity is analogous to doing a crossword puzzle. This is why completing a crossword puzzled demands a relatively narrow range of cognitive skills and as a result stimulates only a limited range of brain regions. An increased amount of experience doing crossword puzzles does not modify the effects of age as measured in tasks requiring reasoning and vocabulary.[18] Mental exercise—brain training—requires a variety of mentally challenging tasks to stimulate the whole brain.

In addition to all the challenges of aging, there are also cognitive gains resulting from a lifelong accumulated body of knowledge that gives us a broad-based perspective on what is important and what is not, enabling us to prioritize our actions and calm down to face a challenge. We also can gain a greater appreciation of our interdependence with others, enhancing our sense of empathy and insight. These skills collectively have been called wisdom.

As we age, we accumulate an increasing number of cognitive templates, which are essentially perspectives on and knowledge of how the world operates. This accumulated knowledge involves a stronger emphasis on pattern recognition than on problem solving. Pattern recognition is a function of the left hemisphere. As a result, there is an increasing reliance on the left hemisphere and a corresponding decreasing reliance on the right hemisphere as we get older.

Creativity and embracing novelty are interdependent. Since novelty is a skill of the right hemisphere, creativity disproportionally involves the right hemisphere. But it would be too simplistic and overly dichotomized to say that there is no left hemisphere involvement in creativity when one is performing creative acts. Familiarity and pattern perception, which are largely left-hemisphere skills, can complement creative acts with details by making them relevant to what we have known and by building on those familiar patterns in the same way a writer uses her rich vocabulary to craft eloquent prose.

Many middle-aged people accumulate knowledge over an entire career and gain a wider perspective. This recognition of gaining knowledge and perspective is valuable. I have made that transition myself, from psychologist to chief psychologist to training director at one medical center to director of training for 24 medical centers. My father transitioned from district attorney to judge. The village elder illustrates the same concept. Once a warrior or farmer, he transformed into a chief, shaman, or village elder to contribute to the community a perspective from his crystallized knowledge.

I have been a lifelong traveler, spending time in approximately 50 countries. I hope to travel to another 50 before I die. Thus, I am personally very pleased to report that traveling promotes brain health. Travel takes us out of our comfort zone and demands that we adapt to new environments. We must make complex decisions that are based on unfamiliar information and interact with people who often do not speak the same language. Traveling to third world countries, which I personally gain the most from, serves as a major wake-up call to acknowledge how easy we have it back home.

Some people benefit from structured programs such as Elderhostel and Osher Lifelong Learning, which offer intellectually driven activities to hundreds of thousands of people. Simultaneously, equal numbers of people are enrolling in university classroom classes as part of their retirement. One of the many benefits of these programs is that they provide the structure and expectation to show up and therefore minimize the chances that you will procrastinate. Structure that includes regularly scheduled classes adds repetition for building in synaptic connections as cells that wire together fire together in the future. Also, because most classes introduce the most rudimentary information and then build more complex information onto that foundation, they build in a broad knowledge base.

To apply the education factor of the formula try these suggestions:

Take a class in a subject in which you have limited knowledge.

Join a book club that assigns nonfiction books.

Learn to play chess and play it often.

Engage in working memory exercises.

Travel to foreign countries, especially in the third world.

Learn to play a musical instrument.

Learn another language.

Take in a museum on a regular basis.

Go to community lectures on a wide range of subjects.

CHAPTER 4

The Diet Factor

From the first moment I saw Scott in the waiting room, it was evident that he had a problem of his own making. He carried a large belly, and his skin looked pasty. During the intake interview he told me that he asked for the appointment because he thought he must be going through a "brain problem." "I just feel dull," he said.

He went on to say that his job of 40 years was "fine" and his relationship with his wife and two grown daughters was "great."

"Maybe it's a sort of male menopause," he said with a puzzled look.

Andropause, the male equivalent of menopause, is marked by a sharp drop in testosterone; by the late fifties a man has more estrogen than testosterone. Scott was 66 years old. Some men experience a much greater drop in testosterone than others. I had his primary care physician check his levels and do a broad-based blood panel. His thyroid levels were within normal levels as were the other measures that could account for those symptoms.

He complained of symptoms that sounded like mild depression by saying, "I should be feeling good, not like my life is ending. I have no energy, and at times I wonder if I've got an early form of

Alzheimer's. My wife and kids complain that I'm forgetful about little things and that I am cranky."

He completed one of our standard depression screening questionnaires, and though it appeared he had a mild depression, he was not suffering from what is called major depression.

One of the dominant themes that jumped out during my review of his daily habits was that his diet was deplorable. He started the day with two cups of coffee sweetened with two heaping spoonfuls of sugar and drank them on an empty stomach. When I asked about breakfast, he said, "Oh, no, I've never been a breakfast person. Besides, I've been trying to lose some weight."

By 10 a.m. he felt light-headed and could "hardly think." For lunch he usually had a hamburger with fries and an extra-large coke from the local McJack Jr.'s drive-through, which he actually did drive through despite the fact that it was only a block and a half away from his office. When I asked why he didn't walk there, he said, "That's just it; I'm too tired. Besides, I usually get the supersized lunch, and it's a pain to carry it back."

He admitted that he drank a few more cups of coffee with yet more sugar during the afternoon "because I'm even more exhausted and need everything I can get." Then he pulled a candy bar out of his pocket. "Sometimes I rely on these."

"How often is sometimes?"

He laughed. "I guess every day."

He told me that after he returns home from work he takes a nap "because I'm wasted; otherwise I don't have energy to sit down with the family for dinner." Then, after dinner, which usually consists of meat and potatoes, he sits in "his" chair in front of the TV and dozes off.

His wife had become so frustrated with his slothlike behavior that she refused to wake him up to go to bed in the evening after he fell asleep. This was the last straw for him and what prompted him to come to see me. When asked why he had not worked closely with his primary care physician, he said, "He told me to lose weight and stop drinking."

He had done me a favor by offering a segue into my next series of questions, which involved alcohol. At this point he looked like he had let the cat out of the bag then began to backpedal.

"Look, I know you people. You don't seem to understand that I'm not an alcoholic. Two beers at night, that's it! Weekends, maybe three. Tops, I promise."

Though his drinking problem was not in the range of alcoholism, it nevertheless contributed empty calories and depleted many neurotransmitters, making his brain function inefficiently to the point where he could not sustain focused thoughts and maintain balanced emotions. His consumption of alcohol combined with a poor diet was a double whammy, disabling his brain with more than a counterpunch. He diet failed to provide his brain with the raw material (nutrients) that his body needed to make neurotransmitters. His drinking depleted the levels of neurotransmitters even more severely. All this made him more fatigued, depressed, and anxious and less able to think clearly. Also, the alcohol was shrinking his dendrites, contributing to the dulling of his brain.

As I explained all this to him, his eyebrows slowly cranked up like a sluggish automatic garage door opener.

"So what am I going to do to chill out after a stressful day?"

"If you change your diet and quit drinking, plus all the other things we are talking about, you'll be able to chill out quite nicely and have more energy for the next day," I told him. I suggested a balanced breakfast, lunch, and dinner each day and no coffee on an empty stomach. All simple carbohydrates needed to be eliminated from his diet, especially sugar. The caffeine in the afternoon and the beer in the evening had to go as well.

Hearing these suggestions was not what he had hoped for. In fact, he admitted that he had counted on receiving a prescription for medication.

"Less is more when it comes to medication," I told him. "And in your case I have not detected that there is any reason that medication is at all necessary. If your diet is balanced, then you will produce the cornucopia of brain chemicals that enable you to think clearly, have balanced positive moods, feel calm when you need to, and be energized during the daytime."

"Look, Doc, I need a quick fix. I can't wait around to see if your health fanatic suggestions work!"

"You're going to see big changes in a matter of days if you give your brain a fighting chance."

Grudgingly, he promised "to try out the health fanatic ideas." We set up an appointment for the next week. I warned him that he would feel worse before feeling better as his body adjusted during the first few days.

When he arrived one week later, he looked sheepishly at me, saying, "All right, I do feel a little better, but at first it was a bear! You didn't tell me how bad it would be."

"Think of it this way: your body had adjusted to being strung out on sugar, caffeine, and a little alcohol. It took a few days to detox yourself."

"So how long must I practice this?"

"How long do you want to feel better? In a few weeks you will be feeling a whole lot better."

Diet Factor Questionnaire

Yes No

☐ ☐ Do you typically crave and consume sweats?

☐ ☐ Do you skip breakfast?

☐ ☐ Are fried foods part of your regular diet?

☐ ☐ Do you avoid fruits and vegetables?

☐ ☐ Are white rice and bread more a part of your diet than whole grains?

Yes No

☐ ☐ Are you generally in the dehydrated range?

☐ ☐ Are sodas normally part of your daily fluid consumption?

☐ ☐ Do you drink alcohol on a regular basis, perhaps more than two drinks daily?

☐ ☐ Are your mealtimes haphazard, with you eating only when hungry?

☐ ☐ Do you snack all day regardless of whether you are hungry?

If you answered yes to any of the above questions you are altering your brain chemistry and impairing your brain functions. The greater the number of questions that you answered yes to, the more you limit the capacity of your brain to function in a healthy manner.

Nathan Goes Natural

Nathan came to see me with complaints of feeling fatigued much of the time and being in a "perpetual brain fog." Working with his primary care physician, we found that most of his labs were in the normal range except his blood sugar, which seemed to be on the rise over the last few years. Also, he appeared to be gaining weight around the waist, which is not uncommon for a man of 55.

When I asked him about his diet, he proudly proclaimed, "I've gone natural." When I asked what he meant by the term *natural*, he said, "Every time I go shopping, I make sure to buy foods that have the label 'natural.' So that I have all the nutrition that I need. So, Doc, you don't need to go there with me; I'm way ahead of you."

For breakfast he had granola from a box that was labeled "natural" with a fruit drink that was labeled as having "all natural flavors." During break time at work he grabbed a "tall skinny latte with of course agave instead of sugar." Lunch usually featured a frozen meal also labeled natural and a natural soda in the midafternoon to "stay hydrated." Dinner usually consisted of pasta.

Trying to avoid sounding politically provocative, I noted that Congress had some years ago been persuaded by the food industry to loosen the monitoring by the U.S. Food and Drug Administration (FDA) along with the labeling requirements. To that end, the use of the term *natural* on labels need not apply to completely natural or organic contents.

As we went over his daily diet, I pointed out that the foods and beverages he was consuming contained large amounts of simple carbohydrates, not only sugars but also white flour. I wondered out loud if the rise in his glucose levels over the last year had something to do with this shift in his diet.

"Maybe I'm needing some of the sugar for a lift because I've been feeling so tired," he suggested.

I told him about how a dietary rush of sugar is generally followed by a crash, and he sat up straight in the chair. I added that his primary care physician and I were concerned about how his blood glucose levels had been rising. The recent symptoms included the fatigue and the brain fog. From a long-term perspective he might be on the way to developing metabolic syndrome and ultimately type 2 diabetes, with symptoms worse than his current complaints.

We worked out a plan to ensure that his diet had *real* complex ingredients. Specifically, all simple carbohydrates were eliminated and replaced with complex carbohydrates, fruits, and vegetables. Over the next few months Nathan, his primary care physician, and I watched as his blood sugar levels normalized while his energy level rose and the brain fog lifted.

Build the Right Diet Foundation

As Nathan discovered, the role of diet becomes increasingly critical as people age. That is also what Scott discovered. Though for years his poor diet did not result in an obvious dramatic effect, his bad habits eventually caught up to him in a dramatic way. His situation was a perfect example of how our bodies are less resilient as well as less resistant to poor diets as we age. Despite the fact that our bodies make some antioxidants, this production declines as we age. We are less resistant to inflammation-producing foods such as sugar and other simple carbohydrates.

Breakfast is the foundation of a balanced diet. Skipping breakfast means your diet loses its foundation and you start the day limping. Far too many people who skip breakfast come to me complaining that they feel dull, forgetful, and unable to think clearly. Some complain of difficulty dealing with stress, anxiety, and/or depression. Often, like Scott, they tell me in the course of the evaluation, "I'm just not a breakfast person."

I routinely ask how long they have had this bad habit of not eating breakfast. Usually the number of years they specify matches the number of years they have been experiencing anxiety, depression, memory problems, and/or general dull thinking.

Failing to break a fast with a nutritious meal is like building a house on sand. A minor amount of stress or a demanding problem results in, at best, cracks in the foundation of the house—your brain's capacity to deal with those demands. Just as you want a firm foundation to build a house, you want a good foundation to start the day for your brain.

Consider breakfast the most important meal of the day. Breakfast provides the meal that ends the longest period without eating, hence the term *breakfast*. It gives your brain a fighting chance to deal with the demands of the day. To be able to think clearly, remember important information, keep your energy high, and maintain balanced moods, eating a balanced breakfast is essential.

Skipping breakfast contributes to the following:

- A feeling of being mentally dull
- Increased anxiety and depression
- Mood swings

- Increased stress reactivity
- Low energy
- Difficulty concentrating

Going without breakfast increases feelings of stress and is associated with high levels of the stress hormones adrenaline and cortisol. High levels of both will make you feel tense and anxious throughout the day. In contrast, eating a nutritious breakfast lowers cortisol levels and lowers susceptibility to colds and upper respiratory tract infections.

Your brain will function far more sharply throughout the day if you consume a nutritious breakfast consisting of protein, complex carbohydrate, and a fruit or vegetable. This balance of foods will help you start the day with the neurochemical foundation you need to thrive instead of feeling exhausted like Scott.

Breakfast provides you with fuel and the feeling of satiety. Your stomach signals that it is full when it secretes a hormone called gastrin, which acts like a neurotransmitter on the vagus nerve, which communicates between the belly and the brain. A hormone called cholecystokinin is released after food is moved into the small intestine. Also, the two neurotransmitters norepinephrine and serotonin are very active in the gut. In fact, there is more serotonin potentially active in the gut than in the brain. When activated, they signal the feeling of satiety. But make sure that the feeling of satiety is not triggered by counterfeit food. If your breakfast consists of foods full of empty calories, your day will start with a whimper.

The timing of when you eat and what you eat can affect your alertness or sedation. Eating several small meals is preferred to eating fewer large meals. Larger meals stress the gastrointestinal track and create adverse systemic effects such as a rapid rise in triglycerides and an increase in blood sugars and can be part of postprandial lipemia (an excessive rise in triglycerides-rich lipoproteins after eating), which is a risk factor for cardiovascular disease and diabetes.

For more energy and less sedation in the afternoon, eat a lunch higher in protein than in carbohydrates. A lunch that is high in carbohydrates will dampen your ability to focus and sharpen your attention. Many professors complain about teaching classes after lunch because students tend to load up on carbohydrates at lunch and become sedated. Make your dinner meal the reverse with the opposite ratio of protein to carbohydrate. You want to be sedated and mellowed out in the evening before going to sleep.

Avoid the Sugar Trap

Sugar is counterfeit food. In American society there is an epidemic of people who consume sugar to an extreme. Soft drinks contain up to four tablespoons of sugar. In Scott's case his daily extra-large Coke is the equivalent of two 12-ounce sodas; in one month this is enough sugar to fill a five-pound bag.

According to the U.S. Department of Agriculture, the average American consumes 120 pounds of sugar each year. This gluttonous, supersized sugar consumption produces four fat-storing periods a day. Each period contributes a gram of stored fat per meal, adding up to 4 grams of fat storage per day.

You may avoid sodas but still not know that your sugar intake is high because the modern diet contains various types of processed foods that often include refined carbohydrates such as white flour. Most of the sugar that people unknowingly consume is in the form of refined carbohydrates such as white bread, pasta, and white rice. To make matters worse, processed foods contain either high-fructose corn syrup or sugar itself.

Your brain uses glucose as its principal fuel. Because glucose must be balanced, your organs (pancreas, liver, thyroid, adrenals, pituitary, and brain) are involved in controlling the amount of glucose in your blood. Keeping the level of sugar in the form of glucose in balance is so important that we have an organ whose principal job is to maintain that balance. The pancreas and its main hormone, insulin, serve to keep glucose in balance and deliver it to cells for fuel.

Low blood sugar results in hypoglycemia, and too much sugar results in hyperglycemia. Both impair your ability to think clearly and maintain balanced emotions. After you eat, your blood sugar rises, signaling your pancreas to secrete insulin, which helps move sugar into your cells. However, if your blood sugar drops below normal levels, your brain sends a distress signal that triggers the release of the hormone epinephrine (adrenaline), which prompts your liver to make more glucose. As a result you may experience nervousness, dizziness and light-headedness, lethargy, weakness, shakiness, and heart palpitations.

The symptoms of low blood sugar are even worse if you tend toward hypoglycemia, and your system is all the more fragile if you have diabetes. You need to be scrupulous about managing your blood sugar. Nervousness and fatigue are more obvious symptoms than are inability to focus attention, loss of short-term memory, and lack of mood stability. These problems are magnified if you consume coffee on an empty stomach the way Scott did.

Sugar is potentially destructive to the body, especially the brain. High levels of sugar contribute to premature aging, and aging makes you less tolerant to sugar in your blood. High sugar consumption contributes to accelerated aging partly because it impairs protein. For example, a process called gycation occurs when sugars attack proteins and block protein from moving freely. Gycation makes membranes "gunked up," causing inflammation and slowing the communication between neurons.

Sugar stiffens protein molecules by creating pigments called advanced glycation end products (AGEs). AGEs act like a chemical glue that fuses molecules, causing a process called cross-linking. Consider what happens to a piece of meat when you leave it too long on the grill. Not only do you brown the skin, you toughen it.

Overcooked meat is cross-linked, making it difficult to cut or chew. When your cells have been cross-linked, many metabolic processes become impaired.

AGEs, also referred to as burned sugar reactions, can damage cells, shortening their life span in a variety of ways. These hard yellow compounds can contribute to Alzheimer's disease through a protein called amyloid precursor protein, which releases beta amyloid and binds to a large cell surface termed a receptor for advanced glycation end product (RAGE).

Ronald Reagan's high sugar consumption may not have caused his Alzheimer's disease, but it did not help him. He loved jelly beans so much that many White House tables as well as the cabinet room table during meetings featured bowls of jelly beans. His sugar consumption may have caused excessive glycation and increased the cascade of AGEs, gunking up his cell membranes and accelerating oxidative stress and inflammation.

Neurons are the least resistant cells and the most easily damaged by AGEs in the body. AGEs cause inflammation and oxidative stress. Inflammation is one of the principal ways neurons become damaged and one of the contributors to Alzheimer's disease. Inflammation is one of the primary causes of neuropathy (damage to the nerves in the peripheral nervous system), which is common in those with diabetes, and is associated with small blood vessel damage leading to vascular damage in the extremities and the delicate glomeruli in the kidneys as well as the retina.

Overall AGEs cause damaging free radicals and inflammation and alter the structure and activities of proteins. They also interfere with communication between neurons. Finally, they lead to structural damage to the mitochondria, the energy factories in your cells that produce the fuel that your cells use. The fuel itself is referred to as adenosine triphosphate (ATP). Consuming the amount of sugar in two soft drinks (75 grams of glucose) triggers free radical products of damaged fatty acids, called isoprostanes, which rise 34 percent after just 90 minutes.[1] Over time even mild elevations in isoprostanes are associated with Alzheimer's disease.[2]

Healthcare researchers have become concerned about elevated sugar. They have improved the methods of measuring its levels in the body, including the glycemic load (GL), which is a measure of glucose levels that reflect what people actually eat. Overall, the higher the GL of a food, the higher the expected rise in blood sugar and the adverse insulin effects of that food. Consuming foods with a high GL leads to a greater risk of obesity, diabetes, and inflammation, all of which have destructive effects on the brain.

There is also a relationship between an increase in GL and another blood marker of oxidative stress called malondialdehyde, which has been shown to damage fatty acids.[3] Since fatty acids are critical to the composition of the brain, this combination of factors is corrosive to the brain and dulls the mind. According to a recent study published in the *Proceedings of the National Academy of Sciences*, middle-aged and elderly people with high blood sugar tend to have a high incidence of swelling in the hippocampus. These findings are consistent with the long-held belief that diabetic patients are at higher than normal risk for developing memory problems. A study performed by Antonio Convit of New York University (NYU) that examined 30 nondiabetic middle-aged and elderly people focused on how quickly sugar is metabolized after a meal. He used MRI scans to examine the size of the hippocampus of his subjects and found that those who metabolized sugar more slowly had a poorer memory and a smaller hippocampus.

Overall, a high sugar intake impairs the ability to think sharply, maintain positive moods, and behave adeptly in social situations. High sugar consumption damages the brain and as a result is associated with higher levels of depression and anxiety. Studies comparing the rates of sugar consumption in countries such as Japan, Canada, and the United States found that Japan has lower consumption rates as well as lower rates of depression. Keeping your blood sugar balanced and sustained is critical to the optimal functions of your brain.

Though simple carbohydrates such as sugar are destructive to the brain, complex carbohydrates are important for providing energy for the body and the brain. Some carbohydrates are good for your brain despite the no-carb fad, but the higher a carbohydrate is on the glycemic index, the lower the value it has in terms of brain health. Carbohydrates that have a low glycemic index—those which contain low levels of fructose—are optimal. In general, the more processed a carbohydrate is, the more quickly blood sugar will rise. In fact, a general rule of thumb is to stay away from processed foods. Processed foods such as prepackaged dinners, white bread, and white rice often include refined carbohydrates, preservatives, and trans fatty acids.

The Diabetes Plague

For thousands of years our ancestors survived and thrived by hunter-gatherer subsistence. Our bodies have not changed, but our diets have, and not for the better. A hunter-gatherer diet consisted of plants, nuts, berries, fish, and lean game. Against that biological reality consider the epidemic of diabetes. The incidence of diabetes has shot up in the United States, climbing to 11.3 percent of adults, or about 26 million people, just in the third quarter of 2009, up from 10.4 percent in the first quarter of 2008. If current trends continue, 15 percent of American adults, or more than 37 million people, will be living with diabetes by the end of 2015.

As with all dementias, the risk of developing Alzheimer's disease grows exponentially with age. Approximately 3 percent of people age 65 are afflicted. By age 75 the incidence jumps to 12 percent, and at age 85 it increases to approximately 50 percent. The risk is greatest for people who carry the apolipoprotein E (APOE) gene. The standard model of Alzheimer's disease is characterized by plaques, tangles, neurotransmitter changes, and neuron death, which all can hasten in those with the APOE genetic predisposition.

Many healthcare professionals refer to Alzheimer's disease as type 3 diabetes. This designation highlights the critical link between diabetes and neurodegenerative disorders. There are two types of diabetes: type 1 and type 2. Type 1 is often called juvenile diabetes, and the main problem is the inability of the pancreas to make insulin. Insulin's main job is to move glucose into cells. When this does not happen, the body functions like a car running out of gas. Type 2 diabetes results from the body's inability to utilize insulin. Normally, when you eat, the pancreas secretes insulin into your bloodstream. As insulin circulates, it acts like a key by unlocking microscopic doors that allow glucose (sugar) to enter your cells to be used as fuel. As your blood sugar drops, so does the levels of insulin. However, this system breaks down if you lose the ability to respond to insulin and don't allow it to bring glucose to cells. This is called insulin resistance. Instead of glucose moving into the cells, it builds up in the bloodstream. High blood sugar results in multiple problems in the heart, kidneys, gums, teeth, extremities, and brain.

Healthcare professionals are now referring to a condition called *diabesity* to emphasize the critical link between obesity and type 2 diabetes. One of the reasons obesity leads to diabetes is that fat cells release a hormone called restin, which makes cells insulin-resistant. Paradoxically, though obese people have an excessive amount of cells, they lose the ability to bring in glucose. Cells experience a famine in the midst of a feast.

Another compounding problem occurs when the pancreas is working overtime to produce very high insulin levels in the blood and seems to run out of steam and finally stops producing insulin. Insulin has been found to serve as a nerve growth factor. The tendency of diabetic patients to become depressed adds yet another factor that impairs memory. The end result is multiple levels of destruction from insulin resistance and too little insulin. Diabetes therefore causes a systemic breakdown of multiple body systems. According to a study conducted by researchers at Cambridge University in the United Kingdom that pooled information from 820,900 people in 100 studies done in Europe and North America, diabetes is associated with a broad range of health problems.

A balanced level of blood sugar is roughly between 60 and 100 mg/dL. If the level is too low, the brain is robbed of its principal fuel. As in a car running out of gas, diabetes drains a person of energy and leads to depression. A 50-year-old with diabetes dies six years sooner than does someone without diabetes. Putting these findings into context, long-term smoking shortens life by 10 years. A person with type 2 diabetes has double the risk of dying of stroke or a heart attack and a 25 percent greater risk of dying of cancer. New research indicates that diabetes can accelerate the development of Alzheimer's disease, too.

Glucose is the brain's principal fuel. It is not surprising therefore that one of the earliest signs of dementia is a decrease in the ability of the brain to use glucose efficiently. This is why neuroscientists are referring to Alzheimer's disease as type 3 diabetes. In fact, people with diabetes have a fourfold increase in Alzheimer's disease.

Three large studies in Japan, Europe, and the United States found that diabetic patients were at least twice as likely to develop Alzheimer's as were those without diabetes. It appears that diabetes slams the brain in three critical ways. First, it causes damage to blood vessels and increases the risk of stroke and heart attack.

One of the clues to the connection between diabetes and dementia involves the way AGEs and glycation (excessive sugar) can accelerate aging. Prediabetic patients and those with diabetes have double the level of AGEs in their blood compared with those without diabetes. AGEs impair the flexibility of small blood vessels, making them narrow, stiff, and less able to deliver blood. Receptors for AGEs exist right on neurons and as a result rev up the beta amyloid cascade, speeding up brain cell death. This is one of the routes to Alzheimer's disease.[4]

People with normal brains and even some with diabetes break down beta amyloid molecules through special enzymes such as insulin-degrading enzyme (IDE). However, many people with diabetes stop making IDE, leaving them vulnerable to misfolded proteins that lead to aging-related neurodegeneration of the Alzheimer's type.

Within each of your 100 billion neurons are microtubules, which like the Tube in London serve as a transportation system to move neurochemicals around in a cell. Neurofibrillary tangles grow inside neurons among the microtubules, which are held together like railroad ties by a protein called tau. As we age, tau tends to get peppered with phosphorous molecules, which makes it misfold, bunching and twisting the microtubules into tangles and creating a train wreck within neurons. Beta amyloid can accelerate the development of tangles.

The connection between the tangles, one of the hallmarks of Alzheimer's disease, and diabetes occurs when too much phosphorus gets attached to tau, producing hyperphosphorylated tau, tangling up the microtubules and creating train wrecks. An enzyme called glycogen synthase kinase-3 beta (GSK-3 beta) has been reported to load too much phosphorus onto tau. Insulin controls GSD-3 beta, and since low insulin is the problem in diabetes, GSK-3 beta runs rampant and allows tau to become hyperphosphorylated, causing the folding of the proteins that leads to Alzheimer's disease.

Plaques tend to form right next to neurons from a segment of a very common protein made in neurons called amyloid precursor protein (APP). Starting out as a very long protein, it soon is snipped into shorter fragments. The neurogenerative problem results from the length of the fragment. If your brain slices off mostly a shorter fragment (called A beta 40, which is 40 amino acids long), you're fine because it produces a gentle, brain-friendly form of beta amyloid. It's the longer APP fragment (called A beta 42, which is 42 amino acids long) that causes trouble for the brain.

This longer version is "sticky" and has a tendency to misfold, producing toxic waste dumps. These poisonous clumps turn into plaques that sit next to neurons, causing destruction in a variety of ways, including revving up free radicals; letting dangerous levels of calcium inside, with the neuron then triggering inflammation; and even switching on neuronal suicide.

Glucose-starved diabetic brains are forced to rely on alternative fuel sources, which can include ketone bodies and lactic acid. Both burn inefficiently, resulting in the release of free radicals that destroy neurons. To make matters worse, diabetic patients are already short on built-in antioxidants such as glutathione; this means that free radicals are allowed to wreak havoc, destroying cells.

Another way glucose-deprived cells rely on destructive methods to gain nourishment is by cannibalizing other cells, including themselves. One of the most energy-hungry areas of the brain is the hippocampal system, making memory one of the first cognitive functions to show signs of impairment. Also, since the hippocampus has more insulin receptors than do most other areas of the brain, diabetic patients tend to experience compound cycles of memory destruction.

One of the systemic effects of diabetes is reduced blood flow to the brain. Plaque causes deterioration of the molecular structure of the blood vessels in the brain that prevents neurons from working properly. As a result of the body's inability to respond to insulin and utilize glucose, the excess floating around increases the chances of plaque building up in the brain.

Diabetes has long been associated with vascular disease. It increases the risk of heart disease, stroke, and vascular dementia. The damage to blood vessels, both small and large, in the brain can be corrosive to neurons and glial cells throughout the brain. The damage occurs to the tiniest blood vessels deep within the brain where networks of axons connect various areas of the brain such as those close to the ventricles. Diabetic brains have been shown to have periventricular white matter hyperintensities, in which axons are stripped of insulating white matter. Imagine the electrical wiring of your house being stripped of the plastic coating covering the wires. The result is electrical shorting out and even electrically triggered fires. This type of brain impairment can cause a wide variety of cognitive deficits.

The link between depression and diabetes has been well established. A person with depression or diabetes is likely to develop the other. Also, there is a higher risk of suicide in those with diabetes. Up to 19 percent of chronically depressed people have shrunken hippocampi as a result of heightened levels of cortisol, excitotoxicty, and blocked neurogenesis.

Stay Hydrated

Adequate hydration is an often overlooked necessity. It is fundamental to a healthy brain. You can go a week without eating but only a few days without taking in fluids. In fact, people who are fasting typically make sure to drink plenty of water.

Consider that our bodies are made up of approximately 60 percent water. It is fundamental to our health. Dehydration causes multiple problems. Cells do not function properly, organs break down, and cells in the brain not only malfunction but shrink. I have seen countless people over the years who complain about anxiety, depression, and lethargy only to find that after I encourage greater water consumption they begin to feel better. They report with delight that they feel not only more energized but also more relaxed. When they discover that they have been chronically dehydrated, they make sure to carry a water bottle wherever they go.

Dehydration impairs the natural transport of minerals and nutrients into brain cells. Brain dehydration eventually leads to major changes in the size, structure, and integrity of brain cells.

Mild to moderate dehydration is likely to cause

- Headache
- Dizziness or light-headedness
- Dry, sticky mouth
- Sleepiness or tiredness
- Thirst
- Decreased urine output
- Few or no tears when crying
- Dry skin
- Constipation

Severe dehydration, indicating a medical emergency, can cause

- Extreme thirst
- Irritability and confusion
- Very dry mouth, skin, and mucous membranes
- Lack of sweating
- Little or no urination; any urine that is produced will be dark yellow or amber
- No tears when crying
- Sunken eyes
- Shriveled and dry skin that lacks elasticity and doesn't bounce back when pinched into a fold
- Low blood pressure
- Rapid heartbeat
- Rapid breathing
- Fever
- In the most serious cases, delirium or unconsciousness

Simple thirst isn't always a reliable gauge of the body's need for water, especially in older adults. A good indicator is the color of the urine. Clear or light-colored urine (like the color of lemonade) means you're well hydrated, whereas a dark yellow or amber color usually signals dehydration.

Replenish Your Brain Chemistry

Your cornucopia of brain nutrients comes from the food you eat. Balanced neurochemistry is dependent on obtaining key nutrients from your diet. A healthy brain has a mixture of macronutrients (carbohydrates, proteins, and fats) and micronutrients (vitamins and minerals).

Aging makes it more difficult to absorb vitamins as well as protein from the diet. As people age, maintaining a balanced diet of whole foods becomes all the more important to maintain a sharper brain. Supplements are not a replacement for a balanced diet. Keep in mind that the following information is meant to drive home the point that what you eat creates the neurochemistry needed to keep your brain sharp.

The neurotransmitters that make your brain function are synthesized from specific amino acids that serve as their building blocks. A poor diet devoid of these critical amino acids will erode your neurochemistry and cause various deficits in memory, attention, and mood. L-Glutamine, for example, is an amino acid found in foods such as almonds and peaches and is synthesized into the neurotransmitter called gamma-aminobutyric acid (GABA). GABA is the principal inhibiting neurotransmitter that helps people stay calm and relaxed. This is the neurotransmitter system that is targeted by drugs such as Valium and Ativan. (I strongly advise avoiding these drugs). For a wide variety of reasons, you need to replenish your GABA levels by dietary means. Good food sources of L-glutamine include beef, chicken, fish, eggs, milk, dairy products, wheat, cabbage, beets, beans, spinach, and parsley.

The amino acid phenylamine is converted into tyrosine, which is a building block for the neurotransmitters epinephrine, norepinephrine, and dopamine. These neurotransmitters are involved in activating attention and give you energy. Good food sources of phenylamine include peanuts, lima beans, sesame seeds, yogurt, and milk.

The amino acid choline is the raw material needed for the manufacture of the neurotransmitter acetylcholine. Choline helps prevent the buildup in the blood of homocysteine, a harmful compound that is associated with cardiovascular disease and osteoporosis. Low levels of choline deplete the neurotransmitter acetylcholine. Because inadequate acetylcholine is associated with memory problems and Alzheimer's disease, some drugs target this neurotransmitter. Good food sources of choline are soybeans, egg yolk, butter, peanuts, potatoes, cauliflower, lentils, oats, sesame seeds, and flax seeds.

Since amino acids compete with one another for access to the brain, the blood-brain barrier allows only a certain amount of particular types of amino acids to pass through at one time. Other amino acids are more abundant in dietary proteins. This is one reason why high-protein meals fail to increase the level of tryptophan in the brain. Because the competition for access to the brain does not favor tryptophan but does favor protein, a high-protein meal in the evening may make it more difficult to sleep. It's best to eat a meal high in complex carbohydrates for dinner.

Just as with amino acids, the foods you eat should have a balanced spectrum of vitamins and minerals. They directly affect your brain chemistry and when in short supply can deplete your neurotransmitters. And just as with amino acids, you should get vitamins from whole foods because food provides more bioavailability—that is, more complete absorption—than supplements can provide. It is also a mistake to take specific supplements without the supervision of your physician. Some vitamins, such as A, can be toxic at high levels. Also, if you take one vitamin alone, it can reduce the levels of another. Don't play amateur biochemist with your brain. A balanced diet through whole foods is the smart strategy.

The B vitamins are critical for your brain in a wide variety of ways. Vitamin B_1 (thiamine), for example, helps convert glucose into fuel for the brain. Low levels of B_1 make you feel dull, tired, and depressed, and you may have attention problems. Consuming alcohol can have a deleterious effect on B_1; even a glass of wine can reduce the absorption of thiamine by the gut. Cooking techniques such as marinating meat in wine, soy sauce, or vinegar can deplete 50 to 70 percent of the meat's thiamine content. It has been shown that the levels of key neurotransmitters such as serotonin and dopamine are reduced by alcohol since alcohol has a corrosive effect on B_1. Reductions in these two neurotransmitters are associated with depression and loss of the anticipation of pleasure and focused attention. The consumption of refined carbohydrates, including sugar, depletes the B_1 supply. Good food sources of B_1 include grains such as wheat germ, brown rice, rice bran, and oatmeal; legumes; nuts and seeds such as peanuts, sunflower seeds, dried soybeans, pistachio nuts, raw peanuts, brazil nuts, and pecans; and fruits and vegetables such as raisins, mushrooms, brussels sprouts, asparagus, peas, millet, cabbage, broccoli, avocados, and plums.

Vitamin B_3 (niacin) is involved in many brain-related functions, including effects on your red blood cells, which carry oxygen to your to brain in the pathways for ATP and ADP–ribose transfer reactions. Moderate levels of B_3 can help lower bad cholesterol (LDL) and boost good cholesterol (HDL), whereas high levels of niacin cause dilation of blood vessels, flushing, itching, and increased blood flow to the brain and decreased blood pressure. Niacin can be manufactured from the amino acid tryptophan, which is also a precursor to serotonin. Since the amount of tryptophan converted to niacin is dependent on your diet, the relationship between niacin and typtophan need to be balanced. Preliminary research has shown that B_3 helps the brain recover from strokes. It has also been shown that it lowers the levels of phosphorylated tau, a chemical related to Alzheimer's disease. Good food sources of B_3 include nuts, meat, fish, eggs, potatoes, beans, and dark leafy vegetables such as collard greens, spinach, and kale.

Vitamin B_5 (pantothenic acid) is critical to the adrenal glands, which among other things secrete epinephrine (adrenaline) to convert fat and glucose into energy. Deficiencies in B_5 result in feelings of malaise and numbness in the feet. Also, B_5 is needed to make stress hormones to keep you energized and focused when you need extra energy. It is also important for the neurotransmitter acetylcholine (critical for memory).

Vitamin B_5 is needed for hormone formation, the uptake of various amino acids, and the neurotransmitter acetylcholine, which is associated with memory. Good food sources of B_5 include animal sources such as tuna, cod, chicken, lobster, turkey, duck, beef, and organ meats such as kidney and tongue, along with eggs (particularly egg yolks) and vegetable sources such as corn, kale, cauliflower, tomatoes, sweet potatoes, broccoli, and legumes.

Vitamin B_6 (pyridoxine) plays many roles, including the synthesis of serotonin and melatonin from tryptophan, epinephrine, norepinephrine, and GABA, and acts as a partner for over 100 different enzymes. Food storage dramatically affects B_6. For this reason it is not a good idea to depend primarily on frozen meals for much of your diet, because the content of B_6 is reduced 57 to 77 percent by freezing vegetables. You should shift to fresh foods whenever possible. Good food sources of B_6 include meats such as chicken, turkey, beef, and pork; fish such as cod, salmon, halibut, trout, tuna, and snapper; vegetables such as bell peppers, spinach, green peas, yams, broccoli, asparagus, turnip greens, chickpeas, lentils, and soybeans; nuts such as peanuts, sunflower seeds, cashews, and hazelnuts; and whole grains.

Vitamin B_7, or biotin, also known as vitamin H or coenzyme R, is a water-soluble B-complex vitamin. Biotin is involved in the metabolism of sugar and the formation of fatty acids. A deficiency of biotin contributes to insomnia, mild depression, anxiety, and oversensitivity to pain. Good food sources of biotin include mushrooms, liver, egg yolks, peanuts, and cauliflower.

B_9 (folic acid) is critical for the division and replacement of red blood cells, protein metabolism, and the utilization of glucose. Low B_9 is associated with brain aging and increased cortical atrophy. The risk of the development of Alzheimer's disease is reduced by as much as 50 percent by eating the recommended daily allowance of folic acid. It breaks down the brain-damaging homocysteine, and vitamins B_6 and B_{12} help dispose of it. B_9 affects DNA synthesis and regulation as well as fatty acid synthesis and energy production and is involved in metabolism in every cell in your body. Good food sources of B_9 include spinach, dark leafy greens, asparagus, turnips, beets, mustard greens, brussels sprouts, lima beans, soybeans, beef liver, brewer's yeast, whole grains, wheat germ, bulgur wheat, kidney beans, white beans, lima beans, mung beans, salmon, orange juice, avocados, and milk. In addition, as a result of the discovery that pregnant women who are deficient in folate during the first month are at risk of giving birth to a baby with spinal defects, grain and cereal products in the United States are mandated to be fortified with folic acid.

Vitamin B_{12} is critical for metabolism in all cells in the body. It combines with folate in the formation of DNA, the genetic material in all cells. It is needed for the synthesis and regulation of fatty acids and the synthesis of red blood cells. According to the Oxford Project to Investigate Memory and Aging (OPTIMA), adults over age 55 with low B_{12} have four times the risk of developing Alzheimer's disease. One of the symptoms of B_{12} deficiency is a red and smooth tongue.

Good food sources of B12 are animal- or dairy-based, and thus vegans should make sure they get enough from other sources. Also, people who have had stomach surgery or are on a chronic dose of ulcer medications may be at risk for low B_{12}. Aging is associated with a stomach increasingly less able to bring B_{12} into the bloodstream. B_{12} deficiencies have been associated with impairments in memory and abstract reasoning. B_{12} is found in some fortified soy-based products as well as clams, mussels, poultry, crab, salmon, eggs, and milk.

Neurons are high energy consumers. Unfortunately, as we age, we burn energy far less efficiently. Just as an older car burns more oil because the rings around the pistons get loose, the gaskets crack, and the crankshaft wobbles, older brains create more toxic waste products as we are increasingly prone to free radical attacks. More mutations in our DNA are feeding back to even more inefficient fuel burning.

As you age, it is critical to bolster your antioxidant defense system to deal with free radicals and prevent their creation. Free radicals cause oxidative stress by stealing electrons from other molecules and damaging cells. This cellular damage can result in decreases in energy levels as well as cognitive and emotional problems. The lack of dietary antioxidants and oxidative stress can add up as one ages. Increases in antioxidants contribute to enhanced memory in older adults.[5]

Our membranes are made up of essential fatty acids (lipid proteins) and possess weaker antioxidant defense than do other cells. They are especially vulnerable to free radical injury. When these fatty parts of membranes are highly oxidized, they may rupture, which technically is referred to as lipid peroxidation. Brain fats need to be nourished and protected from damage by oxidative free radicals. They rely on antioxidant nutrients and enzymes to keep stray electrons from damaging the delicate unsaturated fatty acids of the cell membranes.

One of the areas of the brain that many neuroscientists believe is particularly vulnerable to lipid peroxidation is the hippocampus. Our memory systems are high energy consumers, and brain networks are vulnerable to lipid peroxidation.

Under healthy conditions and when we are younger, a large range of antioxidants help protect us from the destruction caused by oxidation. Four enzymes form part of our natural antioxidant defense system: catalase, glutathione peroxidase, superoxide dismutase, and nitric synthase. Antioxidant vitamins assist these enzymes.

Antioxidants such as vitamins E and C are crucial to maintaining and bolstering this defense system. Vitamin C serves as one of the principal antioxidants and acts as a scavenger of free radicals. Vitamin C is also needed for the manufacture of the neurotransmitter norepinephrine. Good food sources of vitamin C include red berries, kiwi, red and green bell peppers, tomatoes, broccoli, spinach, guava, grapefruit, and oranges.

Vitamin E is a very important antioxidant that protects blood vessels and other tissues from oxidation. Vitamin E works by nesting among fatty acids, phospholipids, and cholesterol molecules. When free radical substances threaten or damage one of the fatty acids, vitamin E traps and neutralizes them before they can damage the cells. Good sources of vitamin E include legumes, walnuts, almonds, sweet potatoes, sunflower seeds, whole wheat, and wheat germ.

Minerals

A sharp brain also requires foods with a balanced level of minerals. Minerals are important for the brain and are categorized as macronutrients and micronutrients. The brain contains more macronutrients than micronutrients.

Macronutrients include magnesium, calcium, sodium, potassium, and chloride. Potassium has been found to be an important part of the dietary effort to lower blood pressure. Good sources of potassium include bananas, oranges, tomatoes, and spinach. Calcium is a macronutrient that is important for development of nerve tissue, maintenance of regular heartbeat, and blood clotting and pressure. It is also involved in the transmission of messages between neurons by triggering the release of neurotransmitters and controlling synaptic strength. Even after the neurotransmitters are released, calcium acts to enhance the strength of the synaptic connection. Good food sources of calcium include bok choy, dairy products, salmon, kidney beans, almonds, and broccoli.

Like calcium, magnesium is involved in the conduction of nerve impulses. Magnesium deficiency can cause irritability, nervousness, and depression. It helps regulate a key receptor in the hippocampus that is important in learning and memory. Adequate magnesium is an essential gatekeeper for the crucial NMDA (*N*-methyl-D-aspartate) receptor, which receives the excitatory neurotransmitter glutamate and is crucial to neuroplasticity. Though many other neurotransmitters get all the press, glutamate is the workhorse in the brain. It is the principal excitatory neurotransmitter. A moderate increase in the level of glutamate facilitates neuroplasticity, which is basic for learning and memory. Magnesium helps the NMDA receptors block background noise and increase neuroplasticity. Good sources of magnesium include wheat and oat bran, brown rice, nuts, and green vegetables.

Because they are found in tiny amounts in the brain, micronutrients are also called trace elements and include, iron, manganese, copper, iodine, zinc, fluoride, selenium, chromium, aluminum, boron, and nickel. These micronutrients can cause problems when found in large amounts in the brain.

Zinc is a key ingredient of copper/zinc superoxide dismutase, a powerful enzyme that detoxifies neuron-attacking free radicals. Deficiencies in this enzyme contribute to the neurological disease amyotrophic lateral sclerosis (ALS), often called Lou Gehrig's disease. Stephen Hawking has ALS.

Zinc has a relatively narrow therapeutic window, meaning that too much and too little can hurt the brain. Thus, as with the other vitamins and minerals, it is best not take a supplement; getting nutrients from whole foods is best. Good sources of zinc include seafood, soybeans, poultry, and dairy products.

Too much iron causes fatigue, weakness, weight loss, abdominal pain, joint pain, diabetes, high blood pressure, and hormonal changes. Iron overload, which also is called hemochromatosis, is a serious condition that can lead to potentially fatal organ damage if untreated. Iron deficiency has been referred to as the most common nutritional deficiency in the world. It leads to anemia with symptoms such as fatigue, shortness of breath, pale skin, concentration problems, dizziness, a weakened immune system, and energy loss. Iron is involved in several important functions. It is involved in the synthesis of neurotransmitters such as serotonin, dopamine, and norepinephrine. It is an important cofactor in the synthesis of the amino acid tyrosine to dopamine and norepinephrine. People with anemia have reduced levels of iron and consequently may also have reduced tyrosine hydroxylase, the enzyme that converts tyrosine to the amino acid levodopa, and thus have lower production of dopamine and norepinephrine, which are important for focus and energy.

Iron acts as a cofactor in many enzymatic reactions needed to produce neurotransmitters such as the cyotochrome P450 enzyme system, which is essential for processing toxic molecules in the brain. It also plays an important role in producing myelin in the enzymes that convert dietary fatty acids into long-chain fatty acids crucial to the brain. Good food sources of iron include dark leafy vegetables, beets, dried beans, dried fruits, eggs (especially egg yolks), iron-fortified cereals, liver, lean red meat (especially beef), oysters, poultry, salmon, tuna, and whole grains.

Add Healthy Phytonutrients

Nutritionists recommend eating fruits and vegetables with the brightest and deepest colors of the rainbow. A class of pigments called carotenoids give many fruits and vegetables their colors, which range from yellow to orange, red, and purple. Carotenoids give carrots their orange color and tomatoes their redness. Carotenoids work as antioxidants to help protect the plant from harmful free radical damage. There are approximately 600 carotenoids. The best known is beta-carotene.

Beta-carotene not only gives carrots and yams their orange color but is critical for the creation of vitamin A, which is also known as retinol. Just as beta carotene helps protect orange, red, and dark green vegetables from the sun's harmful radiation, vitamin A helps cell growth and promotes healthy skin as well as vision, teeth, and bones.

Phytonutrients are substances found in the pigments of many plant foods that have antioxidant abilities. One of the largest groups of phytonutrients is the polyphenol group, which include the flavonoids such as catechins, flavonols, anthocyanins, and isoflavones. Flavonoids have been shown to decrease the oxidation of LDL cholesterol and as a result save blood vessels from fatty deposits and decrease clumping of platelets, thereby reducing the risk of strokes and heart attacks. They also have been reported to reduce inflammation.

There are approximately 6,000 different flavonoids, which come in various types. These compounds are found in a wide variety of foods, including fruits, vegetables, cocoa, cereal grains, soy, and tea. They not only act as antioxidants to protect cells from damage caused by unstable molecules known as free radicals but also bolster the brain by interacting with proteins integral to brain cell structure and function.

Whereas the catechins are found in high amounts in green tea, the isoflavones are found in soy. Flavonols are found in apples, and anthocyanins are found in blueberries, elderberries, and cherries. The catechin in tea contains an antioxidant called epigallocatechin-3-gallate (EECg), which is in much higher levels in green than in black tea. EGCg has been reported to have twice the antioxidant power of the resveratol found in red wine (and the skin of the red grape). The antioxidant benefits include blocking DNA damage, perhaps slowing the aging process, and blocking the oxidation of lipids in the blood, which can provide protection from atherosclerosis. Milk interferes with the absorption of antioxidants in tea.

Blueberries have become popular because some studies have demonstrated that diets enriched with blueberries, strawberries, and spinach are correlated with improved cognition and motor functions.[6] Robert Krikorian of the University of Cincinnati asked subjects older than age 75 to drink two cups of wild blueberry juice every day for 12 weeks. Their recall of words and objects was 30 percent better than that of subjects in the study who received a flavonoid-free beverage resembling blueberry juice. Another study found that pensioners who drank a pint of blueberry juice boosted their memory by up to 40 percent.

James Joseph of the U.S. Department of Agriculture's Agricultural Research Service notes that blueberries not only have antioxidant properties through their anthocyanins and pterostilbene content but also increase levels of enzymes called kinases, which are essential to learning and memory. Anthocyanins make it easier for messages to pass between neurons. Further research has indicated that flavonoids also help regulate other enzymes called phosphatases; the correct balance of phosphatases is critical for maintaining the integrity of synapses.

The antioxidant factor of phytochemicals is called oxygen radical absorbed capacity (ORAC). The fruits with the highest ORAC are blueberries, blackberries, strawberries, raspberries, and plums. Blueberries and blackberries have two times more ORAC than plums.

Soy isoflavones may contribute to memory improvement by acting like weak estrogens that bind to and stimulate estrogen receptors. These receptors trigger modifications in neuronal shape and the neurochemistry of the hippocampus. There is some speculation that flavonoids may stimulate the growth of new neurons in the hippocampus. Flavonoids may also help ameliorate the neurotoxic effects of excess glutamate by preventing binding to its receptors. Finally, flavonoids may oppose the action of enzymes called secretases that are involved in the destruction of neurons and may be elevated in neurodegenerative disorders.

Some of the phytonutrients include lycopenes and resveratrol. There has been a lot of hype about the phytochemical resveratrol in recent years. It is the chemical that is found in the skin of the red grape and is one of the reasons red wine is regarded as healthy.

Yet, as I just noted, the chemical is found in the *skin* of the red grape, and so eating whole red grapes is much healthier than drinking red wine, which contains alcohol. We have a grape arbor that produces an excessive amount of red grapes. Though we live in California's wine county, I eat more of those red grapes than I consume red wine. Although I like a glass of wine now and then, I always have to weigh whether I'd rather get a good night's sleep and enjoy a relaxed mood for the next few days as opposed to having the fleeting good feeling that lasts for an hour after drinking that glass of wine.

According to a study performed by the Harvard epidemiologist Julie Baring on 22,000 male physicians, those drinking between one drink a day and one a week reduced the risk of stroke by 20 percent. But drinking more than one drink a week has no real advantage.

A variety of international studies indicate that wine drinkers are more likely to eat fruits and vegetables and exercise more. They are usually more affluent and get better healthcare. Of course you can drink grape juice or eat red grapes and go without the alcohol to get your dose of resveratrol. Resveratrol is such a hot commodity that the big pharmaceutical companies are trying to develop a resveratrol pill. I am sure that my neighbors in the wine industry will be perturbed when this occurs.

Minimize Alcohol Dulling

Alcohol's initial effects include enhancing the effects of GABA and inhibiting the effects of glutamate. This dual effect accounts for the initial calming effect as well as the blackout effect when alcohol is consumed in excess. Then a few hours later the situation is reversed so that there is less GABA and a surge of glutamate, resulting in increased anxiety and stress.

A phenomenon known as mid–sleep cycle awakening is an illustration of the effect of consuming alcohol in the evening. The GABA effect occurs first, contributing to relaxation and even sedation, while the activating effect of glutamate is dampened. Approximately three hours later the GABA levels are lower and there is a surge in the glutamate level. This process represents alcohol-induced insomnia.

This dysregulation is not confined to just a few hours later in the sleep cycle. When I taught psychological and neuropsychological testing to psychology interns, there was a rule of thumb that went "Don't test a wet brain until three months after the last drink." This is because it takes at least that long (providing a healthy diet and exercise) for the brain to reestablish a healthy new baseline mode of functioning. Testing too early would reveal many of the symptoms of regular alcohol consumption, including such cognitive deficits as the following:

- Performance on tests of visual and spatial perception
- Visual and spatial learning ability
- Ability to make fine motor movements
- Adaptive abilities
- Short-term memory
- Nonverbal abstract learning
- Abstract thinking ability
- Conceptual thinking ability

It was once believed that alcohol kills cells, with one drink destroying as many as 10,000 neurons. It turns out that the old model is far too simplistic. Alcohol actually shrivels dendrites, the part of neurons that reaches out to receive input from other neurons. The greater the amount of dendrites, the greater the potential complexity of cognition. Thus, the greater the amount of alcohol, the lower the capacity for complex thought.

Alcohol can also have a destructive effect on fatty acid pathways. It can do the following:

- Block enzymes needed to form DNA
- Block the enzymes needed to form prostaglandin E_1 (PGE_1)
- Dissolve fatty acids in the brain's membranes and replace them with the poor substitute acid DPA

There is bad news for wine drinkers. Researchers from Germany's Gottingen University compared brain scans from diagnosed alcoholics with those from healthy adults. They found that the size of the hippocampus was largest among nonalcoholics at 3.85 mL. In alcoholics who drank beer it was measured at 3.4 mL. In alcoholics who drank spirits it was measured at 2.9 mL. It was the smallest among alcoholics who preferred wine at 2.8 mL.

A little chocolate every once in a while may be good for you. Though bittersweet dark chocolate can contain one-third of the amount of caffeine in a cup of coffee, it also contains stimulants called theobromine and phenylethylamine, which are naturally occurring amphetamine-like compounds.

A few other compounds found in chocolate include chemicals that may boost the levels of anandamine, a neuromodulator that binds to cannabinoid receptors and therefore may mimic some of the effects of marijuana.

Chocolate also contains a chemical called 1-Me TIQ that may inhibit the development of Parkinson's disease. Chocolate also contains antioxidants. Last but not least, it contains molecules called procyanidins. They tend to link to one another, forming long chains that act as both antioxidants and anti-inflammatories, can block nitric acids decreasing blood clotting, and can relax smooth muscles, all of which could reduce the risk of heart attacks and strokes.

Get Good Fats

Your brain is composed of 60 percent fat. In fact, fat is an important part of a healthy diet despite the one-dimensional fad promoted by food labels that say "fat-free." The truth is that you need the right fats to manufacture cell membranes throughout the body, especially in the brain.

During the last century the amount of essential fatty acids consumed in the Western diet has declined by more than 80 percent. To make matters worse, we consume the wrong fats, including animal fats, vegetable oils, and processed foods. Even the balance of essential fatty acids has changed dramatically. In the past there was a balance between omega-6 and omega-3, but that ratio has been skewed to 30:1. It is not that omega-6 is bad, but it is bad for the brain when the ratio between omega-6 and omega-3 is skewed extremely toward omega-6.

Essential fatty acids are just that, essential to a healthy brain. They serve many critical functions. For example, a healthy neuron can make on average 10,000 synaptic connections with other neurons. The health of the synapses depends in part on essential fatty acids. Neuroplasticity is dependent on the health of the synapses.

The omega-3 fatty acid docosahexaenoic acid (DHA) is found in mitochondria in the cell nucleus (which serve as the energy factories of neurons), synaptosomes (where neurons communicate with one another), photoreceptors (the light-sensitive part of the retina), and the cerebral cortex.

DHA is found in higher concentrations in synaptic membranes than in most tissues of the body. Deficiencies in DHA impair the integrity of synaptic membranes. DHA helps keep cell membranes soft and flexible, which is critical for neuroplasticity. Saturated fats, in contrast, turn membranes rigid, impairing the brain's capacity for neuroplasticity. Soft and flexible membranes are capable of adapting their receptor shapes so that neurotransmitters can fit like a key in a key holder, which results in a neuron firing. DHA is important for holding those receptors in place. But if a receptor becomes rigid from the consumption of saturated fats and trans fatty acids, that receptor is immobilized, unable to wiggle or expand to let the neurotransmitter lock in, consequently impairing the inter-action between neurons. This means that your brain has trouble transmitting information between neurons, making it difficult to think sharply.

For the last two decades many mental healthcare providers have been suggesting that depressed patients take omega-3 supplements because there is a positive relationship between DHA levels and lev-els of serotonin. Serotonin is one of the neurotransmitters involved in mood regulation. DHA aids in the conversion of tryptophan to serotonin and controls its breakdown and reuptake cycles. DHA is also used to manufacture more synapses, which in turn produce more serotonin, making it important in maintaining a stable and positive mood. Good food sources of DHA include salmon, mackerel, sar-dines, herring, anchovies, and bluefish.

The omega-3 fatty acid eicosapentaenoic acid (EPA) is also involved in the activities of neurotransmitters such as serotonin and dopamine and therefore helps with mood regulation. Unlike DHA, it is not found in the brain in significant amounts. DHA provides structural support for cells throughout the body and helps blood flow in the brain and the messenger called *eicosanoids*, which effects inflammation, blood clotting, blood vessel activity, and blood supply. It is found in the same foods as DHA but in higher amounts.

Omega-3 helps prevent excess arachidonic acid (AA) from accu-mulating in tissues. A moderate level of AA is found throughout the body and brain, but you can get too much of it by eating foods with fat from animals such as cows, pigs, chickens, and turkey. A high level of AA acts as a precursor to many highly inflammatory sub-stances. High AA intake later in life increases the risk of developing dementia by over 40 percent. Because of its effect on AA, DHA has emerged as a player in helping to prevent cognitive decline and in the potential prevention of Alzheimer's disease.[7]

When fatty acids such as arachidonic acid are damaged, isopros-tanes appear in tissues and cause free radical activity that chips away at the cell membrane. The levels of isoprostanes are nine times higher one day after a brain injury than they were before the injury.[8] High levels of isoprostanes are found in the cerebrospinal fluid, plasma, and urine of people with Alzheimer's disease; this implies that they are a possible predictor of the disease. Omega-3 fatty acids lower oxidative stress and inflammation.

Omega-3 has also been associated with promoting brain-derived neurotrophic factor (BDNF), which, as was explained in Chapter 2, plays a critical role in neurogenesis and neuroplasticity as a sort of Miracle-Gro for brain cells. BDNF serves as a neuroprotective agent and is critical for memory and new learning. Low levels of BDNF are associated with neurological damage and depression. Inflammation and oxidative stress interfere with BDNF production, but omega-3 can lower both, and the EPA component of omega-3 can help maintain BDNF.

Cytokines can play a major role in inflammation (*cyto* means "cell" and *kinos* means "movement" in Greek). They are proteins, peptides, and glycoproteins that serve as immunomodulating agents such as interleukins and interferons. When essential fatty acids are not balanced, cytokines lead to inflammation and turn the immune system against cells, attacking and killing them. Increases in cytokines are associated with depression, anxiety, and cognitive problems.[9] Another way essential fatty acids lower inflammation is through the actions of EPA in inhibiting cytokines.

Your diet has a major effect on the white matter of your brain. The white matter is comprised of glial cells, so named because researchers initially thought that they served only a support function and were "glue" that held the brain together. Now we know that the various types of glial cells perform many important functions. In fact, they can communicate with one another through calcium waves. Glial cells are more numerous than the neurons that make up the gray matter.

White matter changes near the ventricles, called hyperintensities, can increase as we age. Approximately 25 percent of people over age 65 and 50 percent of people over 75 have some hyperintensities. These white matter changes are often caused by microvascular disease that damages millions of the blood vessels called capillaries, affecting functions such as memory loss, attention, and problem solving. Up to 60 percent of people with Alzheimer's disease have white matter changes.

One of the roles of glial cell is to coat the axons, the parts of neurons that send information to other neurons. This coating is referred to as myelin and makes neurons fire more efficiently. Just as a plastic coating insulates electrical wires on a household appliance and keeps those wires from shorting out, myelin protects axons. Myelin is made of various fats, fatty acids, phospholipids, and cholesterol. In fact, one-fourth of myelin consists of cholesterol. Despite the bad rap, one type of cholesterol is good. The HDL (high-density lipoprotein) type is the good cholesterol. It is the LDL (low-density lipoprotein) type that is the bad cholesterol. Inadequate or damaged myelin impedes nerve impulses. Multiple sclerosis (MS) represents one of the most graphic examples of a demyelinating disease that eventually results in the inability to walk, memory problems, and depression.

According to a study by George Bartzokis reported in the *Journal of Neurobiology of Aging*, the integrity of myelin during middle age is associated with the risk of Alzheimer's disease later in life. Myelin is degraded if there are high levels of LDL cholesterol and/or iron. As cholesterol levels in the brain increase, they eventually promote the production of a toxic protein that attacks the brain.

LDL is the bad cholesterol because it has a tendency to stick to artery walls, leading to cerebrovascular compromises. The HDL type, in contrast, ferries cholesterol from the body back to the liver for processing, preventing its buildup on artery walls. For this reason it is called good cholesterol.

High LDL cholesterol leads to increased vulnerability to strokes and heart attacks. Yet short of those extremes, high LDL can lead to lower cognitive performance among older people because of impaired blood flow to the brain.

The process of going from the clean, smoothly flowing, flexible blood vessels of a child to the plugged-up and stiff-walled vessels of someone with atherosclerosis can result from many bad habits, including a poor diet, no exercise, diabetes, chronic stress, and especially high levels of LDL cholesterol. LDL cholesterol–filled plaque is a sticky yellow outcropping of fat-laden tissue that blocks the free flow of blood, and as a result arteries become stiffer. As a result blood pressure rises, arteries become inflamed, and eventually a stroke can occur.

One of the many risk factors for atherosclerosis involves high levels of the amino acid homocysteine. A healthy supply of B vitamins (including folate, B_6, and B_1) can keep homocysteine in check. But when the body is depleted of B vitamins, homocysteine levels rise, along with the risk of stroke and heart attacks. Short of a stroke, atherosclerosis impairs the brain and accelerates mental decline.

Fats found in peanut butter can increase HDL cholesterol levels without increasing total cholesterol. Increase the monounsaturated fats in your diet, including canola oil, avocado oil, and olive oil. Add soluble fiber to your diet, including oats, fruits, vegetables, and legumes; this will result in both a reduction in LDL cholesterol and an increase in HDL cholesterol. Pure cranberry juice, fish, and other foods containing omega-3 fatty acids can increase HDL levels.

Essential fatty acids can also help the brain facilitate the so-called second-messenger system. This system activates when neurotransmitters penetrate the fatty membrane of the cell and trigger secondary emissaries that reach into the nucleus of the cell, where they turn genes on or off to send back chemicals outside the cell and create more reactions. In other words, your diet affects the way your genes work, and essential fatty acids are critically involved in this fundamental process.

Within each of your cells are microscopic organelles called mitochondria. The function of these tiny powerhouses is to produce adenosine triphosphate, a substance that provides energy to make the brain function. The conduction of neuron signals, the production of neurotransmitters, and a host of other functions will not take place without ATP. Mitochondria have cell membranes richly endowed with essential fatty acids. If those fatty acids are compromised by a diet devoid of essential fatty acids and antioxidants, the mitochrondia will not work properly and can lead to the production of free radicals that may damage their DNA and energy-making ability. Damage to mitochrondria may play a significant role in the development of neurodegenerative diseases. Patients with Alzheimer's disease may have a much higher degree of damage to their mitochrondrial DNA than do people without Alzheimer's disease.[10]

Omega-3 is found in coldwater fish such as salmon, mackerel, herring, and sardines as well as flax, walnuts, sunflower seeds, soybeans, almonds, chickpeas, wheat germ, and bran.

Cut Bad Fats

In addition to the destructive effects of an imbalance between omega-3 and omega-6 and prostaglandins, there are a variety fats you want to minimize or cut from your diet. One such fat is an altered vegetable fat called trans fatty acids.

Trans fatty acids are formed when an unsaturated vegetable fat is heated for long periods in a metal container, as in deep frying. These altered fats are structured differently from those in essential fatty acids such as DHA, which are curved in shape, are flexible, and help maintain the electrical properties of nerve cell membranes. Trans fatty acids are straight in shape, tend to be solid at body temperature, and act like saturated fat, making them corrosive to cell membranes.

Trans fatty acids have become common in the standard Western diet. The usual sources of trans fatty acids include foods prepared with partially hydrogenated oils. It can become difficult to determine if the food you are purchasing at the grocery store contains trans fatty acids. Look for the words "contains partially hydrogenated vegetable oil," which is another way of saying it contains trans fat. Some common sources of trans fatty acids are chips, mayonnaise, doughnuts, cookies, crackers, cakes, shortening, puffed cheese snacks, shortening, margarine, deep-fried foods, some salad dressings, and candy.

Trans fats make up 4 to 7 percent of the typical American diet. By consuming trans fatty acids you decrease the levels of healthy fats. For example, with an increase in trans fatty acids there are corresponding low levels of omega-3 ALA, and the uptake of trans fatty acids into the brain doubles. Also, when levels of trans fatty acids are high, the omega-3 DHA is replaced by an unhealthy substitute in omega-6 called docosapentaenoic acid. This substitution of bad fat for good fat also occurs when one consumes alcohol or excessive omega-6 and/or insufficient essential fatty acids (especially DHA and ALA).

A Rush University Medical Center study involving 4,000 patients examined the relationship between trans fatty acids, saturated fats, copper, and cognitive decline. Increased levels of copper are associated with cognitive decline. The intake of trans fatty acids and saturated fats was associated with high copper levels. Thus, the toxic effect of excess copper is associated with increases in the consumption of trans fatty acids as well as saturated fats, resulting in cognitive decline.

There are several ways in which trans fatty acids dull the brain. They may be taken up directly into nerve membranes, making cells more rigid and inflexible and interfering with the normal functional properties of brain cell membranes.[11] They alter the synthesis of neurotransmitters such as dopamine, impair the brain's blood supply, block the body's ability to make its own essential fatty acids such as DHA, increase LDL cholesterol while decreasing HDL cholesterol, increase plaque in blood vessels, and increase triglycerides, which cause blood to be sluggish and reduce oxygen to the brain.

Additionally, the increased consumption of trans fatty acids causes a major problem with obesity.

Triglycerides are a type of fat found in the blood. When you eat food, your body converts calories it does not need right away into triglycerides, which it stores in fat cells. Between meals, hormones release triglycerides for energy. But if you eat more calories than you burn, your triglycerides levels rise. Elevated triglycerides have been found to be associated with multiple health problems, including an increase in depression. Lowering the triglyceride level is associated with the alleviation of depression.[12]

Practice these dietary guidelines:

A healthy brain diet consists of a mixture of macronutrients (carbohydrates, proteins, and fats) and micronutrients (vitamins and minerals).

Consume whole and balanced foods to build a healthy brain.

Avoid simple carbohydrates. The lower a carbohydrate is on the glycemic index, the better.

Make sure that your fats are balanced and avoid trans fatty acids entirely.

Stay adequately hydrated throughout the day.

Avoid red meat as a regular part of your diet.

Eat fish two to three times a week.

Consume a balanced diet consisting of a complex carbohydrate, a protein, and a fruit or vegetable.

Avoid fried foods.

Avoid highly processed foods.

CHAPTER 5

The Exercise Factor

Diane came to see me complaining that she felt tired and was worried that the constant fatigue was making her mind grow dull. She had gone through menopause roughly 10 years earlier and believed that she'd never emerged from the moodiness and was feeling uneasy like so many of her friends. Nothing in her life was particularly stressful from an objective point of view, but she felt everything was stressful. After her two daughters moved away, she knew that she had far more free time but wondered where it all went.

During her visits with the daughter who was an editor at a publishing house in San Francisco, she often experienced a boost in energy despite the fact that they walked all over the city. When she visited the other daughter, who was married with two children, she experienced no boost in energy but did feel relaxed when spending time with her grandchildren. I pointed out that it was telling that she experienced a boost in energy even after feeling physically tired from walking up and down the hills of San Francisco. In other words, she invested physical energy and got more back in return.

I suggested that she invest in more energy by adding an aerobic boost. She told me that she had been "trying to take care of" herself by taking yoga classes twice a week and was getting all the physical exercise she needed from the yoga.

I told her that we didn't want to replace the yoga with exercise but to add the exercise as part of her day. I had some 40 years earlier gained significantly by learning yoga and visiting ashrams in various parts of the world. It is a wonderful meditative way to stretch and turn on the parasympathetic nervous system as well as reap all the enhancements that meditation can provide to the brain (we will explore those benefits in Chapter 8). However, yoga does not provide the aerobic boost that exercise provides that sets off multilevel biochemical enhancements for the brain, including increasing the release of brain-derived neurotrophic factor (BDNF) to add new neurons. When there is loss of neurons resulting from aging, that addition is particularly important.

Her first response to my suggestion that she add daily aerobic exercise to her life was, "I don't want to go to one of those health clubs with all those people showing off their trim bodies!"

Though she was actually slender, she carried more around her waist than was healthy. She had poor muscle tone and appeared out of breath from the walk from the parking lot to my office. "Is this what happens when you visit your daughter in San Francisco?" I asked.

"At first, yes." She paused for a few moments, looking at me slyly. "So you're saying that I'm out of shape?"

"It looks like you're confirming that from experience. More important, you're also experiencing a boost in energy."

I went on to describe how aerobic exercise can boost various neurotransmitters that calm and sharpen the brain. "You feel mentally dull. Regular exercise provides your brain with the neurochemistry that adds new neurons in the area of your brain that is the key to memory and attention." I went on to describe how brain-derived neurotrophic factor contributes to the formation of new neurons in the hippocampus and prefrontal cortex to make this happen.

"Fine; you say that I need to wear myself out to get these benefits?"

"Actually, you will be strengthening your entire body and adding to the longevity of your brain. And you will feel that the cloudy dullness that you complained about dissipates." I explained that there are many metabolic repair and building processes that result from exercise and that build a stronger and more youthful body and brain.

"I'm not going to one of those health clubs. Besides, I don't have the money for it anyway."

"Walking is the cheapest and most convenient way to exercise. All you need to do is walk fast enough that you find it hard to talk and walk at the same time. Call that the 'talk test.' If can walk every day for 20 to 30 minutes and come back winded and having sweated a little, you get your aerobic boost."

The next challenge was to help her fit walking on a daily basis into her life. It is far too easy for all of us to procrastinate and/or rationalize that we have so many more important things to do. She agreed to structure walking into her late afternoon routine by accepting an invitation that she had previously rejected to walk with friends from work. I was not surprised that at our next appointment she seemed more energized, focused, and hopeful. "I can't believe that one little change in my life has had this ripple effect," she said. "And my moods seem more even. There's one other thing that I didn't expect: I'm feeling much more connected to those two people."

Diane, like most people, agreed in theory that exercise is good for health. Perhaps you too agree but don't know why it is good for your health, let alone your brain. This chapter will explain how exercise sharpens the brain.

Regular exercise now will extend the life of your brain. It will delay the encroachment of dementias such as Alzheimer's disease and give you a cognitive and emotional boost just when you think you are winding down.

Exercise Factor Questionnaire

Yes No

☐ ☐ Do you find yourself procrastinating about exercise, putting it off until you "have the time"?

☐ ☐ Do you rationalize that you need to be fully motivated or that it has to "feel right" before you engage in exercise because it would be inauthentic or you think you would not get enough out of it?

☐ ☐ Do you worry that too much time has elapsed since you exercised that you might as well give up thinking that it will help at this late date?

☐ ☐ Do you worry that you already have health problems that might be worsened by exercise?

☐ ☐ Are you embarrassed about exercising, thinking that you would look ridiculous if others saw you try?

☐ ☐ Do you think that exercise is appropriate for only those who are already healthy?

☐ ☐ When you do exercise, do you go easy on yourself and rarely break out in a sweat?

☐ ☐ Do you regard exercise as just one of the many things that promote health and feel that if you do the other things, you will be okay?

☐ ☐ Do you feel discouraged when you become particularly tired after exercise and less inclined to do it again?

☐ ☐ If you exercise once or twice a week, do you think you've done your duty?

If you answered yes to any of these questions, you are bogging down your body and brain and slowing necessary self-rejuvenation.

Exercise Your Genetic Imperative

The word *exercise* was not in our vocabulary until recent history as we fell into a relatively sedentary life. It was not until roughly

11,000 years ago that some of our ancestors began to subsist in agricultural communities. They traveled in hunter-gatherer bands, walking approximately 12 miles a day in search of hunting and gathering subsistence. We now drive to the local supermarket to hunt and gather food.

Yet the portion of the human genome that determines basic anatomy and physiology has remained unchanged for the last 11,000 years.[1] What has not stayed the same is how much energy we use and how much fuel we consume. The point is that our bodies evolved to move great distances and we have sunk into the couch. If you are like most people, hiking 12 miles would be exhausting without prior conditioning. To make matters worse, many people eat like they are storing up enough energy to move those great distances but don't do the hiking.

Since the basic framework for our physiological gene regulation is similar to what existed during the period between 50,000 and 10,000 BC when our ancestors thrived as hunter-gatherers, our phenotype (that which is actually expressed) of the present day is dramatically different from that of our ancestors, primarily as a consequence of our largely sedentary lifestyle and high-calorie, high-fat, fiber-poor diet. Thus, our current genome is maladapted, resulting in abnormal gene expression, which manifests as multiple acquired diseases. Our genes evolved with the expectation of a certain threshold of physical activity for normal physical gene expression. Regular exercise restores the homeostatic mechanisms toward the normal physiological range of our ancestors. Daily exercise normalizes gene expression.

Many of the genes that were selected for survival when our ancestors had to move great distances to forage for food now shorten survival in the absence of physical activity. In physically inactive people these genes make different quantities of proteins that interact with susceptibility genes for chronic illnesses; over time this can increase the prevalence of chronic illnesses such as atherosclerosis, certain cancers, obesity, and type 2 diabetes.[2]

Consequently, modern Western society is experiencing an epidemic of obesity, including late-onset diabetes, cardiovascular illnesses, and being generally overweight. These are the more obvious problems. The more subtle negative effects occur in the brain. That is what Diane discovered. She was not overweight and did not have major cardiovascular problems such as diabetes, but her physical inactivity was bogging down her brain.

Lack of exercise creates phenotype changes, including the following:

- Decreased size and the strength of skeletal muscles
- Lower capacity of skeletal muscle to oxidize carbohydrates and fats
- Higher insulin resistance
- Greater homeostatic disruption of cellular metabolism in skeletal muscle at a given absolute workload
- Lesser vasodilator capacity in perfusion vessels to the heart
- Smaller maximal cardiac outputs and stroke volumes
- Sarcopenia

Although current hunter-gatherers undergo the same (but slower) age-related losses in hearing and vision capacity that affect those in our generally sedentary society, they rarely develop chronic diseases such as obesity, hypertension, sarcopenia, hypercholesterolemia, nonocclusive atheromata, and insulin resistance.[3] For example, the health differences between two genetically similar but geographically and behaviorally different groups of people demonstrate the dramatic effects of the role of exercise and diet. The Pima Indians are divided by the boundary separating the United States and Mexico. The Mexican Pima Indians expended 2,100 to 2,520 kJ (kilojoules) (500 to 600 kcal) more per day in physical activity, had a diet lower in fat and higher in fiber content, weighed 26 kilograms less, and did not have the diabetes epidemic of their obese Arizona Pima counterparts.[4] The prevalence of type 2 diabetes was six times more for the Arizona Pimas.

Our hunter-gatherer ancestors probably consumed about 3,000 kilocalories per day and used 1,000 kilocalories in subsistence activities, with 2,000 kilocalories used for basal life processes. Today the typical American eats about 2,400 kilocalories and expends 300 kilocalories in physical activity. A mere surplus of 100 kilocalories per day above basal life processes adds pounds of fat each year.

Body weight is determined by a balance between the number of calories consumed and the number of calories expended, that is, used as fuel. Calories are used in several ways: (1) the minimum energy required to keep cells, tissues, and organs alive at rest (similar to keeping a car idling), (2) the energy required to digest food, (3) the energy required to heat the body, and (4) the energy required and used for physical activity. The number of calories required for the first three factors is generally fixed. Consequently, it is the fourth factor (physical activity) combined with the number of calories consumed that determines a person's weight. Further, the fitness level of the muscles affects the basal metabolic rate.

Like the Arizona Pimas, Americans in general are facing a health crisis. According to the Centers for Disease Control and Prevention, 60 percent of Americans are overweight and 30 percent are obese. Collectively these data indicate that physical inactivity and a poor diet are the second major cause of death in the United States. This health epidemic is spreading throughout the world. The World Health Organization reports that 60 percent of people worldwide are overweight.

The weakening of skeletal muscle is a major health threat. The prevalence of weak muscles has been estimated to range from 8.8 percent in people under 70 years of age to 17.5 percent in people over 80 years of age. People with weak muscles have a greater risk of mortality. Whereas contracting muscles increase their glucose uptake, reduced physical activity is associated with a rapid development of insulin resistance.

The Harvard Nurses' Health Study found that those who engaged in less than two and a half hours a week of moderate physical activity such as brisk walking had a greater incidence of major health problems compared with those who undertook more than two and a half hours. For example, those who were relatively sedentary had

- 22 percent increase in breast cancer
- 41 percent greater mortality
- 43 percent increase in coronary heart disease
- 49 percent increase in gallstones
- 85 percent increase in type 2 diabetes
- 85 percent increase in colon cancer
- 92 percent increase in diabetic coronary heart disease
- 115 percent increase in ischemic stroke[5]

A large number of genes in skeletal muscle are activated after exercise. Based on the duration of the exercise, these genes fall into three categories. Stress-response genes are activated during the later phases of exercise. Their protein concentrations rise quickly to high levels and return to normal levels very quickly after exercise. These acutely sensitive genes encode proteins that are part of the general response to stress in all types of cells and include heat shock proteins and some transcription factors—immediate early genes.

The second category is referred to as metabolic-priority genes; these genes are required as a consequence of metabolic stress, such as when muscle glycogen and blood glucose levels are low. These genes can also be expressed at high levels, usually peaking after a few hours and returning to normal levels after 24 hours.

The third category is referred to as metabolic/mitochondrial enzyme genes. These genes encode protein whose function is to convert food to energy. They are produced in much lower concentrations but do not return to normal levels for up to one week. These genes play a role in muscle plasticity, which involves an increase in mitochondrial and capillary concentration.

The glucose transporter-4 gene (GLUT4) can be activated by exercise without the intervention of insulin. GLUT4 enables glucose to cross the plasma membrane from blood into muscle cells, providing a means of fueling active muscle cells and an alternative to having to depend on insulin and the pancreas that produces it. Over time, the lack of exercise causes inactive muscles to gradually become less sensitive to insulin, the pancreas loses the ability to produce enough insulin to compensate, and blood glucose levels rise. This syndrome creates type 2 diabetes. The GLUT4 gene has been referred to as a lifestyle gene because its expression is altered by muscle contraction—exercise. Failure to be active enough to have the GLUT4 gene in the plasma membrane of skeletal muscle predisposes a person to become prediabetic.[6]

Only proteins with a sufficiently long half-life will accumulate with successive episodes of exercise. This explains why it takes weeks to months of aerobic training to improve overall aerobic fitness. Yet there are multiple immediate benefits to even a single episode of exercise. For example, physical activity limits the rise in blood glucose after the next meal. In fact, it is believed that physical activity lowers the glycemic index of carbohydrates by one or more signaling proteins that are activated when insulin binds to a cell.

Overall, this genetic impairment means that there are major health consequences if people do not exercise. The lack of exercise combined with the increasingly poor Western diet results in some genes, such as GLUT4, working to create health problems such as insulin resistance. The overall health benefits of exercise occur over time and can have a dramatic effect on the brain.

Exercise to Treat Chronic Illnesses

Most people agree that achieving physical fitness sounds good in theory. Like Diane, perhaps you don't know why it is critical for sharpening your brain. Exercise will give you a cognitive and energy boost just when you think you are winding down. Exercise sharpens your brain, helps with longevity, boosts your cognitive abilities, and keeps your emotions balanced.

Aerobic exercise produces multiple changes to the brain. It brings immediate additional oxygen and glucose to the brain. When you exercise on a regular basis, your body responds by forming new capillaries to bring that additional blood to brain cells and boosts brain chemicals that protect those cells, as well as strengthening new neural connections.

Exercise provides both protective and enhancing benefits to the brain. Its protective benefits take many forms. For example, chronic inflammation is destructive to cells throughout the body and especially the brain, but exercise lowers inflammatory chemicals, which is very important for the longevity of the brain. One of the many studies demonstrating this protective effect examined the medical records of 13,748 people and found that exercise lowered inflammation, as measured by the level of the chemical C-reactive protein (CRP). Only 8 percent of those who engaged in vigorous exercise had elevated CRP, whereas 21 percent of those who did not exercise had elevated CRP. Even those who engaged in a moderate level of exercise showed less elevation of CRP (13 percent), and 17 percent of those engaging in light exercise showed an elevation of CRP.[7] Overall, the greater the amount of exercise, the lower the level of CRP (Table 5.1).

The reduction of inflammation through exercise occurs at all ages. When 800 men and women between the ages of 70 and 79 were examined, moderate and strenuous exercise was associated with lower levels of CRP.[8] A complete lack of exercise impairs stem cells in the brain and decreases the potential for neurogenesis; in contrast, moderate or vigorous exercise supports neurogenesis.[9]

Table 5.1 Effect of Exercise on C-Reactive Protein

The effect of exercise on C-reactive protein (inflammation chemical).
Degree of physical activity by level of C-reactive protein. Based on study of
13,748 people (Ford, 2002. See note 7.).

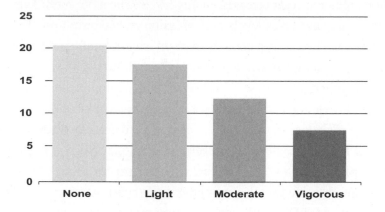

As I write this, I am flying back from Washington after taking part as a panelist in a national Kaiser Permanente–sponsored summit on the multiple medical benefits of brisk walking. Why would a very large medical organization promote walking as a first line of treatment exercise? The experts noted the positive effects of exercise in treatment for diabetes, chronic pain, obesity, heart disease, and depression. A physician from the University of British Colombia reported that the health risks posed by low physical fitness are worse than "smokadiabesity" to emphasize how being out of shape is more devastating to health than are smoking, diabetes, and obesity combined.

Being out of shape is destructive to the brain. According to the National Center for Health Statistics, only 25 percent of Americans are physically active. What is more troubling is that only 10 percent are active enough to achieve health fitness. These statistics underlie one of the main reasons there has been an epidemic in chronic illnesses such as cardiovascular disease and diabetes, both of which are risk factors for dementia.

The epidemic of type 2 diabetes is the result of our high-caloric "supersizing diet" and lack of regular exercise. People with type 2 diabetes live on average six fewer years, and the last few years are complicated by the symptoms of diabetes, including neuropathy, vision problems, and decreased energy levels. The more subtle symptoms include increased levels of depression and cognitive problems.

Regular exercise can not only burn off excess calories and weight but also increase insulin receptor sites throughout the body to aid in the metabolism of glucose. This benefit is quite significant because excess glucose and insulin-resistant receptors are some of the causes of type 2 diabetes. Thus, one of the best ways to prevent the development of type 2 diabetes is to exercise on a regular basis.

If you have a chronic illness, exercise serves as an effective treatment. Aerobic exercise strengthens the heart, helps prevent the buildup of bad (LDL) cholesterol, and improves the functioning of the liver, the pancreas, and other vital organs. Though people with chronic pain, fibromyalgia, arthritis, and similar medical problems often find even the thought of exercise painful, once they get going, their pain levels go down and their motivation to exercise goes up because of the release of endogenous opiates (the brain's own painkillers).

Exercise Away Anxiety and Depression

An accumulating amount of research studies has shown that exercise is very effective in treating depression. These studies have not been confined to the United States but have been conducted throughout the world. Here are some of the findings:

- A Finnish study of 3,403 subjects found that those who exercised two to three times per week were less depressed, angry, stressed, and cynical.
- A Dutch study of 19,288 twins and their families found that those who exercised were less anxious, depressed, and neurotic and more socially outgoing.

- An Alameda County, California, study of 8,023 subjects tracked for 26 years found that those who didn't exercise were 1.5 times more likely to be depressed.
- A Columbia University study of 8,098 subjects found the same inverse relationship between exercise and depression.

A University of Texas study assigned people with major depression to a "dose" of exercise or rest and found that both groups had reduced stress and tension. However, the exercise group reported an increase in positive emotions and vigor.[10]

Blumenthal and colleagues at Duke University Medical Center found that an aerobic exercise program decreased depression and improved cognitive skills in middle-aged and elderly men and women. The study followed 156 men and women who had been diagnosed with major depression. They were assigned to three different groups: mediation, exercise, and combined groups. The exercise group spent 30 minutes walking, bicycling, or jogging three times a week. The researchers found that all three groups improved. In other words, exercise alone was found to be an effective antidepressant.

During the last 20 years studies have been showing that mental health professionals who had grown to believe that psychotherapy and medications are the best treatments for depression should add exercise before medication. Exercise for 30 minutes three times a week has been shown to work at least as well as antidepressant medications such as Zoloft. Researchers at Duke University found that exercise in the form of brisk walking or riding a stationary bike did as good a job as antidepressant medication. Those who continued exercising during the 10-month follow-up did a better job keeping the symptoms from coming back after the depression initially lifted. A review of 14 studies found that aerobic exercise among those with mild to moderate depression was not only more effective than antidepressants but was as effective as psychotherapy. The aerobic exercise entailed walking briskly or running three times a week for at least five weeks.

A wide variety of recent studies have shown that exercise is as effective as psychotherapy for the alleviation of depression. Here are some of the findings:

- An Ohio State University study that involved 45 minutes of walking per day for five days a week (bringing the heart rate to 60 to 70 percent of its maximum) lowered Beck Depression Inventory mean scores from 14.81 to 3.27 compared with no change for controls (depressed nonwalkers).
- A University of Wisconsin study found that exercise (jogging) was effective as psychotherapy for moderate depression.
  - After one year, 90 percent of those in the exercise group were no longer depressed. In contrast, 50 percent of those in the psychotherapy group continued to be depressed.
- A Duke University study found that exercise was as effective as the antidepressant Zoloft.
  - At the 6-month follow-up, exercise was 50 percent more effective in preventing relapse than the medication.
  - The National Institutes of Mental Health panel concluded that long-term exercise reduces moderate depression.

A wide variety of physiological gains produced by exercise help alleviate depression. For example, exercise promotes increased efficiency of the neurotransmitters serotonin and dopamine, which have been associated with lifting depression. In fact, these are some of the very neurotransmitters targeted by the major antidepressant medications. In contrast to medications that have troubling side effects such as insomnia, weight gain, and sexual performance problems, exercise has positive side effects that are the reverse, including better sleep, weight management, and enhanced sexual vitality.

Exercise has great side effects, unlike medication. I often ask, "What do you want, good side effects or bad side effects?" Numerous studies have shown that people suffering from anxiety and/or depression who do regular exercise (often just walking daily) begin to feel better right away. Exercise not only reduces anxiety, it also increases positive feelings. Exercise releases endorphins, neuropeptides that bind to opioid receptors in the brain and have potent analgesic effects.

The studies showing that exercise is effective for mild and moderate depression were accompanied by studies that showed minimal efficacy of antidepressant medication. Beginning in 2000, when an article appeared in the *Journal of the American Medical Association,* articles in a number of other well-respected journals reported that antidepressant medication provided little benefit for mild and moderate depression.

Exercise alleviates depression by a wide variety of means. To take one neurotransmitter as an example, when its levels are low, serotonin has been associated with depression (and anxiety). Serotonin levels increase when the body breaks down fatty acids to fuel the muscles. Fatty acids compete with the amino acid tryptophan (the precursor to serotonin) for slots on transport proteins that increase their concentration in the bloodstream. Once tryptophan pushes through the blood-brain barrier, it is synthesized into serotonin. When you exercise, serotonin also gets a boost from brain-derived neurotrophic factor, as was described in Chapter 2.

Not only is exercise very effective as an antidepressant, there has been mounting evidence that it has strong antianxiety effects. There are multiple ways in which exercise changes the brain and as a result serves as a treatment for anxiety. Exercise lowers blood pressure by increasing the efficiency of the cardiovascular system. Researchers have shown that exercise pumps more oxygen to the brain, which increases the health of the small blood vessels called capillaries.[11] For example, when the heart rate increases during exercise, a hormone called atrial natriuretic peptide (ANP) is produced. ANP tempers the body's stress response by dampening the hypothalamic-pituitary-adrenal (HPA) axis and its fight-or-flight response. ANP does this by going through the blood-brain barrier and attaching to receptors in the hypothalamus to tone down HPA axis activity. It acts on the amygdala and the locus coeruleus to dampen the effects of corticotropin-releasing hormone (CRH), part of the chain of neurochemical processes that induce the fight-or-flight response and anxiety. Thus, ANP defuses some of the main contributors to anxiety, including turning down the flow of epinephrine (adrenaline) and lowering the heart rate.

Built-up stress increases muscle tension, making it difficult to relax. Exercise relaxes the resting tension of muscle spindles, breaking the stress feedback loop to the brain. A good massage breaks the stress feedback loop too. Thus, one could say a good aerobic session accomplishes some of the same benefits in stress reduction as a good massage.

Aerobic exercise can also lower anxiety by dampening the effects of a chemical called cholecystokinin tetrapeptide (CCK-4), which can induce a panic attack even in healthy adults without a history of panic. One study showed that people who engaged in aerobic exercise 30 minutes before the injection of CCK-4 exhibited lower panic-type symptoms compared with those receiving simply a quiet rest before the injection.

There are actually many reasons why exercise is so effective at rebalancing moods. The very neurotransmitters that the psychiatric medications aim to affect are those which are upregulated by exercising, meaning that these neurotransmitters are more available and work more efficiently over the long term. But exercise does this much more efficiently. For example, the major inhibiting neurotransmitter called GABA calms you down. Drugs such as the benzodiazepines, which include Valium and Ativan, are calming because they work on the GABA system. But not only are those drugs very addicting—that is, they entail tolerance and withdrawal—when they wear off, they contribute to what is called anxiety sensitivity, meaning that you feel more anxiety when they wear off than when you began to take the medications. Another side effect of benzodiazepines is depression. Taking these drugs is similar to wading into a warm pit of quicksand.

It feels good initially, but soon you are sucked down into the abyss of depression and anxiety.

These drugs are eventually countertherapeutic because the brain adapts to an abnormal boost to its chemistry. When the brain becomes accustomed to getting a counterfeit version of a particular neurotransmitter, in this case GABA, it produces less of it. It is as if your brain says, "We have plenty of GABA floating around, so stop making so much." Then when the effects of the drug wear off, the brain is in short supply of GABA. Before taking the drug again, you are even more anxious. Every time the drug wears off, you became even more anxious. I have seen scores of patients in the mental health system who mistakenly interpret this syndrome to mean that they have a much greater psychological problem than they previously believed. Benzodiazepines are fool's gold.

Exercise does not have these paradoxical and negative effects. Instead of those negative side effects from the drugs, there are a variety of positive effects. Simply moving your body triggers the release of GABA. Exercise upregulates a cornucopia of neurotransmitters, neuromodulators, and neurohormones that make you calmer, more energized, and more focused. It is well known in popular culture that after a vigorous workout you can experience a "runner's high." The truth is that you don't need to run to get the high. The workout, however, must be aerobic. So-called runner's high results from increased activity of several substances in the brain:

- The neurotransmitters dopamine, norepinephrine, and serotonin
- Endorphins
- Endocannaboids
- Atrial natriuretic peptide, which reduces the hormones in the HPA axis
- Brain natriuretic peptide, which also reduces the hormones in the HPA axis

Exercise lowers the levels of chemicals such as adrenaline and cortisol. This is especially important when they are high in the late afternoon and evening, which results in increased insomnia. Lowering this stress-related chemistry improves sleep. As is described in Chapter 7, if you exercise in the three- to six-hour window before you go to bed, your sleep will be more restful. This is related to lowering stress chemistry and also to a lower body temperature later in the night.

Exercise helps minimize the levels of stress hormones such as cortisol. A high level of cortisol is destructive in numerous ways for the entire body and certainly the brain. High levels of cortisol contribute to abdominal fat (a large belly), which will be described next in this chapter must be avoided to maintain a healthy brain. High levels of cortisol are associated with an increased risk of developing type 2 diabetes and with increased anxiety; 20 percent of cases of depression are destructive to the hippocampus, making it atrophy.

Lose the Belly Fat

Excess body fat can have a destructive effective on the brain. The larger the body mass index (BMI), the greater the risk of developing Alzheimer's disease, according to a 24-year follow-up study conducted in Sweden.[12] A Korean study found that increases in BMI have an inverse relationship to cognitive ability as measured by the Mini Mental State Examination.[13] In other words, as fat increases, cognitive ability decreases.

If you are overweight, it makes a big difference where the extra fat is situated. A large belly is not only very bad for your health but toxic for your brain. Rachel Whitmer, a research scientist at the Division of Research of Kaiser Permanente, led a study that found that people who had large bellies during their fortes had a significantly higher risk of dementia in their seventies. The study involved over 6,000 people and showed that having more fat, principally in the gut, in their early to middle forties increased their chances of becoming forgetful and confused, which are symptoms of dementia, as they aged. The bottom line was that those with the largest guts faced more than twice the risk for dementia compared with the leanest people.

Abdominal fat (gut fat) is much more dangerous than gluteal fat (fat around the buttocks and thighs). People with increased abdominal fat have been found to have high levels of inflammatory cytokines. Abdominal fat leaches out these inflammatory proteins. Inflammation is destructive not only to the organ systems in the abdominal cavity but also to the brain. One of the major risk factors for dementias, including Alzheimer's disease, is inflammation.

The link between a large belly and poor brain health includes multiple health problems. Fat cells are not dormant and inactive storage units. Belly fat generates inflammation. A large gut leaches out toxic chemicals that increase the risk for inflammation, constricts blood vessels, and leads to the breakdown of cell integrity. Fat cells release the same inflammatory chemicals that are released when you have an infection or have been traumatized by an injury. Elevated cytokines are associated not only with inflammation but also with depression through what has been called sickness behavior. Cytokines lower the level of BDNF (Miracle-Gro), a protector of nerve cells and promoter of neuroplasticity and neurogenesis. Accordingly, inflammation is associated with cognitive deficits.

One of the best ways to burn off excess cortisol is to exercise in the late afternoon. While burning off the excess cortisol, you can also slow the atrophy of the key part of your brain for memory—the hippocampus—and even reverse it. You can add new neurons to your hippocampus through the release of brain-derived neurotrophic factor, as was discussed in Chapter 2.

Some of my patients complain that they have stressful jobs and that when they get home, it is difficult to unwind. I always ask them to take a brisk walk or some other form of aerobic exercise after or before dinner. I tell them that if they do this, by bedtime they will be much better able to go to and stay asleep.

Knowing that exercise has antidepressant, antianxiety, and sleep hygiene benefits is one thing. Putting this knowledge to use is another thing. If you are even the slightest bit depressed, you may procrastinate, and procrastination leads to more depression. As is the case with rewiring your brain in general, you must do what you don't feel like doing, and do it often, to stimulate neuroplasticity.

Sometimes taking the first step makes the second step much easier to take. With people who have had a difficult time taking the first step, I take that step with them. We have our session while on a brisk walk in back of my office building, where there are great hiking trails. I go out there at least once and often twice a day for a brisk walk or run. Sometimes I have as little as 10-minute bursts or one 20-minute period of aerobic exercise. One person said, "I wish I could be as relaxed as you sitting there looking so serene!" I quickly noted that I had just come back from my walk and wanted to be relaxed and focused for our session.

An added benefit for me is that the walking trails lead through ponds with many types of water fowl, including swans. For a person like me, who spends a great deal of time in an office, being outdoors, especially in a natural environment, is rejuvenating. On my administrative days, when I am bogged down with a complicated training question, I tell my assistant, "I need to go clear my head with the swans."

Often I tell clients that my assistant and I take such walks as routine part of the day. I ask them to make sure that they do the same thing. It is not uncommon for a depressed client to explain that he or she doesn't feel motivated to exercise. Not trying to be glib, I ask, "How badly do you want to be less depressed or anxious? Enough to do something you don't feel like doing, like taking a brisk walk?" That often works, but when it does not, I sometimes tell a story about a young man who was so depressed that he decided to try to kill himself by running himself to death. He ran a mile thinking that would be enough to cause a heart attack. Shocked that it didn't work, the next day he ran two miles. That didn't work either, so the next day he ran three miles. He began to feel less depressed and realized that he must continue to run not to kill himself but to keep from killing himself.

Everyone who comes to see me with complaints of anxiety and/or depression receives a prescription to exercise in addition to receiving psychotherapy. In fact, Kaiser Permanente now has prescription pads just for exercise, especially walking. On the pad there is a place for the person's name, how many minutes per day, and how many times a week, plus a place for the prescriber to sign. I have been distributing these prescription pads to my colleagues over the last year in an effort to get all of our depressed and anxious patients walking.

Keep Your Brain's Blood Vessels Healthy

Healthy maintenance of the blood vessels in the brain is critical to its longevity. In healthy blood vessels, the amounts of the proteins called collagen (which provides stiffness) and elastin (which provides elasticity) are balanced to provide a supportive yet flexible vessel wall. After age 25, increased amounts of collagen make blood vessels stiffer and less able to narrow or dilate in response to changes in blood pressure.

If there are impairments to the cerebrovascular system up to and including cerebrovascular disease, the normally smooth blood flow through the vessels becomes turbulent, resulting in pools and eddies of blood and damage to the delicate inner lining of the blood vessel. Compromises to the blood-brain barrier block the delivery of essential nutrients and the removal of waste products from the brain, making the aging brain progressively less efficient.

In addition to glucose, the other main fuel for the brain is oxygen. When the delivery of oxygen is blocked or impaired in some way, neurons become impaired and can die. Steady blood flow to the brain is so critical that the brain maintains a mechanism called cerebral autoregulation that ensures that blood flow is reasonably constant despite variations in blood pressure throughout the day. Cerebral autoregulation is involved in changing the diameter of blood vessels: contracting the muscles around the vessels when pressure is low, which increases the flow, or relaxing the muscles when pressure is high, which decreases the flow. Cerebral autoregulation acts on medium-size blood vessels to ensure that throughout the day when a rapid change in blood pressure occurs, you do not lose consciousness or burst a blood vessel.

Maintaining an even blood flow to the brain necessitates a complex network of nerve endings in the muscles around the brain's blood vessels. These nerves use a wide range of neurotransmitters that balance one another's actions in intricate ways to dilate or contract the blood vessels. Exercise promotes healthy cerebral blood flow.

The most dramatic impairment of blood flow in the brain is a stroke. Each year almost 1 million Americans have a stroke, making it the number three cause of death. The southeastern part of the United States is called the stroke belt. African Americans have 80 percent higher rates of strokes than do white Americans. There are two major types of strokes: ischemic and hemorrhagic. Ischemic strokes involve a sudden blockage of a blood vessel so that the area downstream from the blockage is starved of blood and nutrients, including oxygen. Hemorrhagic strokes occur when blood vessels burst like a dam and flood the area around the burst as well as depleting the blood flow to the area of the brain that the blood vessel had been serving with nourishment. Most strokes are of the ischemic type. Before a major ischemic stroke many people experience one or more "ministrokes," also called transient ischemic attacks (TIAs), which occur momentarily with symptoms such as blurred vision, weakness, dizziness, and/or numbness. Whether the stroke is hemorrhagic, ischemic, or a TIA, after a few minutes of being deprived of oxygen, neurons die.

According to the Cardiovascular Health Study, up to a third of the elderly have stroke lesions of which they and their doctors are unaware. This means that millions of Americans have strokelike impairments to their brains that affect their cognitive abilities and mood.

Aside from strokes there are many things that can disrupt the supply of blood to the brain. Collectively they have been referred to as cerebrovascular compromises (CVC) and can include such problems as inflamed or stiff blood vessels and too high or too low blood pressure. A number of health-related factors may contribute to CVCs, including LDL cholesterol, atherosclerosis, platelets, and high stress, which entails elevated stress hormones such as cortisol.

High blood pressure (also called hypertension), a major danger sign for brain health, is the most common cause of CVC. Hypertension is a silent killer because it ups the risk of stroke and/ or heart attack. Short of the extremes of strokes and heart attacks, it leads to brain impairment and has been found to contribute to cognitive deficits.

Because of the multiple destructive effects of hypertension, before a doctor's exam, a nurse checks your blood pressure. Blood pressure is measured by two numbers: the amount of pressure on the "squeeze" when the heart pumps blood out, which is called systolic blood pressure, and the amount of pressure between beats, which is called diastolic blood pressure. The reading is expressed as systolic/diastolic, such as 120/80, which is considered optimal. A reading over 140/90 denotes hypertension. Anything below that number is considered normal.

Build a Healthy Brain

When I was initially studying neuropsychology, I was told that we are all born with as many neurons as we will ever have. The dogma of the day was that we all lose about 10,000 neurons a day. If you want to lose another 10,000, drink a beer or get a fever. That was all wrong.

Although it is true that the brain shrinks with age because there is some atrophy in key areas such as the hippocampus and the dorsolateral prefrontal cortex, new neurons can be born in those areas. As was noted in Chapter 2, the discovery of the birth of new neurons, called neurogenesis, was one of the most revolutionary in neuroscience. One of the main factors associated with the activation of neurogenesis is aerobic exercise. It spurs the release of a protein substance called brain-derived neurotrophic factor (BDNF), which many people call Miracle-Gro. BDNF serves many functions including the following:

- Consolidates the connections between neurons. It helps neurons fire together to wire together.
- Promotes the growth of myelin to make neurons fire more efficiently
- Acts on stem cells in the hippocampus, making them grow into new neurons

The discovery of neurogenesis in the hippocampus and prefrontal cortex (PFC) was revolutionary. It is also great news for people concerned about the aging brain. Despite the tendency to incur some atrophy in the hippocampus and PFC with age, exercise can slow the degenerative process down at least and reverse it at best. People concerned about the longevity of their brains and the integrity of these two areas should take regular advantage of this self-promoting fountain of youth.

In other words, exercise not only arrests the natural aging process but makes the brain of an aging adult younger in the area associated with attention and memory. One study found that brisk walking for just three hours a week was enough to produce neurogenesis in key areas of the brain such as the frontal lobes, the corpus callosum, and the hippocampus.[14] Since this study involved people between the ages of 60 and 79, it illustrates that neurogenesis is indeed possible late in life.

In addition to spurring the birth of new neurons, exercise helps build and maintain the brain in a wide variety of ways. The wide range of benefits includes enhancements to hormones, neurotransmitters, and proteins that build brain cells. For example, beginning in your fifties, you stop producing human growth hormone (HGH), thus accelerating the aging process. HGH is involved in cellular reproduction to help maintain muscles, strength, and stamina. Exercise has been shown to trigger the release of HGH in what has been referred to as the exercise-induced growth hormone response, which contributes to the slowing of the aging process.

Moving from a moderate-intensity workout to a high-intensity workout, for example, by going from jogging to running, puts you into the aerobic range. Your pituitary gland unleashes HGH, which helps layer muscle fiber, burn belly fat, and build brain volume.

This is important because reduction of HGH contributes to the aging process. After age 50 most people stop producing HGH, and as a result the aging process accelerates, as does the loss of cellular reproduction, growth, and repair. Exercise reverses these losses and aids the production of HGH, which helps maintain and develop muscles, strength, and stamina.

The neurotransmitter acetylcholine is critically involved in memory and attention. Acetylcholine is indispensable for the brain and its memory system. Not surprisingly, Alzheimer's disease is marked by a dramatic decline in the level of acetylcholine. Because of this decline, acetylcholine is one of the principal targets of medication in the treatment of Alzheimer's disease. Drugs such as Aricept enhance the activity of acetylcholine.

Healthy levels of acetylcholine are promoted by exercise as well as diet. Since your mind, brain, and body are interrelated, neurons extend their reach from the brain to the muscles at a specialized structure called the neuromuscular junction, where the nervous system uses acetylcholine to communicate to muscles. Research conducted by Jeff Lichtman at Washington University in Saint Louis has shown that muscle fibers contain a scaffold made of special proteins that hold acetylcholine receptors in place. A loss of nerve signals resulting from physical inactivity disassembles this scaffold, causing the loss of acetylcholine receptors. Regular exercise activates muscles, allowing the scaffold to tighten its grip and catch any receptors coming by. Whereas inactivity disassembles acetylcholine receptors, muscular activity (exercise) restores those receptors at the synapse. Thus, exercise boosts acetylcholine activity, which is a critical part of the memory system. This interrelationship between muscle fibers, acetylcholine, and memory is what body workers such as masseuses report that their clients often tell them during a massage. Though it is often called a muscle memory, this does not mean memories are in our muscles but reflects a broad memory system involving mind-body-brain interdependence.

Researchers at the University of California evaluated data from 5,000 women over 65 years of age. The study showed that exercise boosts memory through multiple pathways, including increasing oxygenated blood and glucose to the brain, helping form new capillaries to bring additional blood to the neurons, boosting a wide variety of neurotransmitters that aid in memory, strengthening the connections between neurons, and helping increase the production of new neurons. All these factors improve not only memory systems but also attention, alertness, and other cognitive functions.

A common excuse that people use for not exercising is that they are just too tired. Psychologists have long known that people complain most about fatigue and brain fog around 4 p.m. This is one of the rationalizations used for having coffee or sugar in the late afternoon for a boost of energy. Both are counterfeit forms of energy. A brisk 10-minute walk in the late afternoon will give you 90 minutes of real energy. Boosts in neurotransmitters such as dopamine, norpinephrine, and serotonin will provide you with the neurochemistry to not only boost your energy but keep you calm and focused the rest of the day. I love espresso, but in the afternoon I resist the temptation to drink a cup and instead take a 10-minute run or walk. With my encouragement, my assistant does the same thing each day, not part of her break time but part of the regular day, as an energy boost.

Just as the concept of exercising to get more energy sounds counterintuitive, so does the idea of pushing your body to go farther than you thought it capable of doing. Think again of the body-building phenomenon in which you work out each day with more weight that slightly tears muscles so that they rebuild even stronger. Your brain also has mechanisms that build as you go beyond your previous capabilities.

Fortunately, exercise promotes repair mechanisms to deal with physical stress that not only promote recovery but strengthen the entire body, including the brain. Exercise spurs powerful repair molecules into action, including insulin-like grown factor, vascular endothelial growth factor, and fibroblast growth factor.

This list may seem mind-numbing, so let's take these molecules one by one and highlight why they are important for the brain. Insulin-like growth factor is a protein mainly secreted by the liver and pituitary gland and declines with age. It plays a role in cell development and the prevention of cell death and boosts memory and mood. In the brain it is involved in neural development, including neurogenesis, myelination, neuroplasticity, dendritic branching, and neuroprotection. Beware: if you Google "insulin-like grown factor," you will find a wide variety of companies that want to sell it in a capsule form so that you can build your muscles or slow down aging. What they don't tell you is that an excess of insulin-like grown factor has been associated with various types of cancer. This is another of the many reasons why it is best to be exceedingly cautious about taking supplements.

Insulin-like grown factor is also released by your muscles when you flex them and then travels through the bloodstream into the brain. It is needed to fuel the cells during exercise to increase the production of receptors for insulin. Glucose is the major energy source in the brain, and insulin-like grown factor works with insulin to deliver glucose to cells in your brain as well as managing your glucose levels. It also acts like a sergeant in your body's neurochemical army, issuing orders to ramp up the production of several neurochemicals, including brain-derived neurohrophic factor, which is also called Miracle-Gro because it increases neuroplasticity and neurogenesis. During exercise both brain-derived neurotrophic factor and insulin-like growth factor activate neurons to produce more neurotransmitters such as serotonin and glutamate.

Exercise helps construct and enhance blood vessels to get fuel to your cells, which is critical to a healthy brain. Vascular endothelial growth factor helps build more capillaries. A healthy flow of blood to the brain is critical for the longevity of the brain. It is thought that vascular endothelial growth factor changes the permeability of the blood-brain barrier, which allows other growth factors to engage the brain during exercise; this is ultimately vital to neurogenesis. Exercise restores it for patients with coronary artery disease by helping build new blood vessels (capillaries) to support new cells.

A study performed at the University of Pisa in Italy showed that aerobically fit 63-year-olds protected their blood vessels and kept them dilated. Though with aging the natural system that performs these health-promoting functions that include the way the blood vessels use nitrous oxide diminishes, exercise kept this system going as well as it did in healthy 27-year-olds.

Nitric oxide is a potent antiatherogenic agent, mediating its actions via vasodilation as well as inhibition of platelet aggregation, smooth muscle cell proliferation, and leukocyte adhesion to endothelial cells in the vessel wall.[15] In contrast, a disturbance of the endothelial function from the loss of nitric oxide because of little or no physical exercise results in smooth muscle vasoconstriction.[16]

In fact, exercise promotes healthy blood flow to the brain in a wide variety of other ways, including the following:

- Lowers bad (LDL) cholesterol and raises good (HDL) cholesterol, which prevents arteries from getting stiff and narrow
- Lowers blood pressure
- Makes the heart beat more efficiently
- Boosts the body's sensitivity to glucose, which lowers the risk of diabetes
- Lowers a compound in blood that makes blood clots called fibrinogen and thus lowers the risk of stroke
- Slows the aging-related decline in blood vessels' use of nitrous oxide, which protects against blood clotting and keeps the vessels dilated
- Provides better control of inflammation

Exercise also induces the release of fibroblast growth factor, which helps tissues grow in the body. It is important in the growth of neurons and, along with BDNF, is involved in turning stem cells into new neurons and also in neuroplasticity. The promotion of fibroblast growth factor becomes all the more important as we age. Researchers at Duke University found that the levels of it along with the two other critical growth factors—insulin-like growth factor and vascular endothelial growth factor—decline beginning in middle age. These growth factors are secreted by glial cells, specifically astrocytes, and are critical for enabling stem cells to produce new neurons. The number of astrocytes that produce fibroblast growth factor declines with age. These findings shed light on the mechanisms behind the declining production of new neurons in the dentate gyrus region of the hippocampus. All three growth factors—fibroblast growth factor, insulin-like growth factor, and vascular endothelial growth factor—increase with exercise, along with brain-derived neurotrophic factor.

During exercise oxidative stress occurs at the energy factories within the cells (called the mitochondria) during the conversion of glucose into energy in the form of adenosine triphosphate (ATP), the principal type of fuel that cells burn. This process of energy conversion produces waste by-products called free radicals, which are molecules with a rogue electron that can rupture the cell structure by careening around a cell.

Metabolic stress occurs when the cells can't produce enough ATP because glucose cannot get into the cell or because you have exhausted its supply. Finally, excitoxic stress occurs when ATP can't keep up with the excessive activity of the neurotransmitter called glutamate, which increases with the energy demands of exercising. Excessive glutamate causes excitotoxicity, which is destructive to cells.

Optimally, repetition of a stimulus (practice) lowers the amount of glutamate necessary to make the next transmission. The lowered threshold strengthens the connection (LTP) that had been established initially by a moderate level of activation that was established through the glutamate receptor called **N**-methyl-D-aspartate (NMDA). However, chronic stress overactivates the NMDA receptors, resulting in a destructive process that lets in too much calcium, which generates free radicals. Excitotoxicity, as this is called, kills cells to an extreme degree. An example of what occurs when your brain receives too much glutamate is a bad headache after you eat food with monosodium glutamate (MSG). The MSG overexcites the NMDA receptors, causing excitotoxicity.

These repair factors also work to prevent the damaging effects of chronic psychological stress by keeping the stress hormone cortisol in check. High levels of cortisol have a corrosive effect on the hippocampus, resulting in its atrophy. Since the hippocampus is critical for laying down new memory, chronically high stress can result in a memory deficit. Exercise is an excellent way to burn off excess cortisol and help diminish psychological stress by pumping up the levels of neurotransmitters such as GABA, acetylcholine, serotonin, dopamine, and norepinephrine that keep you calm, positive, and energized.

Exercise also stimulates a variety of genetic transcriptional processes that enhance the health, longevity, and immunological functions in the brain. Exercise-stimulated transcription aids neuroplasticity, including the stimulation of BDNF and vascular endothelial growth factor (VEGF). Brain-derived neurotrophic factor gathers in reserve pools near the synapses when you get your blood pumping during exercise. All this activity stimulates the production of more BDNF receptors, and this enhances memory by promoting neurogenesis in the hippocampus. It helps stem cells divide and differentiate into new neurons and glial cells. These enhancements are important as we age because one of the areas that begin to atrophy later in life is the hippocampus. Also, during exercise, insulin-like growth factor, vascular endothelial growth factor, and fibroblast growth factor push through the blood-brain barrier (the web of capillaries and the high-density cells that protect the brain by screening out intruders such as bacteria) and work with BDNF factor to increase the molecular processes that facilitate memory.

These brain-sharpening benefits of aerobic exercise have been demonstrated in a wide variety of studies. For example, a study carried out at four universities in the United States included 120 older adults between ages 50 and 77 without dementia and randomly placed them in two groups. One group walked around a track for 40 minutes a day three times a week. The other group engaged in stretching and toning exercises. Spatial memory tests and magnetic resonance imaging were performed at the beginning, after six months, and then after one year on the individuals in both groups. The members of the aerobic group increased their hippocampal volume by just over 2 percent. Those who engaged in just the stretching and toning exercises lost 1.4 percent of their hippocampal volume, which is consistent with the decrease seen in normal aging. The tests of spatial memory were consistent with the increased size of the hippocampus. Accordingly, those who engaged in the aerobic exercise improved their memory.

In a University of Illinois–Urbana study, 124 previously sedentary people ages 60 to 79 received aerobic training, did nonaerobic stretching and toning, or did nothing, with the first two groups exercising for one hour three times a week. Again, it was only the aerobic group that showed changes in brain structure as measured by magnetic resonance imaging. Those in stretching group and the nonexercising group showed no changes, whereas the aerobic group members showed substantial increases in gray matter in the frontal lobes and white matter mostly in the corpus callosum, the span of axons that connect the two hemispheres. This increase was significant because the corpus callosum generally deteriorates with age, slowing communication between the hemispheres and slowing thinking as a result. Exercise thus sped up the communication between the two hemispheres and thereby the speed of thinking.

Speed of information processing is a characteristic of fluid intelligence. As was described in Chapter 3, fluid intelligence (intelligence related to speed of processing) generally declines with age but crystallized intelligence (intelligence related to facts and information) remains relatively intact. Aerobically fit older adults show an advantage in fluid intelligence.

The Maastricht Aging Study demonstrated that aerobically fit people age 24 to 76 had higher cognitive speed. Similarly, researchers at the University of Texas found that older aerobically fit women had faster complex reaction times, and 6,979 British men and women between ages 18 and 94 who walked had faster complex reaction times.

Exercise to Minimize Dementia

The long-term gains from exercise exert a protective effect against the clinical symptoms of dementia. Older people who exercise three or more times a week gain an enhanced sense of well-being and a diminished risk of cognitive decline, or a delay in the onset of symptoms of dementia later in life.[17]

Carrolee Barlow of the Salk Institute has argued that exercise rescues brain cells that might otherwise die from oxidative stress during aging. These findings suggest that exercise delays the onset and progression of some neurodegenerative diseases. Even people who already have a dementia process can gain from exercise. A study at the Saint Jude Children's Research Hospital in Memphis found that the effects of exercise can be seen in two months in people with Parkinson's disease. The major impairment factor in Parkinson's disease is a progressive loss of dopamine in neurons in the area of the brainstem called the substantia nigra. Two months of exercise increases neurons, and the greater the amount of exercise, the greater the benefit.

A meta-analysis of the results of 18 studies published between 2000 and 2001 showed that exercise increases cognitive performance in healthy adults between the ages of 55 to 80.[18] The amount of aerobic exercise needed to produce these results is at least 30 to 60 minutes per day three days a week.

Based on the exercise and health data from approximately 5,000 men and women over 65 years of age, those who exercised on a regular basis were less likely to lose cognitive abilities or develop dementia. A five-year study at Laval University in Sainte-Foy, Quebec, showed that the more a person exercises, the greater are the neuroprotective effects, especially in women. Inactive individuals were twice as likely to develop Alzheimer's disease compared to those with the highest levels of exercise, which involved exercising vigorously at least three times a week.

According to a Taiwanese study of 416,000 people who were asked about their exercise habits, 15 minutes a week of exercise cut the risk of death by 14 percent and extended life expectancy by three years compared with those who did not exercise. Each additional 15 minutes of exercise reduced the risk of death by an additional 4 percent.

Overall, there is abundant research evidence demonstrating that exercise can help you sharpen your brain. Exercise is essentially good medicine. The flip side of that is that lack of exercise is bad medicine.

Develop an Exercise Habit

You may be truly convinced that exercise is good for your health, but you need to behave like you believe it. Too many people may put it off as if it were a chore to be done only when it is convenient. Exercise must to be practiced as a regular part of your life to extend the health of your brain, sharpen it, and delay the encroachment of dementia.

Older adults who have not built structured exercise into their lives during their young adult years periodically ask me, "Well, I missed the boat on that one. Is it too late?" Or they may ask, "How on earth can I catch up for all those lost years? Do I have to exercise twice as hard?" It is never too late to start, but the sooner you get started, the greater the benefits to your brain. Start small and build your stamina. Every little bit helps. Even 10 minutes of aerobic exercise a day can give you 90 minutes of energy, provide you with greater ability to focus, and burn off excess stress hormones such as cortisol. For the last few years I have made it a practice to run and walk on the trails behind my office at least once a day. Sometimes I have only 10 minutes to get my heart rate up and spur the release of GABA, dopamine, and norepinephrine to help me feel relaxed, positive, and energized before my next client. Exercise helps me burn off any excess neurochemicals that have been building through the day so that I can be completely present for them.

The Centers for Disease Control and Prevention and the American College of Sports Medicine recommend 30 minutes or more of moderate-intensity exercise on most days, preferably all the days of the week. The exercise may be spread out over the day, such as in 10-minute segments. This exercise may include brisk walking, dancing, jogging, swimming, or bicycling. For weight loss and management, according to the National Institutes of Medicine, you should increase your exercise to 60 minutes of moderate-intensity exercise.

Exercising three or more times a week is the level suggested by the American College of Sports Medicine. Many have called this a public health dose of at least 30 minutes of aerobic exercise, which can involve a wide variety of activities, including brisk walking, bicycling, and running. One study did not find significant differences in alleviating depression in those who exercised three versus five times per week.[19] Similarly, the fitness guidelines of the World Health Organization recommend that adults get at least 30 minutes a day of a moderate workout most days of the week. This can include brisk walking, water aerobics, or bike riding.

Many people, including myself, on workdays break up the 30 minutes of exercise into chunks of 10 minutes spread through the day. Because of the shorter amount of time I exercise, I run at least half the time to get my heart rate up. Like many people, I find it easier to find small chunks of time than longer spans of time. The key is getting the heart rate up enough to break a sweat.

Fitness is a measure of what a person is capable of doing physically. Exercise to promote fitness takes two general forms: aerobic and anaerobic. Aerobic exercise engages large muscles in continuous exertion in such forms of exercise as jogging, bicycling, swimming, hiking, and brisk walking. The emphasis is on exertion—getting your heart rate up high enough that you feel out of breath, sweat, and feel physically exhausted.

The important measure of aerobic fitness many healthcare workers use is the reference point called maximal velocity of oxygen use (VO_2 max). It is measured by an exercise physiologist by clipping your nose shut and asking you to breathe out of a tube that is connected to a computer while you jog on a treadmill. At some point the computer indicates that you have reached your VO_2 max. The higher the reading, the more aerobically fit you are and the less likely you will later die of a heart attack.

Anaerobic exercise is also referred to as strength training for quick bursts of energy that may include forms of exercise such as weight lifting, chin-ups, and push-ups. These forms of exercise are anaerobic because they involve going beyond our capacity to burn oxygen for energy, at which point the body starts to make lactic acid. You know you have reached this point when your muscles begin to burn when you overdo it. My thighs burn when I really push myself while skiing. As we age, we need to continually engage in anaerobic exercise to keep our muscles lean and strong.

At the University of Illinois, Arthur Kramer enrolled 124 sedentary men and women between the ages of 60 and 75 and divided them into two groups. Half of them performed toning and stretching—nonaerobic exercise—and the other half took brisk walks—aerobic exercise. The walkers gradually increased their walks to 45 to 60 minutes. After six months the walkers showed not only more aerobic fitness but a 25 percent improvement in cognitive speed. The toners showed no improvement in either area.

It is best to structure in 30 minutes a day of aerobic exercise. But keep this in mind: 10 minutes of exercise increases energy for 60 to 120 minutes. Also, your mood will be boosted and you will feel as good as you do during any other period of the day.

You may be great at procrastinating or be plagued by being overly busy. You may create a multitude of rationalizations for why you don't have time to exercise. Structuring time to exercise is the way to escape the procrastination problem. You structure eating, sleeping, and going to the bathroom into your schedule, so why not exercise? Do not just think it is a good thing to do if you have time. Make time. Exercise is fundamental to your future health and therefore is a critical part of the Brain Bible formula.

According to I-Min Lee of the Harvard School of Public Health, people who engage in 15 minutes of moderate exercise have a 14 percent lower risk of heart disease compared with inactive people.[20] Many healthcare providers recommend at least 10,000 steps daily as the minimum dose of exercise. Of course, counting those steps would be ridiculous, which is why it is a good idea to purchase a pedometer. A review of 29 studies has shown consistent support for the mental health benefits of aerobic exercise, including attention, memory, and speed of mental functions.[21]

Motivation Tips

Because motivation to start exercising as well as continue exercising is sometimes not there, there are a variety of tips to keep in mind. The American Psychological Association summarized several suggestions from its researchers.[22] Here is a summary:

Make exercise purposeful. University of Wisconsin–Madison exercise researcher William Morgan, PhD, has made the case for "Factor P," putting purpose to your exercise. By hooking your exercise to meaningful activity such as walking your dog, biking to work, or building a stone wall, you can avoid the excuse that you don't have time for a "pointless" activity such as running on a treadmill.

Use cognitive techniques. California State University exercise researcher Robert Thayer, PhD, suggests starting small. By setting your goals small initially, such as saying, "I'm just going to walk a few minutes," you invariably feel like walking more. Another technique is referred to as the cognitive override, in which you remind yourself that a 10-minute walk will give you more energy than a candy bar.

Make exercise a regular part of your day. University of North Carolina at Chapel Hill professor John Silva, PhD, suggests that you assign a specific time of the day for exercise. By structuring exercise into your normal routine, you will be less apt to find that you don't have time.

Be flexible. The chair of the psychology department at the University of Memphis suggests that if you have only five minutes, take a short brisk walk. Later, when you find another 5, 10, or 15 minutes, use those periods too. Vary your routines.

Make it fun. The president of Division 47 (Exercise and Sport) of the American Psychological Association, Kate Hays, PhD, suggests that whatever exercise you choose, make it something that you enjoy. That way you will be more likely return to it.

Exercise with others. By engaging in exercise with others, you make it fun, have a chance to connect with others, and have a motivation to return to it if it is a regular date with others. Consider that though you may feel out of shape now, pushing yourself a little more each time will build strength and endurance. If you walk for exercise with others, do the talk test: walk fast enough that it is difficult to talk and walk at the same time.

Dose yourself. Think that each dose of exercise should boost your heartbeat, make you breathe quickly, and make you sweat. When you feel like having a cup of coffee in the late afternoon, tell yourself, "A walk will give me more energy."

Commit over the long haul. By telling yourself that you will see the benefits of exercise later and that it is cumulative, you can get a daily dose that adds up over time.

Exercising in a stimulating and novel environment is a very effective way to stimulate neurogenesis through the development of new neurons in the dentate gyrus of the hippocampus because it is stimulated by novelty and involved in new learning (memory). Thus, physical exercise and learning work together as a powerful combination to stimulate neurogenesis. Exercise helps make new stem cells, and learning prolongs their survival.

The timing of learning is important. It is best not to try to learn something while jogging on a treadmill. About 30 minutes into exercising blood is directed away from the prefrontal cortex during aerobic exercise to help the body deal with the physical challenge. Because the prefrontal cortex is the executive control center of the brain, you need it to focus your full attention. After you finish exercising, the blood shifts back to your frontal lobes, and with it an increased capacity for focus and learning.

Volitional exercise is not something you mindlessly do out of habit; it is something you decide to do for brain health because of the absence of stress and the inclusion of theta waves, which are the brain waves present when you pay close attention to something. Theta waves are not present when you eat or drink or otherwise are on automatic pilot. Since your frontal lobes do the deciding, activating them represents a key part of neurogenesis. The bottom line is that you can reap the full benefits of exercise if you follow it up by becoming intellectually engaged. Keep in mind that for enhanced memory and cognition, exercise alone won't sustain the new neurons. Otherwise all jocks would be brilliant. You'll need mental exercise plus physical exercise to promote and sustain the new neurons that sharpen your brain. Chapter 3 discusses mental exercise.

Brisk walking is one of the easiest and cheapest forms of exercise because you don't need to be a member of a gym and can do it at any time and in most places. Walking is very good for the brain because it increases blood circulation and with it the oxygen and glucose critical for a healthily functioning brain. It is less strenuous than jogging because your leg muscles don't use extra oxygen and glucose.

Walking is an ideal form of exercise. You can vary your walking speed to achieve different levels of cardio exercise for a brain boost. Even at slower, non-cardio-boosting levels, walking is good for your brain. The popular saying that it is "good to walk to clear your head" makes a lot of sense because less strenuous walking does not disproportionally divert blood with its extra oxygen and glucose to your leg muscles. Walking is an excellent way to oxygenate your brain.

When researchers from the University of California–San Francisco measured the cognitive and related brain functions of approximately 6,000 people who walked at varied levels through the week, they found that those people had better memory skills. For every extra mile walked per week there was a 13 percent less chance of cognitive decline.[23] Those in the higher-energy group saw the least cognitive decline, up to 14 percent.

Brisk walking provides all the benefits of other forms of exercise. For example, a study performed at Duke University Medical Center showed that walking improved learning ability, concentration, and abstract reasoning. Additionally, walking decreased depression and cut stroke risk by 57 percent in people who did it as little as 20 minutes a day.

One way to enhance the effects of exercise is to visualize your accomplishments by using a daily log or journal detailing the speed and the distance of your walk. An exercise program can begin with thinking about exercise. Both thinking about exercise and actually engaging in exercise activate the same neuronal systems. In other words, simply thinking about exercise revs up some of the same neuronal systems that you activate when you exercise. The effects of mentally practicing physical exercise were compared with those of actual physical exercise. By using transcranial magnetic stimulation (TMS) to observe cortical activity and subsequent physical performance, researchers showed that the mental practice not only created changes in the brain but also improved physical performance because the same parts of the brain are activated during mental practice and physical practice. Even after five days of mental practice, physical performance improved. Specifically, five days of mental practice followed by two hours of physical practice improved performance as much as it did among people who engaged solely in physical exercise for five days.[24]

These findings are consistent with the long-held belief in sports psychology that visualizing and mentally rehearsing performance helps improve performance on the playing field. Whether it is mentally rehearsing a home run swing or a killer tennis serve, mental practice improves physical performance.

Though you may find that the faster you can visualize doing something, the faster you can do it, there are limitations to what is possible. For example, if you are right-handed, you'll be better able to imagine moving your right hand than your left. This constraint occurs if you had a stroke and one side of your body is weaker. The side that was not affected is as quick in imagining as well as in actually physically moving because you are using the same brain systems in imagining and actually moving.

Imagining and planning must be followed up by actually engaging in exercise. Most people find that starting out by taking small steps works best to break the procrastination barrier. The key is that you get started now and build on the first step forward by taking the next step. As you prepare for the future, make sure to exercise at least moderately and if possible vigorously.

There are many psychological as well as physical benefits to exercise, including an increased sense of self-esteem and self-confidence. When you are exercising, you can enjoy a meditative and relaxed state of mind. It also offers a distraction from daily stress and anxiety. And if you exercise with other people, you get two of the Brain Bible factors: social support and exercise.

The synaptic connections you make between your neurons and the parts of your brain that are recruited, even in simple tasks, will boost cognitive reserve (a topic that is described in Chapter 3). There are a variety of exercises that you can engage in, including the following:

- Increase your dexterity. If you are right-handed, use your left for simple tasks such as brushing your teeth.
- Listen to music while you exercise.

- Get dressed or wash your hands with your eyes closed.
- Drive to work or the store using new routes.
- Shop at new stores.

To structure exercise into your day, you may chunk it into one specific part of the day or spread it out throughout the day, taking opportunities to get bursts of exercise. To give you an example of this, on my workdays, instead of driving, I walked the quarter of a mile to the hospital. Then, instead of taking the elevator, I would climb the seven flights of stairs and arrive at the ward a little damp under the collar and always felt more relaxed and focused. Try these activities:

If you have a lawn, use a mower that requires you to push it or at the very least walk behind it.

Take advantage of seasonal chores such as raking leaves and shoveling snow.

Use the stairs instead of the elevator.

Sweep the driveway, patio, and walkway.

Take public transportation, walk to the station, and get off one or two stops before your stop and walk home from there.

Make running errands a form of exercise.

Park at the far end of the parking lot and then circumnavigate the shopping mall before entering it.

Go dancing.

Walk the dog briskly.

Bicycle or walk to explore your neighborhood and increase the distance each time.

CHAPTER 6

The Social Factor

Before coming to see me Michael had gone through a difficult divorce. Not only did he have to deal with his marriage coming to an end, he lost most of the friends he and his ex-wife had in common. They had been married for 35 years, and now at age 64 he had few if any social contacts. His only friend was Sam, whom he had accompanied to baseball games during the three years since his divorce. Since he felt jilted by his wife and all their friends, he developed a motto: "No social commitments, no more betrayal."

Trained and employed as a computer engineer, he felt most comfortable with precision. The muddled area of emotion was far too difficult to manage. Though he found himself becoming dull and bored after the divorce, he felt safer not putting himself out there to get rejected. Sure, he spent time with people at work in the break room, but their conversation was always work-oriented. During the first six months after the divorce they asked, "So how are you getting along?" He always said, "Fine, thanks. And you?" apparently thinking that he must express the typical social courtesy. Since no one asked follow-up questions, he wondered if anyone knew how hurt he continued to be from his wife's affair that had led to their divorce. Early on, he did tell Jim and Susan, two coworkers, that he felt deeply wounded and assumed that they would tell everyone else. Yet no one seemed to notice or care, not even Jim and Susan.

By the time he got to me, he appeared moderately depressed.

"Are you feeling depressed?" I asked during our first session.

"Maybe a little. Why? Are you going to lock me away or something?"

"Why would I do that? You're not suicidal, are you?" He looked away, causing me to become concerned.

"I would never do something stupid like that. . . ." After a long pause he said, "But if I became terminally ill and died, I guess I wouldn't be disappointed." Then he laughed and added, "And neither would anyone else."

"Oh, I'm sorry. No one? No family?"

"They're all on the East Coast living their own lives. I suppose they would come to my funeral; that's if I have one. No one would arrange it, I guess. My life is an island with no one on it but me. And I'm not liking my own company."

"No friends?"

"They washed their hands of me right after my wife tried to flush me down the toilet."

He went on to describe how everyone he and his wife knew together had abandoned him and sided with her. The bitter irony, he explained, was that she blamed him for the affair and everyone apparently agreed. When I asked if he actually had asked them, he responded by saying, "No need to. It was obvious."

"Oh, really? How?"

He shook his head and then shrugged his shoulders. "They've all invited her over for dinner. Did I get an invite?" he asked with a fading voice.

"What happened when you called them?"

"Why would I want to get rejected? They know where I am."

As we continued to talk, it became evident that much of his prior social experience had resulted from his wife's efforts. Her departure created a vacuum that he filled with resentment. His loneliness needed to be addressed, but getting there would be tricky. His wife's affair was the place to start.

When I expressed my sympathy for how hurt he must have felt, he looked at me sideways. "So you guys are trained to say such things, aren't you?"

"Is it hard for you to give people a chance?"

"Never again," he said ruefully. "Big risk."

"Isn't there a bigger risk in not taking the risk?"

"What do you mean?"

"Aren't you feeling rejected anyway? Maybe the people at work worry that if they keep asking after you tell them you are okay, you might say, 'I told you I'm fine!'"

"You're taking their side?" he asked, beginning to stir in the chair as if readying himself to bolt.

"Sides? If there were sides, I would certainly be on yours."

He seemed to soften, opening the door enough to tell me more about the relationship and feel empathetically heard. Toward the end of the first session I asked how he felt.

"A little better, I guess. At least I got some of that off my chest and can see that I am not to blame."

"I'll certainly be here if you want to come back."

He nodded yes apologetically. "Make an appointment."

"In the meantime you might consider inviting a few people out for coffee or lunch."

"Shouldn't they be the ones to ask?"

"Maybe since you rebuffed them by saying you were fine, you shut the door."

During our second session we talked about how he had made somewhat of an effort by going out to lunch with his ball game friend, Sam, and then Jim at work. He was surprised that they expressed their support after he told them that he still felt hurt and confused about the divorce.

Knowing that he had great respect for science, I went on to talk about how there are important parts of the brain that thrive on social contact. When they don't get stimulated, they begin to atrophy, and a person can consequently become depressed and cognitively dull. He seemed more alarmed by the cognitive risks than by the risks of depression. We talked about how communication challenges the brain to build extensive circuits to respond to complex social dimensions that extend its life. I told him how people with limited social contacts seem to be vulnerable to the symptoms of dementia earlier than people with robust social networks. In other words, by maintaining an active social life as you age, you help keep your brain sharp. One more piece of information that really got his attention was that loneliness has been associated with the breakdown of telomeres, which, you remember from Chapter 2, are the ends of the chromosomes. Shortened telomeres contribute to accelerated aging.

No person is an island all to herself, that is, no healthy person. That is what Michael discovered. We are social creatures that thrive on positive relationships. Michael had depended on his wife and her social connections for the social nourishment he needed. Over the next few months the major shift for him in therapy was from a passive recipient of sparse social support to an active participant in building a healthy social network of his own. Ironically, he had to lose his marriage and then experience pain from loneliness to learn that he must give as well as receive to enjoy the full dimensions of benefits from relationships.

Social Factor Questionnaire

Yes No

☐   ☐   Do you find that people are more trouble than they are worth?

☐   ☐   Have you found yourself isolating yourself from people more in recent years?

☐   ☐   Do you wait for others to contact you, rarely taking the initiative?

Yes No

☐ ☐ Do you find that your relationships are defined so that you are viewed as a caregiver who never gets cared for?

☐ ☐ In your relationships, do you find yourself thinking that the other person only has his own interests in mind?

☐ ☐ Are you lonely?

☐ ☐ Do you shy away from social gatherings, thinking that more than one person at a time is too complex or bothersome?

☐ ☐ Are you generally the passive one in your relationships?

☐ ☐ Do you regard yourself as too socially awkward to learn to develop and maintain relationships? In other words, why even try?

☐ ☐ Do you feel so wounded by a relationship gone bad or the loss of a loved one that it's too hard to learn to trust again for fear of another loss?

If you answered yes to any of these questions, there is reason to be concerned that you are cutting yourself off from the benefits of the social factor, starving your social brain networks of activation and limiting the benefits that socialization provides.

Rob's Renaissance

With retirement on the horizon, Rob assumed that his social contacts would fade away. He even thought of putting off his retirement because he was worried that he had nothing planned for himself. Since he was a psychologist in our department, one would think that he was psychologically prepared for the transition. One day over lunch he said, "I am really ready to retire, but I couldn't be less ready." Indeed, for the next several weeks after he retired, he came around the department to go out for coffee and lunch with other colleagues. Though everyone seemed pleased to see him, it was evident that they were all sad that he had a difficult time moving on to building a life for himself away from work.

About one month into his retirement over lunch I asked, "So what do you have planned for yourself?"

He shrugged his shoulders. "Well, John, I guess I ought to say 'everything I always wanted to do.'"

"And you're not?"

His sad eyes turned away. "I'm not sure where to start."

"If a client were to say that to you, what would you say?"

"Ha! Now there's the irony. I've been thinking. In our line of work we spend all of our time connecting with people, and so in our off hours it's nice to get away from people to regroup and reflect. Now I'm away and just reflecting. What is it that you have been writing and lecturing about, the social brain networks?"

"Looks like yours are starved."

"Yeah, and I don't like the hunger pain," he said with a characteristic self-deprecatory laugh.

"So what was it that you would say to a client if he were in a similar situation?"

Smiling with his knowing nod, he said, "All right, I guess I'd say 'start small.' My wife has a network of friends, and she seems to not like me hanging around the house hour after hour. That's why I've come around for coffee and lunch with you guys."

"That's the only reason?"

"Hey, now don't get offended," he said with a sly look indicating that he knew was rhetorical, then paused to reflect. "I suppose I could volunteer as a consultant at one of the nonprofits."

"You've been sympathizing with them for years; now they and you can benefit by your involvement."

"Hmm . . . suppose they have no interest?" he said, looking sadly away.

"Right, with all the draconian budget cuts, you think they're going to turn down free help from a psychologist?"

"They could."

"But as you would tell your clients, you won't know unless you try, right? Besides, what do you have to lose by trying?"

The next time I had lunch with Rob, it was he, not me, talking about all the things one can do in retirement.

Avoid Loneliness

To put the power of the social support factor into perspective, consider that for most of its evolutionary history, our species lived a hunter-gatherer lifestyle. Our ancestors thrived because they maintained strong emotional and social ties. They needed one another to stay safe and find food. If, in contrast, an individual was ostracized from the group, he or she was literally doomed to die. Hiking around on the savanna alone meant that individuals did not have the rest of the clan to help them stay safe from predators or reap the benefits of the group's effort to gather food and hunt.

Since we are highly social creatures that have thrived through our capacity to communicate, when we are in healthy relationships, we feel comforted. Alternatively, when we are socially deprived of healthy relationships and lonely, there is a heighted risk for health problems. Loneliness is essentially bad for your health. To put this statement in perspective, the health-related costs of loneliness have been found to be greater than the health-related costs of smoking.[1] In the long run loneliness is as detrimental to longevity as smoking is.[2] Loneliness in older persons almost doubles the risk of developing dementia.[3]

Many studies have shown that mental health risks, including depression, go up dramatically for older people when they are socially isolated and lonely. For example, researchers at the University of Porto assessed 1,000 people age 65 and older and found that the most reliable predictor of psychological distress was the feeling of loneliness. Simply not knowing the neighbors increased the probability of depression.[4] Similarly, a study done by researchers at University

College London assessed 2,600 people 65 and older and found that 15 percent were at risk for social isolation, which was associated with depressed mood and health problems.[5] It is no wonder that interpersonal therapy, which is used to strengthen relationships with friends and family members and build social skills, has been found to be as effective as antidepressants in treating depression.[6]

Consistent with the enhanced quality of life, information derived from the MacArthur Study on Successful Aging revealed that greater emotional support in relationships is associated with better cognitive functioning for up to 7.5 years.[7] The Wisconsin Longitudinal Study showed that the presence of positive social relationships even in the face of economic disadvantage is correlated with resilient individuals and moderated stress levels.[8] This is in contrast to individuals who experience adversity early in life and subsequently have higher stress levels. Indeed, social support has long been known to help people deal with stress and alleviate anxiety and depression.

Several studies have found a strong relationship between loneliness and depression. The Chicago Health, Aging, and Social Relations Study, for example, assessed the social relationships of 229 adults born between 1935 and 1952. The study found that loneliness and depression are related and also that loneliness predicts later increases in depression. The greater the loneliness, the worse the self-rated health.[9] Loneliness was also related to increases in the level of cortisol, one of the major stress hormones.[10]

Lonely and nonlonely people differ in what they perceive as stressful. Loneliness decreases stress resiliency, a measure of how well a person deals with stress in the moment and bounces back from it. Lonely people tend to experience higher levels of stress, more serious difficulties, and less potent "uplifts" than do nonlonely individuals.[11] Loneliness adds to the total stress load and makes a person more susceptible to age-related decreases in stress resilience. On the positive side, social support has been found to lower age-related systolic blood pressure and other health measures.[12]

The benefits of social medicine are evident even at the genetic level. An emerging area of research called social genomics involves molecular biology tools that measure how genes can directly influence what people experience in their social environments. Steve Cole of UCLA has found that the genes that promote inflammation are more active in lonely people and the genes that inhibit inflammation are less active.[13] These findings explain the consistent finding that lonely people are far more likely to have illnesses associated with inflammation such as cardiovascular diseases, neurodegeneration, dementia, and some types of cancer.

In an effort to explore possible reasons why loneliness and inflammation are associated, researchers found that the types of genes that are overexpressed in lonely people originated in a "myeloid" line of immune cells that are quite old in evolutionary terms. These immune cells patrol the body scanning for infection-damaged tissue that inflammation helps repair. In contrast, genes in the B lymphocytes, which are cells that fight off viruses, are quite young from an evolutionary perspective and aid our species as we live in social groups with immune systems primed to fight off viruses shared among people.

Because they spend more time alone and do not need to worry about viruses, lonely people are primed to fight bacteria but not as well prepared to fight viruses, which are generally shared in social situations. People who are more socially connected are better prepared to fight viruses. It's hard to switch gears to fight bacteria or viruses if you are primed one way or the other. This is why some people can fight the flu but sometimes die of pneumonia.

Avoid the Dulling of Your Immune System

The immune system tends to become dysregulated as we age. It is composed of two main components: *cellular* immunity is generally the function of white blood cells called lymphocytes that act directly on an invading antigen, and *humoral* immunity is provided by white blood cells that can produce antibodies.

When your body is attacked by foreign invaders such as bacteria, your immune response is mounted by the complex interaction of these two systems, each of which is composed of three elements, sometimes called the trinities of immunology. B cells are so named because they are derived from bone that secretes antibodies to neutralize the invader. T cells are so named because they are derived from the thymus gland situated just below the throat; they function by direct contact to kill cells attacked by the invader. Accessory cells latch on to foreign invaders and present them to the T cells.

One factor that contributes to the impairment of the immune system as we age is the reduction in the function of the thymus gland, which is responsible for development of T cells. Aging results in T cell deficits, involving a decrease in proportion of some types of T cells relative to other types so that there are impairments in response to viral infections and reduced ability to identify foreign material. Some types of invaders, such as viruses, produce the usual response from the immune system, although that response is slower and less effective so that it takes longer to bounce back and recover from the flu or the common cold. Aging results in disorganization of this highly organized system.

The complement system seems to orchestrate an extreme attack on foreign invaders by using a powerful weapon called the membrane attack complex, which can burn a hole in a cell membrane. In doing so, it exposes the delicate interior of the cell, and this allows calcium to flood in and poison the cell. The complement system also uses one form of glial cells (the white matter) called microglia. Microglia roam the brain looking for problems. When they find a damaged neuron in a variety of forms such as a neuron infested with plaques and tangles, microglia spray nitric oxide, which increases free radicals. The microglia also surround the problem and devour it.

Aging tends to involve a progressive imbalance in the messenger molecules so that the molecules that stimulate an inflammation reaction increase and those that enhance immune function tend to decrease. Both plaques and tangles show many signs of inflammation. For example, plaques tend to show high levels of cytokines, acute-phase reactants, prostaglandins, the membrane attack complex, and microglia, which can release a deadly barrage of neurotoxins.

The interaction between social support and genes associated with cancer has also been explored. Steve Cole of UCLA and Susan Lutgendorf of the University of Iowa found that more than 220 genes are turned on in cancer cells in women with low levels of social support and high levels of depression. This tendency is not found in women with relatively more social support. This is not to say that a lack of social support causes cancer, but it does imply that the physiological infrastructure of a healthy body is undermined by a lack of social support and that people may be more likely to develop cancer if they lack social support. From this perspective we can regard social support as preventive medicine.

What is it about social support that has such a powerful effect on physical and mental health? It would make sense that there are networks in the brain that thrive on social support.

Nourish Your Social Brain

It would make sense, given the highly social nature of our species, that parts of the brain have evolved to become keenly sensitive to the complex nuances in relationships, either enhancing them or detecting the potential for rejection. These brain systems had a direct effect on the survival of our ancestors.

We have the same brain that our ancestors had. Their social brain networks are still operative within us. Consider also that more than any other species, we are born premature. Our period of dependency on our parents before we can live independently is far longer than that of any other species. Our long years of childhood dependency are spent absorbing social influences from our caregivers that shape who we will become as adults. Accordingly, the human brain has evolved with enhanced capabilities to communicate on many levels. To support these complex and powerful social skills, the human brain compared with that of any other species has more extensive socially sensitive neural networks in a wide variety of areas. All these neural networks work together to provide you with the capacity to read another person's emotions and intentions and to regulate your emotions so that you can act appropriately on the basis of the social context of the situation.

Consider the consequences of very poor nurturing social contact during the first few years of life. The test case for socially impoverished early years is the Romanian orphans who have been studied in the United Kingdom, Canada, and the United States because parents in those countries have adopted large numbers of orphans during the last 20 years. After the dictator Ceaușescu was deposed in 1991, approximately 150,000 orphans were found languishing in orphanages. They were kept clean and fed but had very little social contact. They resorted to hand flapping and other primitive self-stimulating behaviors.

Teams of psychologists discovered that the prognosis for later development was much better if an orphan was adopted after just a few months in the orphanage. The longer the children endured the impoverishment, the more impaired they were later in life and the higher was the prevalence of cognitive deficits such as attention deficit disorder (ADD), learning disorders, and poor social skills.

A similar yet far more extensive body of research has focused on the quality of attachment. John Bowlby and Mary Ainsworth as well as a whole generation of later researchers have shown that secure attachment between a child and his caregivers supports dramatically better mental health and cognitive development than avoidant, ambivalent, and disorganized attachment. One of Mary Ainsworth's students, Mary Main, who discovered the disorganized attachment style, said recently that adult attachment patterns mirror those discovered for infant attachment. Secure adult attachment can be acquired through "earned security." In other words, though a person like Michael, whom you met at the beginning of this chapter, may have an adult attachment style referred to as dismissing, he can nevertheless earn security by challenging himself to learn better social skills and essentially rewire his brain so that he can feel more secure and as a result benefit from the activation of his social brain networks.

There are multiple ways in which social support is imperative and can make a person's brain sharper. The power of social support to boost the brain reserve is fueled by the many intellectual and emotional gymnastics that are required when people interact. Think of it this way: each relationship requires that you think and deal with a wide range of different emotions and perspectives on many levels at any one time. Conversations can be exceedingly complex because there are several inferences possible because words are imprecise and both of you must read between the lines of what is being said. On top of that, both of you are paying attention to and communicating with body language, tone of voice, the context of the conversation, and several other dimensions.

Social engagement requires focused attention, decision making, critical thought, creativity, and empathy, all activating your PFC. Each conversation therefore demands that your brain wake up from the tendency to revert to the default mode network of daydreaming, ruminating, and spacing out. By turning on your PFC to pay attention to the person with whom you share the present moment, you can activate many parts of your brain simultaneously.

There is a cast of characters in your social brain. They include the following:

- Polyvagal nerve system
- Orbital frontal cortex
- Amygdala
- Insula

- Cingulate Cortex
- Mirror neurons
- Spindle cells
- Facial expression modules

There are two branches of the autonomic nervous system: the sympathetic and the parasympathetic. The parasympathetic branch acts to balance the excitability of the sympathetic branch, which triggers the fight-or-flight response. The vagus nerve, a long nerve system connecting the brain with many organs in the thoracic cavity such as the heart, lungs, and gut, is involved in the ability to regulate the level of arousal and the parasympathetic nervous system. The vagus nerve has been described as part of the social engagement system. If you have high vagal tone, chances are that you are more engaged in the interpersonal world and can better regulate your emotions.[14] After a stressful event, your body returns to baseline sooner. Your heartbeat does not continue to race, and your gut becomes relaxed again when the situation resolves. If, in contrast, you have low vagal tone, you may have difficulty suppressing your emotions or engaging in sustained shared attention with others. Your heart races, your gut may feel disturbed, and your breathing may quicken.

After a socially stressful event these physiological reactions to stress continue. Having good vagal tone helps you avoid overreacting in an argument with others and triggering the fight-or-flight response. Learning these skills enhances your connectedness with others, which enhances your vagal tone further.

The same polyvagal nerve system that enervates the heart and other organs also enervates the face, so that when your heart is racing, your face will reflect the same degree of discomfort. In this way facial expressions can reveal a person's internal body state.

The ability to control your emotions in social situations is also very dependent on your orbital frontal cortex (OFC), so named because it lies right behind the orbs of the eyes. The OFC thrives on close relationships from infancy on through adulthood. When those relationships are positive, the OFC helps you maintain better control of your emotions. If you stay in practice, your OFC becomes more skilled as you age. However, social isolation tends to deactivate the

OFC and other social brain systems, and as a result you can become less able to regulate your emotions.

The Importance of Empathy

Among the functions of the social brain, especially the OFC, is insight into a person's own behavior and self-awareness, insight into another person's mind (called theory of mind), self-regulation of emotion and behavior, and detection of threat and danger. While your right OFC decodes the mental states in others, your left OFC reasons about those states. When your OFC is working optimally, that is, when it's consistently activated, all these social skills can sharpen your brain. Positive relationships enhance the vagal system and OFC neural networks and boost your sense of well-being.

Two different systems for empathy have been identified. One is referred to as cognitive empathy and the other as emotional empathy. These two empathetic methods of tracking the assumptions we make about another person's emotional states are very useful in social interaction. Cognitive empathy involves an intellectual understanding of what is bothering another person but not feeling the same emotions that person is feeling. There is a cognitive separation of one's own feelings from those observed in another person to gain an understanding of that person's feelings without being swayed by them.

Cognitive empathy, the attempt to understand emotions "objectively," is processed by the temporal-parietal-junction (TPJ) system, which is, as the name implies, situated at the junction of the temporal and parietal lobes. The TPJ is also a hub where many neural circuits converge and diverge. Men have been found to show increased activity in the TPJ compared with women.[15] The TPJ region is also larger in males. Men's brains show an increased activation in the TPJ area during the attribution of emotion to themselves, apparently keeping a boundary between the self and the other person to strengthen the ability to cognitively and analytically find solutions to problems.

Since the TPJ is associated with cognitive empathy, or empathetic understanding of another person's situation, it activates when a person is socially engaged. Loneliness tends to result in atrophy of the TPJ. To make matters worse, loneliness creates a downward spiral so that when you become less socially practiced and more socially awkward, you become less confident. Loneliness results in less activity of the ventral tegmental area, which releases less dopamine, and as a result the nucleus accumbens registers a lower sense of pleasure. Since lonely people activate social brain circuits less, they receive less pleasure from social interaction, and their brains may become less responsive to social interaction if loneliness persists. The TPJ is much less activated among lonely than nonlonely people.[16] As the TPJ atrophies, lonely people are less able to communicate with ease and fluidity because they are out of practice. When a lonely person makes infrequent attempts to interact with others, he invariably is unsuccessful. He finds that this failure reinforces the idea that he is socially inept and perhaps should not even try to be social. Again the concept of use it or lose it is important to keep in mind. Exercising the TPJ may be difficult if it has not been in use, but the more you use it, the more robust and easy to use it becomes. The use it or lose it process works both ways. The more you exercise the TPJ, the more robust the TPJ and its skills are.

Have you ever wondered why you yawn after watching another person yawn, or have you scratched your head after seeing another person scratch her head? Why is it that you can be so engrossed in the trials and tribulations of a character in a movie that you feel you are experiencing the same thing? Those oddities involve another amazing discovery involving the social brain networks: a type of neurons dubbed mirror neurons. They were originally discovered by Giacomo Rizzolatti, who was the lead scientist of the group at the University of Parma in Italy that included Giuseppe Di Pellegrino, Luciano Fadiga, Leonardo Fogassi, and Vittorio Gallese. This so-called Fab Four (not the Beatles) were examining the activity of individual neurons in the brains of macaque monkeys. In the late 1980s they stumbled upon an amazing discovery. When one of them moved his arm, neurons in the monkey's brain also fired in the exact location that controlled the monkey's arm. What made this discovery so puzzling was that the monkey was not moving his arm but was just watching someone moving her arm. In other words, these mirror neurons were mirroring the activity in another individual's brain.

Rizzolatti and his colleagues found that an area in the motor strip of their research monkey's brain, referred to as F5 by neuroscientists, seemed to fire when the research monkey observed the movements in other monkeys. In other words, the monkey's brain fired in the same areas it would have fired in if it had made the same movements itself. The activation of mirror neurons generates "an internal motor representation" of someone else's movements. Looked at another way, these neurons provide "an understanding of the meaning of actions performed by others."

The discovery of mirror neurons led to an explosion of research to explore what these neurons do, where they are situated in the brain, and under what conditions they fire. It turns out that they are primate phenomena and that humans have more mirror neurons than any other species of primates. Also, women have more mirror neurons than men.

Researchers found a neural representation of imitation through the human analogue to F5 that is referred to as Broca's area. Since Broca's area is critical for expressive speech (saying what you want to say), mirror neurons are instrumental in the development of language. As every parent knows, imitation helps children learn language, and this area of the brain helps explain how it occurs.

Emotional empathy involves the capacity to intuit the feelings of another person. Even when the feelings of that person are subtle or puzzling, we can have "gut feelings" about what is going on with her. This capacity involves sharing gestures and facial expressions that reveal how she feels, how she may act, and her intentions.

An area in the cerebral cortex that contains a significant amount of mirror neurons is called the insula (Latin for "island"). The insula provides the link between internal states in the body and thoughts and is an important integration area that gives people the capacity to have gut feelings. The insula also has connections to the amygdala, making a link between the emotions of other people and one's own emotions. When another person makes a particular facial expression that reflects an emotion, you "feel" that emotion.

Mirror neurons allow you to feel what the other person feels without even thinking about it. They constitute an essential part of the brain-based explanation of empathy. When you watch a compelling movie featuring a great actor such as Meryl Streep, you feel what she feels as she deals with challenges.

Emotional empathy is facilitated by the mirror neuron system, which is spread out through many brain regions, including the prefrontal cortex, anterior cingulate, insula, and other areas. Females have been shown to recruit the mirror neuron system to a higher degree than do males during emotional processing in empathetic face-to-face interactions.[17] Young adult women have been found to have a significantly larger gray matter volume in the mirror neuron system than do men. Men have been found to make more accurate judgments than women when subtle or moderately negative emotions are expressed.[18] Overall, studies have shown that females perform better in empathy, interpersonal sensitivity, and emotional recognition than do males, perhaps because of the mirror neuron system.[19]

Mirror neurons help people form relationships and thrive as a result. Experiencing empathy and compassion activates the mirror neuron system and can also stir compassion for oneself. In other words, when you feel loved, you are more likely to love yourself. Also, expressing empathy and compassion illustrates the saying "giving is receiving" and is a brain-based truth. In contrast, insensitivity and selfishness are toxic for your brain and your mental health. You could say that being selfish with others is being selfish with yourself. This turns the concept of selfishness on its head: taking only for yourself makes you lose. By contrast, compassion and loving relationships are good for your brain and your mental health. Jesus asked us to "love thy neighbor"; the Buddha said we should "love all sentient beings"; and Confucius instructed us to treat others as we would have them treat us.

Another socially sensitive type of neuron called a spindle cell allows people to make socially sensitive snap decisions. Your spindle cells provide you with the flexibility to make quick but complex problem-solving decisions in emotionally stirring situations. Discovered in 1881 by Constantin von Economo, these large spindle-shaped cells are found in the insula and the cingulate cortex. These neurons have few branches and differ from most neurons, which are cone- or star-shaped. Spindle cells are thin and elongated and are four times larger than most neurons.

They are found in great numbers in the right hemisphere and are able to connect emotional and social information quickly and efficiently. They actually look like spindles, with a large bulb at one end and a long thick extension. Because they are so long and thick, they are capable of high-velocity transmission.

They seem to be present in the brains of large mammals such as elephants, humpback whales, and gorillas. Whereas 0.8 percent of an elephant's frontal insula contains spindle cells, in the average human 1.25 percent of the frontal insula contains spindle cells. They are very common in humans, less common in other primates, and absent in most nonprimates. The human brain has a thousand times more spindle cells than does that of our closest ape cousin.

Part of the neural network underlying executive attention spindle cells has long axons connecting the anterior cingulate to the anterior insula. These neural networks enable us to have effortful control, which consists of attention, the capacity to shift focus, and the ability to inhibit overly emotional reactions. For example, it is not uncommon for a person to walk into a room occupied by a group of people and instantaneously intuit the emotional climate. In colloquial terms, you pick up the vibes in the room. The group may have just finished a heated argument or awkward moment. When you walk in, you are reading the residual emotional climate.

Because of their location within the frontal insula and anterior cingulate, spindle cells facilitate self-monitoring and help people understand the feelings of others. Thus, they help integrate social awareness and self-awareness. Spindle cells respond extremely quickly and relay information to other socially sensitive neural circuits. They enable people to quickly adjust to changing social contexts, to know who to trust or not trust.

Like many parts of the brain, they develop through a use it or lose it process. Good parenting promotes robust spindle cells; their development has been shown to promote good effortful control of emotions. However, the development of spindle cells is vulnerable to abuse and neglect.

The more you seek out new experiences and rely on social support, the stronger is the wiring among the brain areas involved in reward, emotion, and decision making. Michael Cohen of the University of Bonn found that the more subjects sought out new experiences, the stronger were their connections from the hippocampus to amygdala and to the prefrontal cortex and the mesial striatum, an area involved in emotion and reward.

There is also a biochemistry of social brain networks that activates through positive relationships to give you comfort, keep you calm, and lift your mood. When this cornucopia of neurotransmitters, neuromodulators, and neurohormones is underactivated, you feel less relaxed and more down in the dumps and are more vulnerable to getting ill. This is one of the reasons I call positive relationships social medicine. Neurohormones such as oxytocin are involved in more than childbirth and early bonding. Oxytocin is a neuropeptide produced in the hypothalamus and released by the pituitary gland into the bloodstream. Vasopressin is produced from a gene adjacent to the one that codes for oxytocin. These two hormones are siblings and serve as antagonists of each other. Whereas oxytocin is found in both genders (although much more in females), vasopressin is found principally in males. Vasopressin is a component of the sympathetic nervous system and is associated with an increase in vigilance and emotional arousal.

Women tend to have more oxytocin available, and as they get older, they use it more. Though women generally make more oxytocin than do men, when it is administered intranasally to men, their ability to infer the emotional and mental states of others improves.[20] Men need to be touched two to three times more frequently than females to maintain the same levels of oxytocin.[21]

Oxytocin tends to have a positive relationship with the parasympathetic branch of the autonomic nervous system, allowing you to relax and feel calm, instead of with the sympathetic branch, which makes you anxious when it is overactivated. Consider what happens if after a stressful day you receive a warm hug from your partner. Oxytocin is released in the brain after a 20-second hug from a partner.[22] In the 1960s it was not uncommon for therapists to hug their clients. Now there are strict licensing laws about professional boundaries and the need to protect clients from abuse.

Oxytocin can neutralize stress throughout the hypothalamic-pituitary-adrenal (HPA) axis and can calm the amygdala. One of the early studies on oxytocin showed that men given oxytocin in nasal spray produce less cortisol and have less anxiety.[23] The now classic study performed in Switzerland involved giving intranasal oxytocin to men and then asking them to give away money (which they did) on the assumption that it would be returned. They were more likely to give away maximum amounts of money to a stranger after a squirt of oxytocin.[24]

Another study found that men given intranasal oxytocin had an improved ability to read emotions simply by looking at the photographs of others.[25] During my seminars on how the recent developments in neuroscience can be incorporated in a reconceptualization of psychotherapy, I often joke that many therapists are putting liquid oxytocin in humidifiers in their offices to ensure that their clients maximize trust and turn on the parasympathetic nervous system. To my astonishment, a sizable group believes me. Despite the fact that you can purchase oxytocin on the Internet as "liquid trust," it is not necessarily a trust hormone. However, it is associated with positive upbeat behavior, which is a manifestation of trust and is associated with motivation.

Oxytocin is activated by intimate relationships, especially by touching. For this reason, it has been called the cuddling hormone. When you receive a hug after a tough day, you benefit from a burst of oxytocin, which helps activate your parasympathetic nervous system, including the vagus nerve, which lowers heart rate, increases relaxation, and provides a sense of comfort.

There are gender differences in these social brain networks that affect the way we communicate and deal with stress. Stress seems to have the opposite effect on males and females. After a physical challenge males are more apt to mate. In contrast, females are less apt to mate partly because cortisol seems to block oxytocin receptors.[26] They may need added hugging to raise their oxytocin levels.

Oxytocin production often increases in response to stress and is regulated by estrogen. For women it may act as a signal to seek out social support, whereas men use social support less in response to stress. Women generally respond to stress with a tend and befriend strategy, whereas men are more likely to respond with fight or flight. [27]

Simply expressing empathy increases oxytocin release, and oxytocin production increases the feeling of receiving empathy. For example, one study showed that people experience increases in the feelings of empathy after they express generosity, which also increases oxytocin from baseline levels.[28] You can boost your feelings of empathy for others as well as for yourself at the same time.

Social brain networks are so important to a person's sense of well-being that when you are not socially engaged, you not only become depleted of their many benefits but even go through withdrawal. For example, when a person is romantically rejected, intense withdrawal occurs with a sharp reduction of dopamine. In contrast to the intoxicating experience of falling in love, when dopamine levels are high, a drop in dopamine results in feeling dull and unfocused. Also, with rejection your amygdala becomes activated, making you more anxious.

The less social nourishment you receive, the more depleted and underactivated your social brain networks become. One in five Americans experiences loneliness. As was pointed out earlier in this chapter, researchers have found that loneliness is a significant health risk, and the health-related effects can be as detrimental in the long run as those of smoking.[29]

Nourishing your social brain networks can require that you step out of your comfort zone and into a new comfort zone. By practicing the following, you will be able to reap the truth in the concept that giving is receiving:

- Cultivate empathy for those in need.
- Convey compassion for your family and friends.
- Develop intimacy with your friends and family.

Smiling, Laughter, and Humor

Exercising your social brain networks can begin by observing others. Even seeing others smile can activate positive emotions through mirror neuron activation. Research has shown that seeing smiles for as little as a second before the presentation of neutral stimuli promotes a positive reaction to those stimuli.[30] Seeing others smile triggers the release of dopamine, the neurotransmitter associated with the anticipation of pleasure.[31]

Smiling can kindle positive moods just as frowning can kindle negative moods. This occurs because the nerves that extend to the facial muscles from the brain fire in both directions. Bilateral smiling reflects left PFC as well as right PFC activation. There is a bidirectional feedback process between the face and the social brain networks so that smiling can kindle positive mood states. Even during periods of stress, smiling can speed the recovery from cardiovascular symptoms of negative emotions.[32]

A client of mine was surprised to discover this phenomenon. Jane came to me during the first few years of her retirement and complained that she had lost all her social contacts. She felt isolated and lonely. Though she was still invited to staff parties, she declined, saying, "I don't want people to see what I have become. Besides, what do you want me to do, put on a happy face?"

"Exactly," I responded. I went on to describe the two-way-street flow of neurological information between the face and the brain. Smiling will make her feel more pleasure. And there is a social feedback benefit as well; when she smiles, others will too, thus helping her smile back authentically. She would receive not only a kick start to her own positive emotions but also an added boost from the positive emotions reflected back to her from others. When I explained this to Jane, it seemed to be the clincher to encouraging her to socialize again.

Then Jane had second thoughts: "This all sounds too simple. What if I or someone else is pretending to smile? What if they are smirking?"

"You raise an excellent point," I responded. "Smirking, in fact, is not smiling." I went on to describe how smirking (an asymmetrical lift to the left side of the mouth) is associated with right frontal activation and negative emotions, whereas bilateral (both sides of the face) smiling is associated with left frontal activation and positive emotions.

In fact, that is not the complete story. How do you know that another person's smile is authentic? Building on the discovery of the orbicularis oculi muscles by the French neuroanatomist Guilliame Benjamin Amand Duchenne (1806–1875), Paul Ekman described authentic smiles as Duchenne smiles, or D smiles. Non-D smiles do not involve the orbicularis oculi muscle (the happiness muscle), and therefore there are no crow's-feet around the eyes. Whereas D smiles involve the eyes and bilateral lifts of the corners of the mouth, non-D smiles don't involve the eyes and are asymmetrical. D smiles are associated with the left PFC and positive emotions, whereas non-D smiles are associated with the right PFC and negative emotions.[33]

But what if the person had Botox injections around the eyes so that you can't detect a D smile? Do people who have Botox injections experience the same degree of joy when smiling? An interesting series of studies were described in *Scientific American Mind* that found that the answer is no. Remember that there is a bidirectional flow of emotional information. Putting on a happy face actually does help a person feel happier. If you can't put on a *full* happy face, you cannot experience the complete emotions of a smile. Another fascinating discovery about Botox came up in a series of studies showing that people with Botox injections around the eyes are also less likely to be able to read the emotions of others. This demonstrates that in addition to a bidirectional flow of information between a person's face and that person's brain there is a bidirectional flow of information between another person's face, yours, and your brain.

Sharing a laugh with someone can improve not only your mood but also your health. Indeed, there is truth in the saying "laughter is the best medicine." Laughter involves breathing in and out, which promotes differential effects on the autonomic nervous system. Breathing out, as is the case with laughter, triggers the vagus nerve and the parasympathetic nervous system and promotes a drop in heart rate and blood pressure and increases relaxation.[34] It's rare to hear someone laughing on the inhale; laughter is generally done on the exhale.

There are a wide variety of other benefits to laughter, such as the following:

- Improving cognitive function
- Exercising and relaxing the muscles

- Increasing heart rate and blood pressure
- Decreasing cortisol levels
- Increasing natural killer cell activity
- Altering gene expression
- Stimulating the dopamine reward system
- Increasing longevity [35]

Laughter triggers what has been dubbed the laughter module, which is involved in the planning of movements. These neuronal tracks lead to the insula (triggering its mirror neurons and internal visceral reactions) and the amygdala (emotional reactions).[36] Hearing another person laugh triggers the same neuronal circuits so that both people share a moment of mirth: a cooperative bond and shared understanding. Though they know nothing about mirror neurons and laughter circuits, television producers of sitcoms add laugh tracks not only to indicate when to laugh but to prompt you to laugh with the track. The same phenomenon occurs in viewing movies with other people. This is why comedy films receive better reviews from people who see them in a theater rather than at home on DVD.

Whereas smiling expresses instant emotion, laughter offers through multiple channels an invitation to share a state of mind; sharing humor broadens the dimensions of connections between you and the other person. A healthy sense of humor can liberate a person from the day-to-day tension and worry that contributes to stress buildup. When you and the other person share a humorous insight or a funny take on a situation, both of you detach from the tension and lighten up as you come together.

The most liberating type of humor is being able to laugh at oneself. By avoiding taking yourself too seriously you can break the tension between you and another person. Laughing at yourself liberates you from micromanaging each of your minor flaws. Acceptance of them is critical to mental health. My 108-year-old aunt died a few days before I wrote this section. She had a wonderful sense of humor and a zest for life. Her ability to laugh at herself was as amazing as her sharp mind. Despite failing hearing and vision, she had a robust sense of humor. The last time I saw her, she joked, "My brain is in better shape than my eyes and ears!" She also was incredibly warm and engaging, wanting to keep up with the latest details on all her family members and always showing compassion to those who came to visit.

The Brain Benefits of Partnering

As a species that thrives in a social environment, we are generally monogamous. Our brains have become keenly sensitive to each stage of a romantic relationship. When these brain networks are activated, we feel physically and mentally enriched. When they are underactivated or when our romantic relationships are in trouble, these brain systems deactivate and we experience increased stress.

Early in a relationship, intense romantic love (infatuation) promotes a sort of neurological basis for seeing with rose-colored glasses. During the falling in love stage of a relationship the amygdala and the right PFC are deactivated.[37] This explains why during the infatuation phase both people fail to see the red flags of possible risky behavior and/or potential flaws in the other person.

I am not trying to reduce love to biochemistry. Nevertheless, it is important to recognize that the mind and the brain and the heart are parts of the same unified system. The infatuation phase of a romantic relationship, the falling in love phase, takes place when there is good chemistry between the two people. At the sight of the person, your prefrontal cortex says, "Pay attention; she or he is attractive," triggering your ventral tegmental area and substantia nigra to discharge dopamine, the neurotransmitter that is involved in the anticipation of pleasure. After the charged encounter with the person, your hippocampus codes in this pleasurable memory. When you see that person again, your nucleus accumbens, the pleasure and addiction center, gets activated by more dopamine. When you are separated too long, you may experience a crash or withdrawal that is almost like a drug withdrawal. Activation of the reward systems tends to make you see things with rose-colored glasses, and your septal region (another pleasure center) becomes activated after the dopamine release and the excitement. Meanwhile, there is a deactivation of the amygdala and fear with an increase in potential blindness to red flags of major flaws in the person. Your relatives may say that person is totally wrong for you, but you are blind to this feedback.

After the infatuation phase, both of you eventually realize that the other is a mere mortal with human flaws. You hope that your partner will accept your flaws, but you may run the risk of not being able to reciprocate those expectations. One hopes that both of you face the reality that a lasting relationship requires commitment, consistent effort, acceptance of imperfections, and willingness to put your partner's needs foremost in your mind.

There are multiple neural networks involved in deepening the love between you, including activating the vagus nerve, which is especially activated by oxytocin, lowering heart rate and increasing relaxation and giving you a sense of comfort with the other person. Activation of the reward system in the brain, including the medial insula, caudate, putamen, and ventral anterior cingulate, is associated with long-term committed love.

Partners in a long-term relationship run the risk becoming lazy and allowing the relationship to grow stale. The staleness and loss of the feeling of excitement in the relationship can be explained neurochemically with the concept of tolerance. Here dopamine receptors downregulate (decrease in number). Couples need to create novelty to stimulate dopamine by doing things together that are out of their usual routine.

The sensual side of the relationship is very important, and too often partners lose their commitment to make an effort to keep this side of the relationship alive and healthy. This can be considered a measure of novelty. Couples that do not make the effort to cultivate their sexual relationship run the risk of falling into a sense of staleness in the relationship whatever their age. The preponderance of routine and lack of desire wear on the relationship. Willingness to explore new ways to excite and engage in a rich sensual relationship provides a psychophysical foundation for intimacy.

Men have two and a half times the brain space in the hypothalamus devoted to sex drive. They have far more sexual thoughts than do women, and many of these thoughts involve visual images. Also, their visual system (the occipital lobes) plays a much greater role than is the case for women.[38] Sexual thoughts float through the male mind as often as every 52 seconds, whereas for a woman this occurs perhaps once a day and on more heated days three or four times. During andropause and menopause sexual thoughts drop dramatically, especially for women. With the decline in sexual thoughts for both men and women there is an increased interest in cuddling. There is a neurochemistry associated with the deemphasis on sex and the increase in cuddling, which includes more emphasis on oxytocin.

Healthy relationships involve the physical, emotional, and intellectual aspects of the relationship. Unhealthy relationships put undue emphasis on just one of the three, forcing the physical, emotional, or intellectual side of the relationship to make up for the impoverishment in the other two.

The National Social Life, Health, and Aging Project examined 3,000 adults ages 57 to 85 years, with a significant minority representation. Many health and social network dimensions were assessed. The study found that health and sexuality reinforce each other. In other words, as sexual activity increases, so does health status. Sexual expression is a key contributor to healthy aging.

A healthy marriage serves as a buffer against stress by functioning as a form of emotional regulation. A study using functional magnetic resonance imaging (fMRI) showed that women with high relationship satisfaction who were exposed to stressful imagery were less subjectively bothered by the threat when they held their husbands' hands.[39] But when they held the hand of a stranger the benefit was absent. When they were in the presence of their husbands, their brains registered less threat-related neural activity in areas such as the right insula, right superior frontal gyrus, and hypothalamus. Extending this level of social support over a lifetime bolsters resiliency to stress and the ability to deal with chronic illness. Potential losses of these relationships can be debilitating to overall health.

However, both partners in couples with relationships marked by chronic conflict tend to have higher levels of stress neurochemistry, including elevated levels of epinephrine, norepinphrine, and adrenocorticotropic hormone.[40] There also tend to be increases in inflammation in high-conflict couples. The conflict level has even been shown to influence how fast wounds heal.[41]

Avoid Destructive Relationships

Though social support is good for your brain, there are some relationships that are bad for your mind and therefore your brain. These, of course, include the obvious destructive relationships of abuse, both verbal and physical. There are also codependent relationships, which involve clear exploitation and enabling. You know how to avoid these relationships, but what about relationships that are not overtly abusive yet lack reciprocity? These relationships can undermine the concept of social support and can be corrosive to your health.

A relationship lacking in reciprocity puts your needs on the back burner and the other person's needs up front. The most insidious of these relationships occurs with passive-aggressive people who pretend to care about you but spend most of their time inviting you to feel sorry for them about their latest petty concern. Because they drain you of energy, these relationships dull rather than sharpen your brain. The neurochemistry of this type of social stress impairs healthy brain circuitry and tears it down. The levels of stress hormones such as cortisol go up, leading to multiple adverse effects. Meanwhile, you receive minimal or no boost from the social brain networks that normally help you feel connected, healthy, and calm.

I call this type of relationship a black hole. As in space, where anything close to the powerful gravitational force of a black hole is pulled into its center, black hole passive-aggressive people suck you into a universe with one central focus: them. When you don't maintain your own clear boundaries, your life becomes unimportant in that type of relationship. So how can you identify black hole relationships, especially since they can be so subtle? The telltale mode of operating by such a person often involves consistently playing the victim to gain sympathy. If he or she pretends to be interested in you but never does anything that demonstrates it, the relationship revolves around a black hole.

Neither of you actually receives healthy benefits from such relationships. Just as codependent relationships with people who are using drugs and/or alcohol zap you of energy while enabling the person abusing substances to continue his or her reckless and self-destructive behavior, codependent relationships with passive-aggressive people enable the person to continue to regard himself as the center of the universe, and all the energy gets sucked into his black hole.

One of the most subtle and insidious black holes involves the persistent and perpetually negative person. These people constantly ask those around them to pep them up, look on the bright side, and be responsible for their feelings. It can be exhausting spending time with them because you are in a position to regulate their mood. They also spend a great deal of time in their default mode network (DMN) ruminating about themselves and who didn't give them what they want and feeling resentful about it. By the way, a particular pattern of DMN has been identified that is characteristic of depression. We can extrapolate from that research to assume that a passive-aggressive person may pretend to engage you while she is really off ruminating and feeling "depressed."

Empathy and compassion are very healthy feelings and the basis of the major religions. When these feelings are inspired by someone worthy of receiving them, they can be a powerful way to experience the truth in the maxim that giving is receiving. In contrast, when you are preyed on by a black hole, your sympathy is being exploited; you are receiving no reciprocal social support from such a relationship, and the relationship actually takes energy away from your effort to nurture and care for yourself. The social brain networks thrive on healthy, reciprocal relationships, whereas unhealthy relationships deprive these networks. From our first hours through our last, the experience of being truly cared for and loved and having caring and loving relationships helps us feel secure and develop frustration tolerance while contributing to greater longevity.

Both giving and receiving empathy are beneficial. Giving is, in fact, receiving when you consider that mirror neurons allow you to experience what another person experiences. As people feel your empathy, your mirror neurons help you feel what they feel. In other words, as they feel comforted, you feel vicariously comforted. Imagine two mirrors facing each other and reflecting each other's reflection; applying that concept explains what you will experience on an emotional level when you convey empathy.

Putting the Social Factor into Practice

A social support network can become increasingly challenging to access, build, and maintain while we age, for a variety of reasons. Unfortunately, older people are valued less in employment situations. Many are in the process of retirement or have already retired and lose the social contacts they had at work and must make a greater effort to reconstruct social support systems.

As you age, you may find it more difficult to meet new people and maintain social relationships. Often as we age friends move away to be closer to their families, some die, and still others are reluctant to engage. Therefore, I often tell clients who have found that their social contacts have withered away to structure into their social contacts activities such as clubs, political organizations, community groups, Sierra Club hikes, volunteer jobs, book groups, and religious institutions to provide a regular dose of social support. When you schedule in time with people, you build in an expectation to follow through. This makes it more difficult to procrastinate or tell yourself that you have something else you must do.

By adding other Brain Bible factors to the social factor, you will gain far more than you will if you focus on the social dimension alone. For example, while you spend time with family and friends, you can easily add in physical exercise, diet, and a stimulating intellectual conversation. For example, you have not seen your sister in a while, and so you invite her and a friend to join you for a vigorous hike. Your reunion with your sister is comforting, and you enjoy catching up on what she and her family have been doing since you last talked to her. You also take the opportunity to get to know her friend and the autobiographical aspects of her life. The three of you begin to huff and puff your way up the trail to your destination. You reach a spectacular picnic spot where everyone unpacks his or her potluck food item. Following your plan, all of you have brought the healthiest food you have read about recently. During lunch your sister's friend leads you into a conversation about new developments in neuroscience that have shed light on the variety of ways to promote better brain health. She says, "In fact, we are doing four things that promote healthy brains right now: socializing, exercising, sharing education, and eating nutritious food. If we had done this hike after dinner, we would have promoted a good night's sleep! Shall we do that next Saturday?"

Try the following:

Volunteer during a political election.

Volunteer for a private nonprofit agency.

Join a book group.

Meet with friends for a regularly scheduled breakfast, lunch, or dinner.

Take part in a Sierra Club or Audubon Society hike.

Join a bridge or other game group.

Go to a structured, regularly scheduled dance class.

If you are partnered, vary your activities and go out on regularly scheduled "dates."

Go to a comedy club with friends.

CHAPTER 7

The Sleep Factor

Emily had tossed and turned most nights since her late fifties. Now, at age 62, she felt that she was condemned to a life of insomnia despite trying everything she had heard would help her get to sleep. She tried a variety of over-the-counter sleep aids that worked for the first few nights, but she felt very groggy in the morning and had a fuzzy head until noon. During those mornings she drank more coffee to compensate for a brain that seemed like it was running on half of its cylinders. And the irritability! Twice she barked at a coworker who had done nothing more than pour himself the last cup of coffee from the staff break room coffee pot.

Two glasses of wine each evening helped her relax, but by the time she got to bed that relaxation had burned off like butter in a hot frying pan. Indeed, she felt that her life had become far too stressful to promote even the semblance of relaxation. Finally, she decided to get help. When she sat down for her first session, she said, "I've got chronic insomnia, but I think it's a symptom of something else. Maybe you can help me deal with the stress in my life so I can get some sleep."

She went on to describe how her job as a claims adjuster in an insurance company had grown more demanding over the last few years. She could never seem to get all her work done, whereas some of her coworkers had no apparent problems. She wondered if she was getting more cases than her coworkers. When she counted cases to compare, she was baffled to find that she and the other six claims adjusters had the exact same number. Then she thought that her cases might be more complicated. That hypothesis was not correct either because cases were assigned randomly as they came in. Why were her coworkers processing claims twice as fast as she was? That was what her supervisor wanted to know when she was brought to his office. Her first thought was that she was being harassed; she thought they might be planning to force her to quit so that they could bring in a younger worker. Only her supervisor had been with the company as long as she had. He said something that got her wondering: "Look, Emily, we started together and I hope we retire together. Something is up with you, and it's my hope that you can get some help."

"So that's why I'm here," she said to me, shrugging her shoulders. "He's right, but I don't know what it is."

She and her husband of 35 years were just entering a time in their lives when they could afford to live comfortably and travel. If she could just deal with the feeling of being stressed and get some sleep!

As she described her life at work and home, it dawned on her that most other people would not consider what she had to deal with a reason for being stressed out. In fact, they would regard her life as generally normal, and some might think it was idyllic.

I asked her how many hours she was sleeping at night, and as she pondered the question, she shook her head. "All together, you mean? I guess two or three."

It is common for people to be convinced that they are not sleeping when they are in fact in stage 1 sleep. Therefore, I speculated that she was getting another two hours of sleep but was unaware of it. If this was the case, she was getting four or five hours of sleep per night. Nevertheless, the next morning she would have higher levels of stress neurohormones such as adrenaline and cortisol floating in her system. The elevated stress chemistry essentially impaired her prefrontal cortex's ability to deal effectively with the demands of the day by impeding her decision-making abilities and affecting her decisions about how to process the claims, an activity she had performed without a problem in the past. The ineffective decision making probably increased her frustration and initiated the release of more stress hormones. All this had increased her subjective feelings of higher levels of stress.

This self-perpetuating cycle ramped up self-perpetuating stress. After I explained how this cycle had to be broken, she said, "Can't you just give me some sleeping pills? I've heard all older women go through this." What she did to try to resolve her insomnia in the past only served to prolong it.

"I even try to bore myself to sleep by watching old movies during those wee hours of the night."

"You've got a TV in your bedroom?"

"Yeah, doesn't everyone? What does that have to do with anything?"

I told her that she had to create in her bedroom an atmosphere in which only one of two things occur: sleep or making love. If it represented an entertainment zone or a place to discuss household finances with her husband, she would increase her tendency to experience more nonsleep time.

"Getting the TV out of my bedroom is not the magic pill, Doctor."

"You're right; it's just one of many things we want to do all at one time. There is no magic pill. Let's take the high level of stress hormones—"

"Right," she interrupted. "Give me something that will cut them out of my life."

"One of the most effective ways to burn off stress hormones like cortisol is to exercise, and if you do it in the late afternoon or early evening, you get the maximum sleep benefit." I went on to describe how the normal cycle of cortisol involves a slow rise in that hormone around 5 a.m.; it increases as we start the day and then tapers off in the afternoon. In fact, it's around 4 p.m. that some people reach for a cup of coffee because of that decreased amount of energy. For people who have higher levels of cortisol in the morning because of chronic insomnia and/or stress, the drop-off in the late afternoon does not generally occur, especially if they do not exercise. I also told her about the importance of low body temperature at night. One of the reasons many people wake up in the middle of the night is that their body temperature is too high; it should be lower. To promote sleep she could promote a cooler body temperature by making sure she didn't put too many blankets on her bed and keeping the window cracked. If she exercised three to six hours before bedtime, she would not only burn off the stress hormones but also push up her body temperature so that later it would drop down naturally during her sleep cycle.

"I don't want to waste time after work by going to some expensive gym. Besides, I've never been good at sports or anything athletic."

"Walking is the cheapest and easiest form of exercise, and you can do it almost anywhere and anytime. I would recommend that you take a 20-minute brisk walk after dinner."

"But what about my downtime? I usually like to catch up with friends on e-mail and Facebook until I go to bed. It relaxes me."

I told her that looking at the computer screen is essentially like looking at light. When she looks at the computer screen, the retina at the back of her eye sends a signal to her pineal gland in the center of the brain, telling the gland that it's daytime now and not time to secrete the sleeping hormone melatonin, thus increasing or creating insomnia.

As with Emily, one of the most common complaints of people as they age is diminishing quality of sleep. They complain of difficulty falling asleep and staying asleep and then awakening in the morning feeling unrefreshed. This is partly because older people spend less time in stage 3 and 4 slow-wave sleep.

Sleep Factor Questionnaire

Yes No

☐ ☐ Do you have a television set in your bedroom?

☐ ☐ Are you in the habit of checking your e-mail and working on the computer late in the evening before bed?

☐ ☐ Do you and your partner engage in major conversations and even arguments in bed before you go to sleep?

☐ ☐ Are you in the habit of having caffeinated drinks after lunch?

☐ ☐ If you wake up in the middle of the night, do you find yourself becoming angry and concerned that the next day will be a waste?

☐ ☐ Do you consume simple carbohydrates in the evening?

☐ ☐ Do you drink alcohol in the evening?

☐ ☐ Do you drink most of your fluids in the evening?

☐ ☐ Do you skip dinner, eating your last meal in the afternoon?

☐ ☐ Is your bedroom warm and/or do you make sure you have plenty of blankets on the bed?

If you answered yes to any of these questions, your sleep may be impaired, with adverse consequences to your brain.

Minimize Your Sleep Debt

If the body, including the brain, is not allowed to rebuild its resources in response to stress, it breaks down and accelerated aging occurs. One major way to impair its ability to rebuild its resources is lack of sleep. Researchers have shown that when people were restricted to four hours of sleep per night for six nights, they had lower glucose tolerance, elevated evening cortisol concentrations, and increased sympathetic nervous system activity.[1] The effect of sleep debt mirrors the aging process. Thus, aging combined with sleep debt intensifies the aging process.

One of the factors associated with poorer sleep among the elderly is increased sensitivity to stress hormones. Older adults, especially men, appear to become more sensitive to the stimulating effects of corticotropin-releasing hormone (CRH) and cortisol. Compared to young and middle-aged men, when older men are administered CRH, they sleep less and less deeply. Those with insomnia tend to secrete the highest amount of cortisol, particularly in the evening and nighttime hours.

With aging, and more pronounced in women than in men, high body temperature, prolactin levels, and cortisol levels complicate sleep. With men there appears to be a greater likelihood of daytime sleepiness and tiredness.[2]

Sleep deprivation can lead to a heightened risk of insulin resistance, type 2 diabetes, and high blood pressure, all serious threats to the brain. The endocrine system and metabolic changes resulting from sleep deprivation mimic many of the hallmarks of aging and also increase the severity of medical conditions such as diabetes.

A study performed at University College London Medical School found an association between middle-aged adults sleeping less than six or more than eight hours per night and a decline in brain function. The magnitude of the impairment is comparable to being four to seven years older. It appears that an average of seven hours seems to be optimum, though there are people who function well with less or more.[3] Various studies have shown that sleeping too little or too much increases mortality and the chance of having a heart attack, stroke, and other health problems.

Six hours of sleep is reported as the minimum biological requirement and for this reason is referred to as the core sleep. During core sleep you receive all of your slow-wave sleep and half of your rapid-eye-movement (REM) sleep.

One of the most common complaints of people as they age is diminishing quality of sleep. Most surveys indicate that with aging there is a general increase in awakening throughout the sleep cycle. One of the reasons for the disruption of sleep is associated with the potential increase in medical problems and aging. Other factors include the following:

- Increased sympathetic nervous system activity with elevated norepinephrine
- Daytime napping
- Less exposure to light during the daytime
- Less exercise
- Depression
- Breathing irregularities
- Higher body temperature

Some medical conditions can disrupt the length and quality of sleep. For example, sleep-disordered breathing in the elderly is common and is also associated with cognitive impairment and dementia. In a study that followed almost 300 people with an average age of 82 over several years, it was found that roughly one-third had sleep-disordered breathing, including sleep apnea. Those with sleep-disordered breathing had almost twice the risk of cognitive impairment or dementia compared with those with normal breathing patterns. Sleep-disordered breathing results in hypoxia: less oxygen supplied to the brain. When this occurs, cells become impaired and die.

Obstructive sleep apnea is a disorder of interrupted breathing when muscles relax. It usually is associated with fat buildup or loss of muscle tone with aging. During an episode of obstructive sleep apnea, the inhalation of air creates suction that collapses the windpipe, blocking the airflow for 10 seconds to 1 minute while the sleeper struggles to breathe. When oxygen levels fall, the brain responds by waking the person enough to tighten the upper airway muscles and open the trachea (windpipe), leading to a gasp or snort and then resumption of normal breathing. This cycle can occur hundreds of times a night.

Sleep-related respiratory distress (SRRD) and periodic leg movements (PLM) are two factors that tend to complicate sleep as people age. The incidence of SRRD increases with age, especially with sleep apnea. Alcohol consumption, especially in males, has been associated with age and also is associated with upper airway collapse.

Sleep apnea is a possible contributor to the sundowning syndrome. Because of the fatigue associated with sleep apnea, by the late afternoon energy levels can become decreased. According to Thomas Daily, chief of pulmonary medicine at Kaiser Permanente in Santa Clara, California up to 36 percent of Americans experience sleep apnea. Lifestyle changes such as losing weight, sleeping on the back, using a mouthpiece, and if recommended by your doctor, using a continuous positive airway pressure (CPAP) machine can deal effectively with sleep apnea. The decline in cognitive functioning is associated with sleep apnea, including difficulty concentrating, irritability, and depression. Also, there is an increased risk of stroke.

Sleep-disordered breathing affects up to 60 percent of the elderly. The problem is not necessarily the fragmented sleep itself or its duration but hypoxia, or lack of oxygen supply to the brain. Sleep-disordered breathing may increase the risk of later developing dementia. In a recent study, researchers followed approximately 300 women with a mean age of 82 with no signs of dementia.[4] In that group, 193 had normal sleep patterns and 105 had a form of sleep apnea defined as 15 or more events per hour of interrupted sleep, resulting in lower oxygen levels to the brain. Five years later, the researchers assessed their cognitive status, including memory and attention. Those with sleep-disordered breathing had almost twice the risk of cognitive impairment or dementia as those without sleep-disordered breathing.

Sleeping is not one-dimensional process. There are qualitative differences among the types of sleep. Since the 1930s researchers have been able to identify different types and stages of sleep. As measured by the electroencephalogram, three types of sleep—fast-wave, slow-wave, and dream (REM) sleep—have been identified (see Table 7.1).

Table 7.1 Stages of Sleep

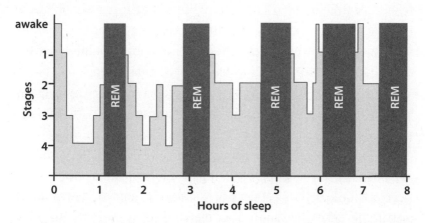

Stage 1 is a transition state between waking and sleeping. In this stage the brain waves are fast and are referred to as low-amplitude high-frequency waves. In fact, they look very similar to the waking state, as you can see in Table 7.1. If you wake up from stage 1 sleep, you'll probably report that you were not really asleep.

In stage 2, sleep is relatively light and the brain waves are referred to as theta waves. Many insomnia patients complain that they do not sleep when in fact they are experiencing stage 2 sleep. This stage occurs increasingly as you age. You spend half the night in stage 2 sleep. Stage 2 sleep also increases during periods of stress, whereas slow-wave or deep sleep decreases.

Stages 3 and 4 are considered deep sleep. During these phases of the sleep cycle you produce slow brain waves referred to as delta waves. Deep sleep boosts the immune system while allowing body functions to slow down. If you are deprived of deep sleep, your immune system tends to be suppressed and your body aches. Stress increases the release of noreprinphrine and epinephrine, and they also decrease the amount of slow-wave sleep. If you are sleep-deprived, the first stage of sleep to rebound is deep sleep, indicating its importance to your overall health. Older people spend less time in stage 3 and stage 4 slow-wave sleep.

The decline in slow-wave sleep may occur earlier than age-related decline in other bodily functions. There is a simultaneous increase in stage 1 sleep. These trends are greater for men than for women. Seniors who are in better physiological condition and are described as fit have higher levels of slow-wave sleep.

Dream sleep occurs during a stage called rapid-eye-movement sleep. REM sleep was identified by sleep researchers 70 years ago who found that people who were awakened during a period of sleep marked by rapid eye movement reported vivid dreams. REM sleep is composed of low-amplitude and high-frequency brain waves. REM sleep is called paradoxical sleep because body functions are at almost wakeful levels of activation. Your metabolism goes up during REM sleep, and energizing neurotransmitters are active. You may dream that you're running and most of your organs function as if you were doing exactly that, but your limbs do not move. As is the case with slow-wave sleep, the time you spend in REM decreases as you age.

Though you generally go through REM periods every 90 minutes, most of REM sleep occurs later in the sleep cycle. It accounts for 25 percent of total sleep time in healthy adults. In contrast, the slowest-wave sleep occurs earlier in the sleep cycle. Table 7.1 illustrates a typical night of sleep.

Your sleep pattern and circadian rhythm follow daylight length. Also, the routines that structure your life around eating, working, social contacts, and exercise play a role in sleep hygiene. Sleep is affected by light and darkness. When light comes in through your eyes, the retina signals the pineal gland that it is daytime. The pineal gland, which is positioned in the middle of the brain, will respond to light by suppressing its release of the sleeping hormone melatonin and indicate that it's not time to sleep. In contrast, when it's dark, the retina sends information to the pineal gland that it is night and time to sleep, and so it should produce melatonin to induce sedation.

Since the amount of light you are exposed to during the daytime affects your sleep, maximize your exposure to bright light in the daytime to set your body clock to match the natural day-night cycle. If you experience insomnia, don't use your computer in the late evening because you're essentially looking at light. This light tricks your brain into adjusting to a daytime pattern and suppresses the pineal gland's secretion of melatonin, which you need to be able to go to sleep. Since your body clock, referred to as your circadian rhythm, can become maladapted to the actual day-night cycle, you need soft light a few hours before going to sleep.

The stress hormone cortisol affects your circadian rhythm. It is secreted in about 10 bursts every day, with most pulsates occurring between 4 a.m. and noon. This time span is effective in getting a person up in the morning, out the door, and engaged in the day. From an evolutionary perspective, being alert the first thing in the morning kept our species alive. Because our ancestors spent thousands of years in a hunter-gatherer subsistence lifestyle, they needed to begin to be vigilant around dawn, when most predators were on the prowl.

Before 4 a.m. there is a six-hour period with almost no cortisol bursts, which aids in sleep. Alternatively, when you are stressed out, your cortisol levels do not level out, resulting in greater potential for insomnia. Another way the human biological clock promotes sleep at night is that the kidneys slow the rate of urine production overnight. These natural biological rhythms are easily disrupted as people age.

Your circadian rhythm is tied not only to the exposure to light but also to body temperature. Ideally, when you go to sleep at night, your body temperature should be in the process of dropping. Just before you get up from bed, your body temperature is on the rise. When you get out of bed in the morning and expose yourself to light as well as moving your body, you promote a further rise in body temperature.

If you have insomnia, you may have difficulty regulating your body temperature. Your body temperature may actually increase at night when it should be going down. This may occur if you fail to get any exercise in the daytime. By exercising during the three- to six-hour window before you go to sleep you can promote a dip in your body temperature at night.

Sleeping for Brain Health

Sleep is critical for the maintenance of the brain. It serves critical functions, and without an adequate amount of regular sleep there are multiple health deficits. For example, sleep has been shown to be crucial for gene transcription involving synaptic consolation, protein synthesis, and myelin formation. As was noted in Chapter 2, myelin forms the critical white matter of the brain, and without it neurons would not fire efficiently, as in multiple sclerosis, a demyelinating neurological disease. Sleep is critical for the synthesis and transportation of cholesterol, and cholesterol consitutes a significant proportion of myelin.

Sleep deprivation can lead to weight gain even after one week's time because of an increase in production of a hormone called ghrelin, which promotes appetite and food intake. Simultaneously, there is a decline in the production of the hormone leptin, which curbs appetite. To make matters worse, increased appetite related to sleep loss is associated with the consumption of starchy, high-carbohydrate foods, sweets , and other high-calorie foods. Consumption of these foods by sleep-deprived people can be 33 to 45 percent higher than it is in non-sleep-deprived people. Unfortunately, the increase in appetite does not include hunger for fruits, vegetables, and high-protein foods.[5]

Sleep is critical for consolidating memory. Deep sleep is critical for consolidating explicit memory, and REM sleep is critical for consolidating procedural memory. Sleep deprivation has also been shown to compromise attention, new learning, and memory. The longer you are deprived of sleep, the more compromised your cognitive skills are.

Synaptic consolidation is critical for the formation of memories. During sleep unstable memory traces are reconfigured into more permanent ones for long-term storage.[6] The experiences of the day are reactivated and consolidated during sleep.[7]

The saying "Why don't you sleep on it?" actually reflects wisdom. Not only do you arise with vitality in the morning, your enlarged fresh perspective is based on consolidating important memories gained the previous day. It's because of this extension of the neuroplastic process begun during the day and extended through sleep that you can arrive at new insights. In fact, throughout history there have been anecdotal stories of great insights having been gained after a good night's sleep. For example, Dmitri Mendeleev conceived the idea of organizing the chemical elements according to their atomic weights in what is now referred to as the periodic table. Otto Loewi reported that he woke during the middle of the night with the insight of how neurons communicate through chemical messengers that are now referred to as neurotransmitters.

A single night of sleep deprivation produces a significant deficit in hippocampal activity during episodic memory encoding, resulting in worse subsequent memory retention. Only with more than 6 hours of sleep does memory improve over the 24 hours after a learning session.[8] Adequate sleep changes memory, making it more robust and resistant to interference in the coming day, thus stabilizing memory. During sleep the brain dissects memories and retains only the most salient details, helping you remember important aspects of the information. Sleep also plays a crucial role in retaining emotional memories. From this perspective it makes sense to never go to sleep angry. Emotional memories create a long-lasting and potentially traumatic representation of distressing experiences.

Sleep deprivation impairs not only memory but also the later capacity for memory. As was noted in Chapter 3, one of the most revolutionary findings in neuroscience was the recent discovery that new neurons can grow in the hippocampus in the area called the subventricular zone of the dentate gyrus. Studies have shown that sleep deprivation impairs the ability of these stem cells to become new neurons.[9]

Improve Your Sleep Quality

Insomnia is quite common, especially in aging people. Most people have had insomnia at least once in their lives, and for many it's an ongoing problem. Up to half the population reports trouble sleeping once a week, and 15 percent have trouble sleeping two or more nights a week. As was noted earlier in this chapter, sleep problems are especially common among people who are aging and are experiencing anxiety or depression. If you're tense and preoccupied, it's difficult to unwind and sleep. Stress raises the levels of the activating neurotransmitters norepinephrine, epinephrine, and cortisol. Normally these neurotransmitters subside at night. If you experience stress, anxiety, or depression, you may keep yourself charged up and tense by thinking about what is waiting for you the next day.

There are several things you can do to improve the quality of your sleep. The first step in sleep hygiene is to eliminate factors that impair your sleep. Some people try to improve their sleep by using techniques that actually exacerbate their sleep problems.

Many factors contribute to insomnia, including, aging, medical conditions, and drugs. Because as we age the quality of our sleep deteriorates, bad habits that contribute to insomnia add up: dietary practices, bedtime schedules, and environmental factors.

There are many types of insomnia and many causes. Some of the causes are self-induced. Some are obvious, and some are paradoxical. Take caffeine and alcohol, for example. One of the ways caffeine causes insomnia is by blocking the receptor for a neurochemical called adenosine, which promotes sleep. Adenosine levels in the brain are quite vulnerable to caffeine several hours after consumption. Many people experience insomnia because of the caffeine they consume in the late afternoon, incorrectly thinking that since it was consumed many hours before bedtime, there will be no problem. Even if they do sleep through the night, the depth of their sleep is shallower than it would be if they had had no caffeine because adenosine is responsible for promoting slow-wave sleep.

Types of Insomnia

According to the American Sleep Association, the following disturbances are indicative of primary insomnia:[10]

Frequency: insomnia is experienced three or more nights per week.

The duration of insomnia is more than one month.

Time awake after sleep onset is more than 30 minutes; this is referred to as early insomnia. Total sleep time is less than 6.5 hours, and sleep efficiency is lower than 85 percent.

There are problems initiating and maintaining sleep.

Daytime fatigue and/or cognitive impairment is associated with the sleep loss.

As a consequence of the light sleep, spent mostly at stages 1 and 2, these people wake up in the morning feeling like they need more sleep. Since stage 4 sleep is critical for boosting the immune system, they may be more vulnerable to catching whatever virus is floating around.

According to common folklore, alcohol is a sleep promoter because drinkers are somewhat sedentary for the first two or three hours. But after two or three hours of drinking alcohol, the lights go on in your brain and can't go off. This also contributes to *midsleep cycle awakening* because the alcohol prevents the sedative effects during the middle of the sleep cycle. As a result, it may take an hour or two to go back to sleep. Up to 10 percent of all sleep maintenance problems are caused by alcohol. If you have sleep problems, you should not drink alcohol several hours before bedtime, if at all. Generally, alcohol reduces the deepest stage of sleep (stage 4) and REM sleep.

The brain is light-sensitive, and the presence or absence of light affects sleep. When the retina (which is actually part of the brain) signals the pineal gland, which is positioned in the center of the brain, the light cue tells the pineal gland not to secrete the sleeping hormone called melatonin. When it is dark and there is no light signal, the pineal gland secretes melatonin to help you go to and stay asleep. Therefore, bright light in the evening and before you go to bed will trick your brain into keeping you awake because it prepares you for daytime and wakefulness instead of preparing you for sleep.

Several medical conditions either cause or exacerbate insomnia. Work with your doctor to receive comprehensive, thorough treatment for the following conditions:

- Parkinson's disease
- Fibromyalgia
- Kidney disease
- Hyperthyroidism
- Bronchitis
- Arthritis
- Cancer
- Asthma
- Hypertension
- Heart disease

A wide variety of medical treatments also can cause insomnia. Many physicians don't have or take the time to warn their patients that the medications they prescribe can cause insomnia. The following list is just a sample of medications that contribute to insomnia:

- Decongestants
- Corticosteriods
- Diuretics
- Heart medications
- Parkinson's medications
- Asthma medications
- Appetite suppressants
- Kidney medications

It has been estimated that 95 percent of sleep problems go undiagnosed because physicians don't ask about them. Because insomnia is so common, you would think physicians are prepared to help improve the quality of their patients' sleep. Unfortunately, most physicians are not well trained in sleep issues according to a study performed by the dean of sleep research, William Dement, who found that most physicians receive on average just 40 minutes of training in the study of sleep in their medical education. Most of that training is directed toward what sleep medication to prescribe for insomnia; usually these doctors prescribe benzodiazepines despite the fact that most medical journals recommend a nondrug approach to insomnia.

Unfortunately, over-the-counter sleep drugs and physician-prescribed benzodiazepines have been the treatment of choice for millions of people. Benzodiazepines contribute to shallow sleep and minimize deep sleep. They also lead to addiction and tolerance, in which more of the drug will be needed to achieve the same sedative effect, and when patients withdraw from the drug, they experience even more insomnia.

Many over-the-counter drugs contain Benadryl and produce some sedation. Like benzodiazepines, over-the-counter sleep aids suppress deep sleep and also lead to tolerance and withdrawal. Despite the fact that these sleep aids have a significant placebo effect, they cause grogginess and difficulty concentrating the next morning.

A very common medication prescribed by psychiatrists for sleep is actually an old tricyclic antidepressant medication called trazodone. One of its side effects is sedation. When taken at below-antidepressant levels, it is effective in promoting sleep, but patients often complain about feeling zonked the next day. There are a wide variety of other side effects as well as contraindications to taking this medication. Make sure to talk to your prescribing doctor about all these concerns.

Though they contribute to sedation over the short term, sleep medications are ineffective in treating insomnia over the long term. Two major surveys of hundreds of studies showed this ineffectiveness and stated that these drugs are contraindicated for the treatment for long-term insomnia. Because they are highly addictive and produce tolerance and withdrawal, many people are reluctant to quit because when they stop taking the medication, they experience greater anxiety and insomnia, making it even harder to sleep. Withdrawal from benzodiazepines should be supervised by a physician. Stanford University researchers have shown that adults age 55 to 75 who exercise for 20 to 30 minutes in the afternoon reduce the time it takes to get to sleep by half. Comprehensive studies have shown that exercise increases overall sleep quality by promoting not only sleep time but also slow-wave sleep.[11]

By exercising three to six hours before bedtime you can promote sleep by cooling your body temperature when it's especially critical: during the middle of the sleep cycle. Exercise elevates heart rate and body temperature and gives them enough time to return to baseline before bedtime.

Another key way to keep your body temperature low at night is to make sure your bedroom is cool. Warm bedrooms promote light and/or disrupted sleep. Taking a hot bath helps not only as a wind-down activity but also by raising body temperature while you are in the tub and then lowering it sharply by bedtime.

For these reasons, avoid bright light–oriented activities such as computer use before bedtime because light overrides drowsiness. Staring at the computer screen for long periods involves looking at light, which signals the pineal gland that it is daytime and it should not secrete melatonin.

The timing of exposure to natural light is part of sleep hygiene. Expose yourself to bright light in the late morning to encourage lowered body temperature in the middle hours of the sleep cycle and promote staying asleep. If you wake up in the very early morning and can't get back to sleep—this is referred to as *early morning awakening*—you should expose yourself to bright light. This will ensure that your pineal gland will not produce melatonin throughout the day and that your body temperature will be lowest when you sleep.

Your diet in the evening has a major effect on the quality of your sleep. Foods rich in tryptophan (an amino acid that converts to serotonin and from it to melatonin) contribute to sedation. In contrast, consuming protein-rich foods makes you less sleepy because the plasma-rich large neutral amino acids win the competition for access to your brain. Simple carbohydrates such as white bread and sugar can contribute to sleep problems too because they result in increased blood glucose and shallow sleep or even awakening during your sleep cycle. By contrast, complex carbohydrates such as whole grains, including wheat, can be sedating because there will be a slow and sustained rise in glucose.

Changes in vitamins levels can also affect sleep. For example, B vitamins, calcium, and magnesium may inhibit sleep. It's best to get these vitamins and minerals from a balanced diet of whole foods.

Novel sounds can disturb your sleep. It's best to minimize nonrepetitive sounds that invite your attention because the brain is primed to pay attention to novelty. In contrast, white noise such as a fan is monotonous and can serve as a good screen for other noises, such as barking dogs. Some people keep a fan on all night long to provide white noise. Another useful technique is to use good-quality earplugs to filter out noises. Make sure the television is anywhere but in your bedroom. If someone is in another room watching it, ask her to turn it down or off well before bedtime because it will periodically grab your attention and wake you.

The context of going to sleep and your attitude affect whether you can get to sleep. For example, your bedroom should promote sleep. Your bed should be for two purposes only: sleep and sex. It should not be used as an entertainment zone or a place to discuss household finances. Even when the television is turned off or when you are not discussing finances or family issues, the context in which those activities occur in your bedroom can impair sleep. Think of it this way: since your neurons that fire together wire together, making memory possible, using your bedroom for activities besides sleep can spur those associations. In contrast, if your bedroom is used to relax to go to sleep, the associations are built on sleep promotion.

If you toss and turn for more than an hour, you should get up and go to another room. Getting out of bed allows your body temperature to drop and shifts the neurodynamics of lying there thinking about the fact that you're still awake.

There are several ways to improve sleep, including exercise, diet, light exposure during the day, and keeping the bedroom cool at night.

Your attitude toward your sleep deprivation affects the way you will feel the rest of the day. Though when you awaken from a sleep-deprived night you probably feel worse immediately, you generally feel better as your body temperature rises, you're exposed to light, and activity energizes your body. Also, your mood will be lower and you'll continue to feel poorly if you think the loss of sleep is a major problem that cannot be resolved.

Don't try too hard to go to sleep. Your brain activity increases when you worry about not getting enough sleep. Research has shown that trying to fall asleep promotes muscle tension and elevated heart rate, blood pressure, and stress hormones. A vivid example of how this occurs was demonstrated in one study that offered participants a chance to compete with others for a cash prize awarded to whoever could get to sleep the fastest. The participants took twice as long as they usually did to fall asleep.

Sleep scheduling is another way to reestablish a normal sleep pattern. By adjusting the time you go to bed—for example, by staying up considerably later than usual—you'll build up sleep pressure to go to sleep and stay asleep through the night. This is the case because if you're sleep-deprived, you will fall asleep earlier the next night to catch up on lost sleep. When insomnia has become a habit and you assign considerable importance to the problem, it's usually a good practice to establish a schedule that is commensurate with reconditioning your sleep cycle. The commonsense practice of sleeping in in the morning is likely to make it more difficult to sleep the next night. Sleep scheduling, by contrast, requires that you get up in the morning at the usual time despite the amount of sleep you managed the previous night. Instead of going to bed earlier, you'll be going to bed later.

Calculate how many hours you actually sleep on average and then add an hour to the total. Use this formula to schedule how much sleep time you should allow yourself. For example, if you averaged five hours of sleep for the last month despite staying in bed for eight hours, you can allow yourself six hours of potential sleep time. If your normal wake-up time has been 6 a.m., you can go to bed at 11:30 p.m. You should use this schedule for at least four weeks. Your goal will be to fill up most of that bedtime with sleep. Eventually your body temperature will adjust and the sleep pressure will build up so that you can make another adjustment to add another hour to be able to sleep for seven hours.

This approach is useful if you have chronic insomnia, not if you have experienced a night or two of poor sleep. If you're a chronic insomniac, the task is to repair your sleep cycle architecture. If your sleep cycle is out of sync, sleep scheduling helps move it back into sync to reestablish more normal neurodynamics. By practicing sleep scheduling, you'll increase sleep efficiency.

Laurie's Improving Sleep

Laurie told me that she had been plagued by insomnia her entire life. Even when she did sleep, it always felt like she was on the threshold of wakefulness. To compensate she attempted to maximize the time in bed so that she could "grab whatever sleep is possible."

She also spent a great deal of time in her bedroom on the bed, reading, watching television, and talking on the phone. Her bed had multiple contexts; it was a place for entertainment, socializing, and, most important, frustration. When I suggested that she reserve her bed and bedroom for only sleep and sex, she protested, "It's my space to get away!" She went on to describe how the rest of the house was very busy and that her husband and teenage children made relaxing there impossible.

"The paradox is that you don't feel tired enough to sleep," I told her. I went on to describe the difference between relaxation and sleep pressure. Although it is always good to relax, if that is her primary effort, she leaves little room to build up sleep pressure.

We talked about how the window of time that she allows for sleep is so wide that sleep occurs sporadically. By condensing the time she spends in bed, and for that matter in her bedroom, she will build up biological pressure to fill the narrowed time with better-quality sleep. I described the stages of sleep and how the goal is to improve the depth of her sleep so that she can feel rested. Also, by compressing the time that she is in bed, she will allow herself the sleep she needs, not the moving in and out of sleep.

At first, it was hard for her to conceptualize that she could possibly gain sleep by allowing herself less time in bed, and the loss of a place to retreat such as her bedroom was troubling. We worked together to structure in downtime away from her bedroom. Also, she realized that she had actually been hiding out from her family.

Next, I introduced the sleep scheduling details, asking how many hours she actually slept on average, and then added an hour to the total. Next we used this formula to schedule how much sleep time she should allow herself. As she filled up the time in bed with sleep, we added a half hour. The first week was rough, as she was not confident that the plan made sense. To her surprise, in the second and third weeks it seemed like there were some incremental improvements, so that by the fourth week, with more time in bed actually sleeping, her mood increased along with her energy level.

Negative sleep thoughts like those Laurie experienced push temporary insomnia into long-term insomnia. They are essentially inaccurate ideas about sleep that create a self-fulfilling prophecy. If you believe these negative sleep thoughts, you'll have more difficulty falling asleep again because of the buildup of stress. These thoughts will result in negative emotions such as anger and result in all the biochemical changes associated with anger, which are activating, not sedating. The sequence starting with negative sleep thoughts sets off a chain of events that result in insomnia.

Identify your false thoughts and replace them with accurate information about sleep. For example, if you wake up in the middle of the night, you may interpret your wakefulness in one of the following ways:

- I may get back to sleep or I may not. Either way it isn't the end of the world.
- This isn't great, but at least I've gotten my core sleep.
- If I don't get a good night's sleep tonight, I will tomorrow night.

Adopting these thoughts will help you get back to sleep if you wake up. By adopting reasonable thoughts about sleep, you'll take the pressure off yourself and relax enough to get to sleep. In addition, while you're lying in bed, use the opportunity to relax. Relaxation methods such as diaphragmatic breathing help quiet the mind. Relaxation during the day will help you sleep at night. Relaxation methods work best if practiced twice daily, once during the day and once before bed. They serve to reduce the effect of stress.

There are a wide variety of techniques to help you achieve a healthy sleep pattern. Follow these guidelines:

Don't do anything in bed other than sleep (except for sex). Don't watch television, balance the checkbook, discuss finances with your spouse, or argue in bed. Make the bed carry only one association—sleep.

If you can't sleep, get up and go to another room.

Don't try too hard to go to sleep. It will increase your stress and lead to a paradoxical effect. Try telling yourself, "It's okay if I get just a few hours of sleep tonight. I will catch up the next night." This change in expectation will free you to be able to relax and get to sleep. The harder you try to go to sleep, the harder it will be to induce sleep.

Avoid drinking large quantities of liquid at night. This will lower the sleep threshold and cause you to wake up to urinate.

Avoid bright light at least a few hours before going to sleep. Don't work on the computer into the evening.

Do all planning for the next day before you get into bed. If you think of something you need to do the next day, get up and write it down. This will help postpone thinking or worrying about anything until the next day.

Avoid all daytime naps. Think of naps as a way to steal sleep from the nighttime.

Try eating a light snack with complex carbohydrates before bed. Foods rich in L-tryptophan are advisable. Don't eat anything with sugar or salt before bed.

Avoid protein snacks at night because protein blocks the synthesis of serotonin and as a result promotes alertness.

Exercise from three to six hours before bedtime.

If noise bothers you, use earplugs.

Avoid alcohol for five hours before going to bed.

If you're troubled by chronic insomnia, try the sleep scheduling technique.

Try relaxation exercises. They will help you go to sleep or go back to sleep if you awaken during the night.

Keep your body temperature low. Don't overcover. Crack the window to get cool fresh air into the bedroom.

PART THREE

Putting It All Together

CHAPTER 8

Moderate Your Stress

Steve carried a cup of coffee in one hand and an iPhone in the other, checking his e-mails as we walked into my office for our first meeting. The social courtesy that we all expect was not there; it was subordinated to a half smile as he said, "Let me send this off and we can talk." A few moments later he put the phone on the arm of the chair and said, "Okay, I wish we had more time, but I have a conference call at eleven. So where do I start?" He gave a sarcastic laugh. "I'm pretty stressed and need something for my brain. I just picked up your book *Rewire Your Brain*, and as soon as I have the time I may take a look."

He went on to describe how as the CEO of a telecom start-up he was "burning out before I'm done." He glanced down at his phone again as if he were expecting it to respond. After a sip of coffee he asked, "So what do I do?"

"Looks like you're spinning your wheels."

He shrugged his shoulders and then glanced at his phone. After another sip of coffee, he said, "If people would do their jobs, maybe I can slow down." Picking up the phone again, he texted something with his thumb more quickly than I thought possible.

"Can I ask you a favor?" I said, searching for some eye contact. "Could you put the phone in your pocket so we can talk?"

"So talk," he said with a sigh. Then he looked again at his phone, then at me. "All right, I'm sorry."

"You're a busy guy."

He laughed. "Yeah," he said as he held up the coffee cup. "Without this liquid energy it would all fall apart."

After some gentle inquiry he told me that he rarely eats breakfast and grazes at lunch and that dinner with his wife seems to be the only time he sits down long enough to eat. "She thinks I'm a bit snappy. But she doesn't get how stressed I am. If you can get me some Ativan or something like that, I'll go away and get out of your hair."

"Maybe we can work together so that you don't feel like you need Ativan. In fact, the Ativan will make things worse in the long run," I said. I went on to tell him that the long-term use of benzo-diazepines such as Ativan is countertherapeutic and that there are plenty of healthy things he can do right away to minimize the free-floating anxiety he had told me about. Later, after an immediate dietary change and some well-timed exercise, his sleep improved and his anxiety lessened, though it still bothered him. I invited him to the anti-anxiety class that I teach weekly, where he learned several anxiety reduction techniques along with much about his brain. One evening in class he said, "This meeting ought to be called 'The User's Manual for the Brain.'" As the CEO of his company, he began to help his employees stay healthy so that they could contribute more while changing their attitude about the company.

Reducing Chronic Stress

All the healthy brain factors I have described in the previous chapters may sound deceptively simple yet reasonable enough, but you may regard them as things to do when you have the time and during periods without stress. Ironically, your stress level actually increases if you do not attend to these factors. For all my clients, whether they are anxious or depressed, I consistently ask them to cultivate these factors simultaneously because the research suggests that together they lessen anxiety and depression. Nevertheless, I recognize that it is difficult to engage in healthy behaviors when you are feeling stressed. For this reason, this chapter will address stress head on because there are many assumptions about stress that are frankly misinformed and if believed make stress more difficult to manage.

In his book with the apt title *Why Zebras Don't Get Ulcers*, Robert Sapolsky points out that humans are the only species that creates stress by simply thinking. Since we have a larger cortex, we can use it to worry. To drive home this point, he described how stampeding zebras use all their stress hormones to get away from the charging lions. Maybe lame Uncle Henry who can't keep up with the fleeing herd then falls victim to the lions. When the rest of the herd gets to a water hole after the stampede, they don't obsess about being the lion's next dinner. One zebra does not say to the other, "Those lions had their eyes on me, not Uncle Henry. I know I'm next! I'm not going to get to sleep tonight." Humans may have such a conversation and probably will worry about being the lion's next dinner. With a larger cortex we have the capacity to generate our own stress as well as to neutralize it.

The popular mindset is that all stress should be avoided. The truth is that that mindset should be avoided because it is wrong for many reasons. First, the term *stress* itself is one-dimensional and does not fit the complexities of human experience. When a person comes to me asking for help to achieve a "stress-free life," I often say, "Why? Do you want to be dead?" Before we call a situation stressful, we often feel a little anxiety. A periodic and moderate degree of stress is actually good, not bad. Without a moderate degree of stress we wouldn't arrive at work on time or get to the grocery store to pick up food when the refrigerator is bare. A moderate degree of anxiety turns on the prefrontal cortex to help us adapt to the world and be successful in reaching our goals.

The term *stress*, popularized by Hans Selye during the middle of the last century, is more appropriate for describing physical stress on a bridge to measure the weight that it can endure. Stress researchers such as Bruce McEwen of Rockefeller University propose that we use the term *allostasis* instead of the word *stress* because it better describes how well each individual deals with the demands of life as well as her capacity for resiliency. Like shock absorbers on a car that allow you to drive down a bumpy road without breaking an axle, allostasis is the process of maintaining stability through change. Instead of pulling over and saying, "I can't drive on this terrible road because of all the bumps and holes!" you continue driving, being careful to maintain a safe speed and when possible steering around the major holes. A resilient person continues what he is doing despite the fact that it may be challenging. In fact, he may do it because it is challenging. And that is healthy!

Allostasis also involves constant adjustments at moderate levels of stress. There are many parts of the body and brain that, like a thermostat, help keep stress within a tolerable range. The hippocampus, for example, has a large number of cortisol receptors that when activated by a moderate amount of cortisol during a brief period of stress act as a thermostat, providing a negative feedback system, such as telling the stress system, "Okay, we have enough cortisol; shut down the supply!" In this way, the amygdala and the hippocampus work in balance. The amygdala can ramp up the stress response, and the hippocampus can tone it down. That is the case, of course, only if the stress is in the moderate range. Aristotle long ago said, "Everything in moderation, nothing in excess." That concept could not be more for true for stress.

Allostatic adjustments are adaptive over the short term. Cortisol helps orchestrate adjustments by enhancing or inhibiting gene transcription, regulating brain-derived neurotrophic factor (Miracle-Gro), and upregulating amygdala activity when needed. Moderate levels and short-term bursts of cortisol target prefrontal systems involved in adapting to stress and regulating emotions.[1]

Another way allostasis is involved in moderating stress levels is through the autonomic nervous system. The two branches of the autonomic nervous system are the sympathetic branch and the parasympathetic branch. The sympathetic branch activates when you meet a potentially dangerous situation such as a grizzly bear prowling around your camp. The parasympathetic branch calms you down after the bear lumbers away. Optimal brain health is promoted by a balance of sympathetic and parasympathetic nervous system activity. When dealing with a significant challenge, you need to be charged up, and you need to be able to calm down afterward.

If I step off the curb without looking both ways and then at the last moment spot a semi truck heading toward me, the sympathetic nervous system activates the flight part of the fight-or-flight response. Once I flee back onto the curb safety and need to get back to a relaxed state, the parasympathetic nervous system gets my heart rate and breathing back down to the normal range.

The vagus nerve system is a major part of the parasympathetic nervous system. If you have what is called high vagal tone, you are able to calm your heartbeat through all the parts of your parasympathetic nervous system. If you have low vagal tone, your parasympathetic nervous system does a poor job of calming you down long after you are safely back on the curb. As was described in Chapter 6, this polyvagal system has been called the social engagement system because the vagus nerve system enervates not only the organs in the thoracic cavity such as the heart but also the face. When your heart is racing, you are likely to have an anxious look on your face. If someone you trust gives you a hug, you release oxytocin and your vagus nerve system responds by calming you down.

If your "vagal break" is impaired and you have trouble calming your heart long after you are safely back on the curb, the sympathetic branch of your autonomic nervous system dominates. Just as there are two parts of your autonomic nervous system, the sympathetic and the parasympathetic, there are many parts to your sympathetic system. The best known is the so-called fight-or-flight response. If you happen to walk down a dark urban street alone late at night and three menacing-looking men approach, your hypothalamic-pituitary-adrenocortical (HPA) axis response system kicks into gear. Your amygdala signals potential danger by telling your hypothalamus to secrete corticotropin-releasing hormone, signaling your pituitary, which responds by releasing adrenocorticotropic hormone, which bursts into your bloodstream and signals your adrenal glands (on top of your kidneys) to release adrenaline. Your heart rate quickens while the size of your blood vessels changes to prepare to flee or fight. Then, about 30 minutes later, if those menacing guys are still following you, your adrenals release cortisol, keeping you on full alert.

The stress response system works quite well with periodic and moderate levels of stress. Take, for example, the level of the neurotransmitter norepinephrine. When the norepinephrine level is moderate, it has a high affinity for the alpha-2A receptors, which elicit alert wakefulness and facilitate optimum activation of the prefrontal cortex to better regulate your behavior and attention and suppress the potential overactivity of the amygdala. In contrast, when you are highly stressed, there is an excessive release of norepinephrine engaging the alpha1 and beta adrenoreceptors, which impair prefrontal cortex functions and disinhibit the amygdala. In this case the amygdala can hijack the prefrontal cortex with excessive norepinephrine and take it offline, even promoting irrational behavior.

The term *allostatic load* refers to being stressed out or chronically stressed. Allostatic load occurs when a person does not possess the energy or has not recouped enough to deal with the demands she is facing. With prolonged allostatic load, as when stress tips too far into the excessive range, a flood of cortisol destroys the thermostat like a heater that can't shut off. The excess cortisol is corrosive to the hippocampus and leads to its atrophy, and the amygdala responds to the excess cortisol by becoming hyperactive.

Normally your hippocampus gradually decreases in volume as you age and also loses receptors for cortisol. This makes it less able to recognize an elevated level of cortisol and turn off its production the way a thermostat signals the heater to turn off when the room reaches a certain temperature. Unfortunately, just as your hippocampus is less able to recognize cortisol, it is also more vulnerable to its ill effects. As a result, your hippocampus is less able to code in new explicit memory. The bottom line is that excessive or chronic stress can become bad for your memory.

You may not be one of the millions of people who have experienced trauma, chronic stress, and/or depression, but it is instructive to understand how the feedback systems of those people have broken down, resulting in a smaller hippocampus and a hyperactive amygdala. With the excessive amygdala activity, they suffer from all the consequences of excessive stress hormones flooding their bodies and brains and have a diminished ability to shut it off.

High levels of cortisol impair the ability to think clearly and focus on what is important in your environment. Even the cell structures of neurons become more vulnerable with excessive levels of cortisol. When a healthy young brain is exposed to excessive cortisol, a process known as compensatory synaptogenesis occurs as undamaged nerve cells sprout to restore dendritic spines' density and length and restore or replace synaptic contacts. With aging brains, however, compensatory synaptogenesis occurs much more slowly. In other words, it's more difficult for aging brains to recover the repair process after excessive exposure to cortisol. The progressive process of damage to neurons has been referred to as a cascade of neurodegeneration that involves impairment of glucose transport into brain cells, destabilization of calcium balance, and a greater degree of the oxidative process. All these adverse processes result in accelerated aging.

Resiliency may become compromised with aging for a variety of reasons. Maintaining routines provides structure, but people tend to become less flexible and adaptive as they age if their routines are disrupted or when they feel pressured for time. Without healthy coping skills they may be more prone to overreact to stress because the internal stress regulation system may be less efficient after the stressful or unplanned event fades and it takes longer to bounce back to baseline.

Difficulty bouncing back after a stressful event involves the dysregulation of stress chemistry. Normally short-term acute stress results in the usual chain of events in which corticotropin-releasing hormone (CRH) is released by the hypothalamus, which stimulates the pituitary gland to release adrenocorticotropic hormone (ACTH), which in turn stimulates the adrenal glands to release cortisol, at which point one of the effects of cortisol is to reduce the release of CRH. Unfortunately, during aging this very effective negative feedback system tends to break down, and it takes longer for an older person to bounce back to his baseline mode of functioning after experiencing stress. This loss of the negative feedback system results in both an overall increase in the secretion of cortisol and a delay in the return to baseline after a person experiences stress.

It also makes a major difference to your brain if the stress is short term or long term. Short-term stress helps learning and performance, but long-term stress erodes both. Short-term stress turns on the prefrontal cortex, whereas long-term (chronic) stress tends to turns it off. Short-term stress can be adaptive for the brain, but long-term stress can break down homeostatic structures in the body and brain, including the immune system, cardiovascular system, and gastrointestinal system. Long-term stress has also been associated with hyperinflammation, metabolic syndrome, and various chronic diseases. The consequences of the chronic nature of the stress impair the body and weaken the brain's ability to bounce back.

By contrast, short-term acute stress jolts your body and brain to marshal the resources for a resilient system. You become better able to deal with a similar threat in the future, much as with a vaccination, in which the injection of a weaker version of a virus challenges your body to produce antibodies for repair and to fight off the virus when you are exposed to it again. Your body can resist the virus because it has rebuilt its defense system. In the same way short-term stress helps prepare you for the next stressful situation.

There are individual differences in how well a person deals with stress, all the way to the chromosomal level and the pace of aging. Long-term chronic stress contributes to cellular aging in a number of ways, even at the chromosomal level as measured by telomere length. For example, chronic stress has been associated with the shortening of telomeres in a study of younger and older women caring for dementia patients.[2] In a study of 20- to 50-year-old mothers who had been caring for a chronically ill child, telomere length in the peripheral blood monocular cells was associated with the duration of caregiving.[3]

Not all stress is experienced in the same way, and these differences have an effect on the pace of premature aging. One way to classify these differences is referred to as perceived stress. In other words, how much stress a person feels she is experiencing is based on what she regards as stressful and her capacity to deal with it. In the study described above, telomere length shortened as the level of perceived stress rose. Those with the highest level of perceived stress were noted to have an age-related telomere length 9 to 17 years above that of those with the lowest perceived stress levels. They also had significantly associated lower telomerase activity.

Your stress response system also includes the role of your immune system. Interleukin-6, a cytokine, plays a role in mediating the effects of the acute stress phase and is elevated in response to inflammation. Acute-phase proteins also become elevated and act to remove cellular debris, inhibit pathogen growth, and promote bacterial destruction. One class of acute-phase proteins includes protease inhibitors, including C-reactive protein, which is often used as a marker of heightened inflammation. It acts to limit tissue damage incurred from excessive inflammation. As was described in Chapter 5, one powerful way to lower inflammation, as measured by C-reactive protein, is aerobic exercise.

All these factors are activated with acute stress over the short term by priming the immune system into a state of readiness to combat potential injury and infection. If the stress is very intense and/or chronic, a wide range of symptoms occur that have been dubbed sickness behaviors and include decreased food and water intake, increased sleepiness, and decreased activities, including less social engagement. In other words, if you tend to slack off on your healthy brain factors when you need them the most, things get much worse.

The experience of stress ramps up so that the more you experience stress, the more likely you are to experience it in the future. Chronic stress elevates proinflammatory cytokines, which prime stress systems so that a subsequent stressor results in a more rapid induction of cytokines.[4] Depression, too, has been associated with elevations in inflammation as measured by large nuclear factor kappa B and the serum interleukin-6 (IL-6) response to stress.[5] A person with a history of higher levels of depression and stress is at greater risk for exaggerated and prolonged inflammatory responses.[6]

The proinflammatory cytokine IL-6 has been associated with chronic illnesses such as arthritis, cardiovascular disease, osteoporosis, and type 2 diabetes.

In a study that compared over 100 caregivers to the same number of noncaregivers, it was found that IL-6 among the caregivers was four times that of the noncaregivers (see note 6). What is most troubling is that once the caregiving ended, the rate of annual change in IL-6 production was the same. Up to three years after bereavement the rate of IL-6 production remained the same as that of current caregivers. It is common in normal bereavement that the levels of anxiety and depression heighten among widows and widowers during the first few months. Though levels of depression and anxiety appear to recede after one or two years, the rate of IL-6 production does not appear to recover.

Moderating your stress levels so that these destructive processes do not occur necessitates that you engage in the healthy brain factors even when you do not feel like it and especially when you are chronically stressed. In fact, I often say to patients, "You're going to have to do things that you don't feel like doing to rewire your brain so that you will feel better."

In addition to all the brain-healthy factors described in this book that make you less vulnerable to stress, there are a wide variety of relaxation techniques to deal with stress, and many of them are similar to those that have been used throughout history. It has only been during the last century that some of them have been identified as effective stress busters. For example, prayer and meditation have been practiced within religious cultures and conceptualized within specific theologies. Yet they have been shown to help relieve stress not only because of the belief in a higher power and the comfort that brings but also because they activate the parasympathetic nervous system to relieve stress.

Many of the relaxation techniques that were developed to deal with stress and anxiety by psychologists during the last century actually incorporated some of the same factors but without the religious overtones. All the relaxation techniques include a focus on breathing in a way that promotes relaxation. Other common factors include a focus on observing the body, imagery, suggestions, and absorption in a soothing activity.

Practice Relaxation Techniques

Do not wait until you are stressed out to incorporate relaxation exercises into your life. Practice them before you are stressed out so that it will be easier to use them when you are stressed later. I recommend using a hybrid of all the following approaches:

- When using deep breathing exercises, consciously slow your breathing and focus on taking regular and deep breaths; put the emphasis on the exhale.
- Use progressive relaxation (also called Jacobson's progressive relaxation or progressive muscle relaxation). With this method, you focus on tightening and relaxing each muscle group. Progressive relaxation is often combined with guided imagery and breathing exercises.
- Focus on the physical sensation, including your breathing or heartbeat, while you picture your body as warm, heavy, and/ or relaxed. This technique was highlighted in autogenic training by German psychologists in the 1930s.
- Using guided imagery or visualization, focus your attention on pleasant images or places that you find serene to replace negative or stressful feelings and relax.
- With self-hypnosis you can produce the relaxation response with a phrase or nonverbal cue such as a suggestion to later reengage in life with a positive attitude.

Other stress-busting activities may or may not appear at first glance to address stress directly, but the side effects are stress-relieving. Here are some examples:

- Engage in a hobby.
- Read novels.
- Spend time at spas or gyms.
- Spend time in nature.
- Try light yoga. The combination of deep breathing techniques and stretching poses makes yoga a great parasympathetic activator.
- Sniff scents. Studies suggest that aromatherapy can relieve stress. Certain aromas, such as lavender, have been reported to reduce stress levels.

- Listen to music. Research points to multiple ways in which music can help relieve stress, from triggering biochemical stress reducers to assisting in treating the stress associated with medical procedures.
- Laugh. Laughter, as was noted in Chapter 6, can reduce the physical effects of stress, such as fatigue, on the body.
- Get a massage. Getting a massage may do more than alleviate physical pain.
- Sex. Studies have shown sex can actually decrease the physical symptoms of stress by lowering blood pressure and boosting oxytocin.
- Hug someone. Hugging may actually reduce blood pressure and also boost oxytocin levels in adults.
- Engage in an art project.
- Take a walk. A quiet, meditative stroll can defuse stress, especially when you step outdoors.
- Kiss someone. Kissing lowers cortisol while boosting oxytocin.

Practice Being Here Now

Meditation with a focus on the present activates the parasympathetic nervous system without the practitioner realizing it. During the last 50 years many of these meditative techniques have been compared and measured in terms of their relative effects on diminishing stress, promoting mental health, and having beneficial effects on the brain.

To highlight one approach that integrates many of the elements in the others, Michael Posner and his colleagues assessed the effects of Integrative Body-Mind Training (IBMT), a meditation technique developed in the 1990s in China. It emphasizes focused attention combined with a balanced state of relaxation, which helps with posture relaxation, balance, and mind-body harmony. They randomly assigned participants to either IBMT or relationship training for five days for 20 minutes per day. Participants in IBMT showed more improvement in executive attention and one general marker of lower cortisol.

During the last 20 years stress reduction therapy groups have employed techniques to improve attention skills directed at being in the present moment. Within the large mental health system in which I work, which includes 24 medical centers, each center operates psychotherapy groups for people with anxiety and depression that have a mindfulness emphasis. One could call these "be here now groups." These groups treat anxiety and depression in this way to help those who are anxious because they are focused on the fear of the future and those who are depressed and ruminating too much about the past.

More than 40 years ago a book titled *Be Here Now* by Ram Dass looked like a product of the late 1960s, but the central concept is timeless. In fact, being focused on the present moment has been a concern of many of the world's religions. When Siddhartha Gautama, known as the Buddha, was asked, "Are you a god?" he answered, "No, I am just awake." Being awake means that you are here now.

Many people stumble through life on autopilot and rarely are in the present moment. They experience only fleeting moments of wakefulness to the present. Instead, they worry about the future or ruminate about the past, spiking up their stress levels. Stimulus-driven attention grabs our attention all too frequently, and we experience a kind of subclinical ADD. Cultivating a sustained present focus can be difficult in Western society, which is drifting into a culture infused with ADD. Movies in the past featured actual conversations with entire paragraphs spoken; nowadays a real in-depth conversation is seldom heard in a movie. Instead, many movies and television shows feature multiple car crashes, guns blazing, and people "breaking bad." When I wrote *America's Meltdown: The Lowest-Common-Denominator Society* more than 10 years ago, movies contained more complex scripts, relatively speaking. Thus, when I advocate working on staying in the present, it is with the acknowledgment that there are counterforces at play. Yet to keep sharp you will need to cultivate a greater ability to stay in the present despite these counterforces.

The key is to recognize that there is no here there. Yet many people spend a great deal of time trying to get to some point in their lives, such as retirement. It is as if there were some point in your life that when you get there, all will be good. Even when they reach that destination, people focus on the next destination, such as a special vacation as if there will be bliss when it arrives. But the problem with this logic is that there will always be another destination that we crave, such as a particular event within the vacation.

While one is at that destination or at any point in time, for that matter, improving the ability to string one working memory into another seamlessly allows one to act in the present. The continuity among a string of working memories represents an immersion in the actions within the unfolding present. The present moment is not a static phenomenon but a constantly evolving present moment. Your present moment skills improve when you take part in the constantly unfolding process by immersing yourself in the action. The pre-Socratic philosopher Heraclitus said, "You can't step in the same river twice, for it is always changing."

Our participation in the always changing world was captured in the well-known Zen saying "Zen is not like chopping wood. Zen *is* chopping wood." The act of being present while doing can be described as an aspect of mindfulness. There is a leaning into life in the present moment instead of passively leaning away from life. Acting deliberately allows you to cultivate these attention skills as well as your nonjudgmental observation ability. This is what mindfulness means.

As I write these pages at Camden Bay in Maine, sailboats and large cabin cruisers chart their ways into and out of the harbor. Seagulls soar overhead in search of scraps of food left by humans. Despite the beauty of the scene, like anyone, I experience the intermittent feeling of being here, punctuated by drifting off into my default mode network of daydreaming, planning ahead to a seminar I am to do tomorrow, or ruminating about something that occurred during my seminar on Cape Cod a few days ago.

It certainly is easier to be present in an environment such as Camden Bay with all of its delights, including the scent of the salt air and periodic cool breezes. Yet my working memory and the attention to the now, which I am constantly attempting to expand, are vulnerable even in the best of times and the most captivating places. A woman with a cell phone walks by, and after the brief distraction I bring myself back to my present instead of someone else's present. I shift back to the present moment, attending to my body, the sun on my back, the sound of wind in the trees, and the light reflecting off the water on the hulls of the boats moored in the many docks in the harbor.

Despite the gross overuse and the often presumptuous connotations of the word *spirituality*, actively being present, feeling compassion for the interdependence of all things, moderates stress and sharpens the brain. While actively and mindfully working to improve our brain health, we boost our resilience against stress and sharpen our brains. Can we be completely awake in the now? Though there are no Christs or Buddhas among us, we can certainly try to awaken to the present unfolding moment and compassionately share the world while sharpening our brains together.

CHAPTER 9

The Brain Bible
Seven-Day Jump Start

This book has ventured into social neuroscience, cognitive psychology, nutritional neuroscience, developmental psychology, mind-body medicine, gerontology, sleep research, and a variety of other sciences in an attempt not only to highlight the factors that help keep the brain healthy but to gain an appreciation of the importance of each of them and provide ways to apply these factors to your daily life.

Even after reading this book and, I hope, agreeing in principle that all the brain-healthy factors make sense, you may think that you don't have the time to get started. Cultivating a healthy brain as you age need not seem like a chore or an inconvenience. Why not make keep your brain healthy by doing things you enjoy every day? Only bad habits can stand in your way, such as feeling that spending time with other people is too much of a bother, that physical and cognitive exercise takes too much work, that the unhealthy food you have grown to love is too good to give up, and that your evening routines are so ingrained that to change them would require restructuring other parts of your life.

Your brain has the ability to jump-start new habits. Bear with me as I discuss one more brain circuit to describe how habits develop.

Your prefrontal cortex maintains connections through its dopamine circuits to the habit brain that is organized within the basal ganglia (an area below the cortex). The dorsolateral prefrontal cortex, as you learned in Chapter 2, is critical for executive functions, including planning and flexible decision making; it connects with the part of the basal ganglia called the head of the caudate nucleus, which projects back to consolidate new habits involving executive functions. Another part of the PFC involves the anterior cingulate cortex, which, as you also learned in Chapter 2, is critically involved in attention and motivation; this area also has a dopamine circuit to the body of the caudate nucleus. Yet another part of the PFC, the orbitofrontal cortex, which is essential for social and emotional intelligence, projects axons from its dopamine neurons to the lower caudate as well as the amygdala and is involved in reward-based addictions and social habits. These three habit loops return to the same areas of the prefrontal cortex, and they all contribute to developing new habits that involve thinking, motivation, and social experiences as well as the feeling of reward derived from the new habits (Trafton, Gordon, and Mistra, 2011).[1] In other words, after you decide to establish a new habit such as one of the brain-healthy factors and make a concerted effort to practice the new habit by increasing it on a regular basis, it eventually becomes rewarding and enjoyable. So how do you get started with your new positive habits when you do not feel like doing things that you know in the long run will make you feel better when stressed? The answer is to focus your attention on the present moment and place all the Brain Bible factors center stage in your mind; you will find that it is hard to give it up because it has become a habit, a good one!

Structure the Brain Bible Factors into Your Life

You can build each of the critical brain factors into your daily routines so that they become habits. As was described in Chapter 2, when you decide to do what you do not feel like doing, it becomes something that you do with ease, effortlessly, and begin to crave. This can certainly happen with the healthy brain factors. I am fortunate to have witnessed countless clients, friends, relatives, and myself gain from establishing regular habits associated with these factors so that they become cravings. When exercise is inconvenient, such as after a series of long flights or meetings, my body feels deprived, and so upon landing I take a very long walk, which also ensures that I get a good night's sleep. When I find that my daily activities do not provide an opportunity to learn something new and I feel intellectually malnourished, I make sure to structure a time each morning to read and learn to enjoy something new. When I am socially deprived, I feel it, and so I make my schedule include time with family and friends. The importance of social nourishment is shared. The social activity need not always include the same people or the same activity. For example, I am fortunate to have a group of friends we refer to as the Gang of Four, or simply the GOF. We have been getting together on a regular basis for close to 20 years, hiking in such places as the Grand Canyon, Escalante Canyon in Utah, the Lost Coast in the far north of California, and the Sonoma and Marin beaches. When too much time goes by without our getting together, all of us comment that we need a GOF fix. Close personal relationships are a staple of a healthy life.

Making the decision with your executive brain to establish regular habits consistent with these factors can begin by asking yourself some basic questions. When you ask yourself what you value most in your life, wouldn't you answer family, friends, and your health? Taking this one step further, wouldn't you acknowledge that your health is significantly affected by diet, exercise, and sleep? Finally, doesn't your life become larger and more interesting with lifelong learning? When practiced together, these are the most beneficial for the health of your brain.

If you find it difficult to build these factors into your day, try structuring them in incrementally. Simultaneously, monitor your progress. Below, you will find a weekly Brain Bible Activity Log in which you can record and monitor your daily dose of each of these factors. I recommend copying this page so that you can use it on a regular basis. For now, to get started, use the sheet for a seven-day jump start. After you jot down what you did each day, at the end of the week review your efforts and increase the time and/or effort in subsequent weeks. You should see progress not only in terms of applying all the factors each day but also in the quality of your effort. For example, in the first week you may have noted that you walked around the block on the first day and on the next day you walked farther.

Brain Bible Activity Log

Education: learn something new each day

Monday _____

Tuesday _____

Wednesday _____

Thursday _____

Friday _____

Saturday _____

Sunday _____

Diet: be mindful of your nutrition intake each day

Monday _____

Tuesday _____

Wednesday _____

Thursday _____

Friday _____

Saturday _____

Sunday _____

Exercise activities: get up and do something physical this week

Monday _____

Tuesday _____

Wednesday _____

Thursday _____

Friday _____

Saturday _____

Sunday _____

Social activities: get out and talk to people this week

Monday _____

Tuesday _____

Wednesday _____

Thursday _____

Friday _____

Saturday _____

Sunday _____

Sleep hygiene: how did you sleep last night?

Monday _____

Tuesday _____

Wednesday _____

Thursday _____

Friday _____

Saturday _____

Sunday _____

Combine all the factors each day for a full dose of brain health. For example, when exercising, add factors such as sports games, which by necessity involve other people, whether tennis, badminton, volleyball, or basketball. Everyone shares in the physical effort, and you get to know or get to know better those who are playing the games. Some of you may not be as strong players as others, but you receive encouragement or praise when you manage a shot or an assist. Building team spirit builds social ties and provides the social factor while you are exercising together. After the game everyone can enjoy a hearty laugh and a nutritious meal together. You not only have worked up a healthy appetite, you can enjoy the social cohesion of eating together.

There is much to be said about the multiple benefits of sitting down and sharing a meal with others. Throughout history reference has been made to breaking bread together, sometimes as a spiritual sacrament such as the image of the Last Supper or in the form of the Eucharist. Eating together, meeting for lunch, going out for dinner, and sharing the search for the best restaurants or the best recipes for dinner parties combine the diet factor and the social factor. Taking a walk after dinner can factor in exercise and improve your sleep at night. Add in a thought-provoking conversation at dinner or during the walk and you have all the factors. After the day and evening exercise and social events, if you read an intellectually stimulating book before bed, you will have included all the elements of the formula for the day.

All the factors of the formula enhance one another. The quality of your sleep is affected by the quality of your social support system, your diet, and whether you treated yourself to physical and cognitive exercise. For example, a series of studies on the effect of loneliness on the quality of sleep have shown that loneliness contributes to disruptions in sleep and more frequent microawakenings during sleep despite an equivalent number of nighttime hours of sleep between lonely and nonlonely individuals.[1]

Another way to combine the social factor with the education factor is to share the learning experience with other people in a class. If you take a brisk walk before the class, you will receive the aerobic boost necessary to release brain-derived neurotrophic factor (Miracle-Gro) and as a result aid the eventual production of new neurons in your hippocampus when you engage in the cognitive exercise as you learn. Here you will add three of the factors.

Maintaining your complete attention in the present moment while engaging in each of the factors allows you to take complete advantage of their full benefits. The most obvious example of applying a present focus to each factor is social engagement. It is extraordinarily difficult, if not contradictory, to spend time with another person and drift out of the present moment into your default mode network by ruminating about the past or daydreaming about the future. Similarly, exercising a focus on the present moment will help you avoid tripping or getting hurt while running or walking. Certainly learning (education) requires attention, which is the gateway to acquiring memory. It is difficult to fully appreciate the taste and aroma of food if you are not in the present moment. Finally, going to sleep is hampered by worrying about the future or ruminating about the past. Staying in the moment allows you to relax enough to go to sleep.

Notes

Chapter 2

1. The Seattle Longitudinal Study, one of the largest and longest studies performed in this area, examined what happens to people when they age. The study followed 6,000 people since 1956 and found that people in their late forties and fifties performed better on many cognitive tests than they had in their twenties. Specifically, they did better on tests involving problem solving, vocabulary, spatial organization, and verbal memory. The only two areas where they did worse were related to how quickly they could multiply, add, subtract, and divide (mathematical ability) and their perceptual speed, which was measured by how fast they could push a button when prompted.

    Other studies have shown similar results. For example, middle-aged and younger pilots and air traffic controllers were put in flight simulators to see how quickly they responded to demanding tasks and emergencies. Again, younger people were found to have faster reaction times, but older people did as well or better at the job at hand, especially at keeping the planes apart. Thus, apart from speed, you have the opportunity to use your brain more efficiently and display greater mental skills than you could during your younger years.

2. The right hemisphere is more active when you're learning something new. Once the knowledge is learned and becomes routine, the left hemisphere comes more into play. This is one reason language is processed by the left hemisphere.

3. Samani NJ, Boultby R, Butler R, Thompson JR, Goodall AH (2001). Telomere shortening in atherosclerosis. *Lancet* 358:472–473; Sampson MJ, Winterbone M, Hughes JC (2006). Monocyte telomere shortening and

oxidative DNA damage in type 2 diabetes. *Diabetes Care* 29:283–289; Von Zglinicki T, Saretzki G, Docke W, Lotze C (1995). Mild hyperoxia shortens telomeres and inhibits proliferation of fibroblasts: A model for senescence? *Exp Cell Res* 220:186–193; Honig LS, Schupf N, Lee JH, Tang MX, Mayeux R (2006). Shorter telomeres are associated with mortality in those with APOE epsilon4 and dementia. *Ann Neurol* 60:181–187.

4. Significant individual differences in the shrinkage rates were observed between people in the dorsolateral prefrontal cortex, cerebellum, and all white matter areas. Those with hypertension, for example, showed relatively significant shrinkage in the corpus callosum.

5. Valliant, G. (2003). *Aging Well: Surprising Guideposts to a Happier Life from the Landmark Harvard Study of Adult Development*. Little, Brown and Company; reprint edition.

6. https://www.alz.org/downloads/facts_figures_2012.pdf

7. Maguire EA; Gadian DG, Johnsrude IS, Good CD, Ashburner J, Frankowiak RS, Firth CD (2000). Navigation-related structural change in the hippocampus of taxi drivers. *Proc Natl Acad Sci USA* 97:4398–4403.

8. Green DW, Crinion J, Prince CJ (2007). Exploring cross-linguistic vocabulary effects on brain structures using voxel-based morphometry. *Bilingualism, Language, and Cognition* 10:189–199.

9. Pantev C, Engelien A, Candia V, Elbert T (2001). Representational cortex in musicians. Plastic alterations in response to musical practice. *Ann N Y Acad Sci*. 930:300–14.

10. Schneider P, Scherg M, Dosch HG, Specht HJ. Gutschatt HA, Rupp A (2002). Morphology of Heeschl's gyrus reflects enhanced activation in the auditory cortex of musicians. *Nat Neurosci* 5:688–694.

11. Pascual-Leone A, Torres F (1993). Plasticity of the sensorimotor cortex representation of the reading finger in Braille readers. *Brain* 116:39–52.

12. Draganski B, Gaser C, Busch V, Schuierer G, Bogdahn U, May A (2004). Neuroplasticity: changes in grey matter induced by training. *Nature* 427, 311–312. doi: 10.1038/427311a.

13. Schoenbaum G, Setlow B, Ramus SJ (2003). A systems approach to orbitofrontal cortex function: Recordings in rat orbitofrontal cortex reveal interactions with different learning systems. Behav Brain Res 146:19–29.

14. Schoenbaum G, Setlow B, Nugent SL, Saddoris MP, Gallagher M (2003). Lesions of orbitofrontal cortex and basolateral amygdala complex disrupt acquisition of odor-guided discriminations and reversals. Learn Mem10:129–140.

Chapter 3

1. Vaillant G (2003). *Aging Well: Surprising Guideposts to a Happier Life from the Landmark Harvard Study of Adult Development.* New York: Little, Brown.

2. Steptoe A, Hamer M, Butcher L, Lin J, Brydon L, Kivimaki M, Marmot M, Blackburn E, Erusalimsky J (2011). Educational attainment but not measures of current socio-economic circumstances are associated with leukocyte telomere length in healthy older men and women. *Brain, Behavior, and Immunity*, 25: 1292–1298. 10.1016/j.bbi.2011.04.010.

3. Katzman R (1993). Education and the prevalence of dementia and Alzheimer's disease. *Neurology* 43:13–20.

4. Stern Y (2002). What is cognitive reserve? Theory and research application of the reserve concept. *J Internat Neuropsychol Soc* 8:448–460.

5. Ibid.

6. Roe CM, Xiong C, Miller JP, Morris JC (2007). Education and Alzheimer disease without dementia: Support for the cognitive reserve hypothesis. *Neurology* 68(3):223–228.

7. Van Praag H, Kempermann G, Gage FH (2000). Neural consequences of environmental enrichment. *Nat Rev Neurosci* 1(3):191–198.

8. Snowdon DA, Kemper SJ, Grainer LH, Wakstein DR, Markesbery WR (1996). Linguistic ability in early life and cognitive function and Alzheimer's disease later in life: Findings from the Nun Study (comments). *JAMA* 275:528–532.

9. Baddeley AD (1992). Working memory. *Science* 255:556–559.

10. Klingberg T (2008). Prefrontal cortex and basal ganglia control access to working memory. *Nat Neurosci* 11:103–107.

11. Conway AR, Cowan N, Blunting MF (2001). The cocktail party revisited: The importance of working memory capacity. *Psychom Bull Rev* 8:331–335.

12. Kingberg T (2009). *The Overflowing Brain: Information Overload and the Limits of Working Memory.* New York: Oxford University Press.

13. Verghese J, Lipton RB, Katz, MJ, et al. (2003). Leisure activities and the risk of dementia in the elderly. *N Engl J Med* 348:2508–2516.

14. Willis SL, Tennstedt SL, Marsiske M, Ball K, Elias J, Koepke KM, Morris JN, Rebok GW, Unverzagt FW, Stoddard AM, Wright E, ACTIVE Study Group (2006). Long-term effects of cognitive training on everyday functional outcomes in older adults. *JAMA* 296(23):2805–2814.

15. Erickson KI, Colcombe SJ, Wadhwa R, Bherer L, Peterson MS, Scalf PE, Kim JS, Alvarado M, Kramer AF (2007). Training-induced plasticity in older adults: Effects of training on hemispheric asymmetry. *Neurobiol Aging* 28:272–283.

16. Mirmiran M, van Someren EJ, Swaab DF (1996). Is brain plasticity preserved during aging and in Alzheimer's disease? *Behav Brain Res* 78:43–48.

17. Verghese J, Lipton B, Katz MJ, et al. (2003). Leisure activities and the risk of dementia in the elderly. *N Engl J Med* 348:2508–2516.

18. Hambrick DZ, Sathouse TA, Meinz EJ (1999). Predictors of crossword puzzle proficiency and moderators of age-cognition relations. *J Exp Psychol Gen* 128:131–164.

Chapter 4

1. Sampson MJ, Gopaul N, Davies IR, Hughes DA, Carrier MJ (2002). Isoprostanes: Direct evidence of increased free radical damage during acute hyperglycemia in type 2 diabetes. *Diabetes Care* 25(3):537–541.

2. Domenico Pratico D, Christopher M Clark CM, Feyan Liun F, Joshua Rokach J, Trojanowski JQ (2002). Increase of brain oxidative stress in mild cognitive impairment: A possible predictor of Alzheimer disease. *Arch Neurol* 59(6):972–976.

3. Hu Y, Block G, Norkus EP, Morrow JD, Dietrich M, Hudes M (2006). Relations of glycemic index and glycemic load with plasma oxidative stress markers. *Am J Clin Nutr.* 2006 Jul;84(1):70–6.

4. Victoroff J (2003). *Saving Your Brain.* New York: Bantam.

5. Krikorian R, Shidler MD, Nash TA, Kalt W, Vinqvist-Tymchuk MR, Shukitt-Hale B (2010). Blueberry supplementation improves memory in older adults. *J Agric Food Chem* 58:3996–4000.

6. Joseph J, Shukitt-Hale B, Denisova NA, Bielinski D, Martin A, McEwen JJ, Bickford PC (1999). Reversals of age-related declines in neuronal signal transduction, cognitive, and motor behavioral deficits with blueberry, spinach, or strawberry dietary supplementation. *J Neurosci* 19(18):8114–8121

7. Morris MC, Evans DA, Bienias JL, et al. (2003). Consumption of fish and n-3 fatty acids and risk of incident Alzheimer disease. *Arch Neurol* 60(7):940–946.

8. Domenico Pratico D, Christopher M Clark CM, Feyan Liun F, Joshua Rokach J, Trojanowski JQ (2002). Increase of brain oxidative stress in

mild cognitive impairment: A possible predictor of Alzheimer's disease. *Arch Neurol* 59(6):972–976.

9. Reichenberg A, Yirmiya R, Schuld A, Kraus T, Haack M, Morag A, et al. (2001). Cytokine-associated emotional and cognitive disturbances in humans. *Arch Gen Psychiatry* 58:445–452.

10. Benzi G, Moretti A (1995). Are reactive oxygen species involved in Alzheimer's disease? *Neurobiol Aging* 16(4):661–674.

11. Schmidt M (2006). *Brain-Building Nutrition: How Dietary Fats and Oils Affect Mental, Physical, and Emotional Intelligence*, 3d ed. New York: Frog Books.

12. Glueck CJ, Tieger M, Kunkel R, Tracy T, Speirs J, Streicher P, Illig E (1993). Improvements in symptoms of depression in an index of life stressors accompany treatment of severe hypertriglyceridemia. *Biol Psychiatry* 34:240–252.

Chapter 5

1. Cavalli-Sforza LL, Menozzi P, Piazza P (1994). *The History and Geography of the Human Genes*. Princeton, NJ: Princeton University Press; Cordain L, Gotshall RW, Eaton S III (1998). Physical activity, energy expenditure, and fitness: An evolutionary perspective. *Int J Sports Med* 19:328–335.

2. Booth FW, Neufer PD (2005.) Exercise controls gene expression: The activity level of skeletal muscle modulates a range of genes that produce dramatic molecular changes—and keeps us healthy. *American Scientist* 93 http://www.americanscientist.org/.

3. Eaton SB, Strassman BI, Neese RM, Neel JV, Ewal PW, Williams GC, Weder AB, Eaton SB, Lindeburg S, Konne, M, Mysterud I, Cordain L (2002). Evolutionary health promotion. *Prev Med* 34:109–118.

4. Esparza J, Fox C, Harper IT, Bennett PII, Schultz LO, Valencia ME, Rasussin E (2000). Daily energy expenditure in Mexican and U.S. Pima Indians: Low physical activity as a possible cause of obesity. *Int J Obes Relat Metab Disord* 24:55–59.

5. Hu FB, Manson JE, Stampfer MJ, Colditz GA, Liu S, Solomon CG, Willet WC (2001). Diet, lifestyle, and the risk of type 2 diabetes mellitus in women. *N Engl J Med* 345:790–797; Leitzman MF, Rimm EB, Willet WC, Spiegelman D, Grodstein F, Stampfer MJ, Colditz, GA, Giovannucci E (1999). Recreational physical activity in women. *N Engl J Med* 341:777–784.

6. Booth FW, Neufer PD (2005). Exercise controls gene expression: The activity level of skeletal muscle modulates a range of genes that produce dramatic molecular changes—and keeps us healthy. *American Scientist* 93. http://www.americanscientist.org/

7. Ford ES (2002). Does exercise reduce inflammation? Physical activity and c-reactive protein among U.S. adults. *Epidemiology* 13:561–568.

8. Geffken DF, Cushman M, Burke GL, et al. (2001). Association between physical activity and markers of inflammation in a healthy elderly population. *Am J Epidemiol* 153:242–250.

9. Van Praag H, Shubert T, Zhao C, Gage FH (2005). Exercise enhances learning and hippocampal neurogenesis in aged mice. *J Neurosci* 25:8680–8685.

10. Bartholomew JB, Morrison D, Ciccolo JT (2005). Effects of acute exercise on mood and well-being in patients with major depression. *Med Sci Sports Exerc* 37:2032–2037.

11. Swain R, Harris A, Wiener E, Dutka M, Morris H, Theien B, Konda S, Engberg K, Lauterbur P, Greenough W (2003). Prolonged exercise induces angiogenesis and increases cerebral blood volume in primary motor cortex of the rat. *Neuroscience* 117:1037–1046.

12. Gustafson D, Lissner L, Bengtsson C, Björkelund C, Skoog I (2004). A 24-year follow-up of body mass index and cerebral atrophy. *Neurology* 63(10):1876–1881.

13. SK, Nam HS, Son MH, Son EJ, Cho KH (2004). Interactive effect of obesity indexes on cognition. *Dement Geriatr Cogn Disord* 19:91–96.

14. Colcombe SJ, Erickson KI, Raz N, Webb AG, Cohen NJ, McAuley E, Kramer AF (2003). Aerobic fitness reduces brain tissue loss in aging humans. *J Gerontol A Biol Sci Med Sci* 58:176–180.

15. Wroblewski L, Lissin L, Cooke JP (2000). Maintaining the endothelium: Preventive strategies for vessel integrity. *Prev Cardiol* 3:172–177.

16. Hambrecht R, Wolf A, Gielen S, Linke A, Hofer J, Erbs, S, Schoene N, Schuler G (2000). Effects of exercise on coronary endothelial function in patients with coronary artery diseases. *N Engl J Med* 342:454–460.

17. Larson EB, Wang L, Bowen JD, et al. (2006). Exercise is associated with reduced risk for incident dementia among persons 65 years of age and older. *Ann Intern Med* 144:73–81.

18. Colcombe S, Kramer AF (2003). Fitness effects on the cognitive function of older adults: A meta-analytic study. *Psychol Sci* 14(2):125–130.

19. Dunn AL, Trivedi MH, Kampert JB, Clark CG, Chambliss HO (2005). Exercise treatment for depression: Efficacy and dose response. *Am J Med* 5(28):1–8.

20. Lee IM, Rexrode KM, Cook NR, Manson JE, Buring JE (2001). Physical activity and coronary heart disease in women: Is "no pain, no gain" passé? *JAMA* 285:1447–1454.

21. Smith PJ, Blumenthal JA, Hoffman BM, Cooper H, Strauman TA, Browndyke JN, Sherwood A (2010). Aerobic exercise and neurocognitive performance: A meta-analytic review of randomized controlled trials *Psychosom Med* 72:239–252.

22. Weir, K. (2011). The exercise effect: Evidence is mounting for the benefits of exercise, yet psychologists don't often use exercise as part of their treatment arsenal. Here's more research on why they should. *The Monitor on Psychology* December 2011, Vol. 42. No. 11.

23. Yaffe K, Barnes D, Nevitt M, Lui LY, Covinsky K (2001). A prospective study of physical activity and cognitive decline in elderly women. *Arch Intern Med* 161(14):1703–1708.

24. Pascual-Leone A, Nguyet D, Cohen LG, et al. (1995). Modulation of muscle responses evoked by transcranial magnetic stimulation during the acquisition of new fine motor skills. *J Neurophysiol* 74:1037–1045.

Chapter 6

1. House JS, Landis KR, Umberson D (1988). Social relationships and health. *Science* 241:540–542.

2. Hawkley L, Cacioppo J, Masi C, Berry J (2006). Loneliness is a unique predictor of age-related differences in systolic blood pressure. *Psych Aging* 25(1):132–141.

3. Wilson RS, Krueger KR, Arnold SE, et al. (2007). Loneliness and the risk of Alzheimer disease. *Arch Gen Psychiatry* 64:234–240.

4. Paul C, Ayis S, Ebrahim S (2006). Psychological distress, loneliness, and disability in old age. *Psychology Health Med* 11:221–232.

5. Iliffe S, Kharicha K, Harari D, Swift C, Gillman G, Stuck AE (2007). Health risk appraisal in older people. The implications for clinicians and commissioners of social isolation risk in older people. *Br J Gen Pract* 57:277–282.

6. Hollon SD, Thase ME, Markowitz JC (2002). Treatment and prevention of depression. *Psychol Sci Public Interest* 3:39–72.

7. Seeman TE, Lusignolo TM, Albert M, Berkman L (2001). Social relationships, social support, and patterns of cognitive aging in healthy, high-functioning older adults: MacArthur Studies of Successful Aging. *Health Psychology* 20(4):243–255.

8. Singer B, Ryff C (1999). Hierarchies of life histories and associated health risks. *Ann N Y Acad Sci* 896:96–115.

9. Lyyra TM, Heikkinen RL (2006). Perceived social support and mortality in older people. *J Gerontol B Psychol Sci Soc Sci* 61:S147–S152.

10. Adam EK, Hawkley LC, Kudielka BM, Cacioppo JT (2006). Day-to-day dynamics of experience—cortisol associations in a population-based sample of older adults. *Proc Natl Acad Sci USA* 103:17058–17063.

11. Cacioppo JT, Ernst JM, Burleson MH, McClintock MK, Malarkey WB, Hawkley LC,Kowalewski RB, Paulsen A, Hobson JA, Hugdahl K, Spiegel D, Berntson GG (2000). Lonely traits and concomitant physiological processes: The MacArthur Social Neuroscience Studies. *Int J Psychophysiology* 35:143–154.

12. Uchino BN, Kiecolt-Glaser JK, Cacioppo JT (1992). Age-related changes in cardiovascular response as a function of a chronic stressor and social support. *J Pers Soc Psychol* 63:839–846.

13. Cole SW, Hawkley LC, Arevalo JMG, Cacioppo JT (2011). Transcript origin analysis identifies antigen presenting cells as primary targets of socially regulated leukocyte gene expression. *Proc Natl Acad Sci* 108:3080–085.

14. Porges WW (2003). The polyvagal theory: Phylogenetic contributions to social behavior. *Physiol Behav* 79:503–513.

15. Schulte-Ruther M, Markowitsch HJ, Shah NJ, Fink GR, Piefke M (2008). Gender differences in brain networks supporting empathy. *Neuroimage* Aug 1; 42(1):393-403.

16. Cacioppo JT, Hawkley, LC (2009). Loneliness. In MR Leary, RH Hoyle (eds.), *Handbook of Individual Differences in Social Behavior*. New York: Guilford.

17. Schulte-Ruther M, Markowitsch HJ, Shah NJ, Fink GR, Piefke M (2008). Gender differences in brain networks supporting empathy. *Neuroimage* Aug 1; 42(1):393-403.

18. Yuan J, Luo Y, et al. (2009). Neural correlates of the females' susceptibility to negative emotions: An insight into gender-related prevalence of affective disturbances. *Hum Brain Mapp* 30(11): 3676–386.

19. Cheng Y, Chou KH, et al. (2009). Sex differences in the neuroanatomy of human mirror-neuron system: A voxel-based morphometric investigation. *Neuroscience* 158(2):713–720.

20. Domes G, Heinrichs M, Michel A, Berger C, Herpertz SC (2006). Oxytocin Improves "mind-reading" in humans. *Biol Psychiatry* Mar 15; 61(6):731–3.
21. Uvnas-Moberg K (2003). *The Oxytocin Factor: Tapping the Hormone of Calm, Love and Healing.* Cambridge, MA: Da Capo Press.
22. Light KC, Grewen KM, et al. (2005). More frequent partner hugs and higher oxytocin levels are linked to lower blood pressure and heart rate in premenopausal women. *Biol Psychol* 69(1):5–21.
23. Heinrichs M, Baumgartner T, Kirschbaum C, Ehlert U (2003). Social support and oxytocin interact to suppress cortisol and subjective responses to psychosocial stress. *Biol Psychiatry* 54:1389–1398.
24. Kosfeld M, Heinrichs M, Zak PJ, Fischbacher U, Fehr E (2005). Oxytocin increases trust in humans. *Nature* 435:673–676.
25. Domes G, Heinrichs M, Michel A, Berger C, Herpertz SC (2006). Oxytocin Improves "mind-reading" in humans. *Biol Psychiatry* Mar 15; 61(6):731–3.
26. DeVries AC, DeVries MB, Taymans SE, Carter CS (1996). The effects of stress on social preferences are sexually dimorphic in prairie voles. *Proc Natl Acad Sci USA* 93:11980–11984.
27. Tamres L, Janicki D, Helgeson V (2002). Sex differences in coping behavior: A meta-analytic review and an examination of relative coping. *Pers Soc Psychol Rev* 6:2–30.
28. Barraza JA, Zak PJ (2009). Empathy toward strangers triggers oxytocin release and subsequent generosity. *Ann NY Acad Sci* 1167:182–189.
29. Cacioppo JT, Hawkley LC (2009). Loneliness. In MR Leary, RH Hoyle (eds.), *Handbook of Individual Differences in Social Behavior*. New York: Guilford.
30. Dimburg V, Ohman A (1998.) Behold the wrath: Psychophysical responses to facial stimuli. *Motivation Emotion* 20:149–82.
31. Depue R, Morrone-Strupinsky J (2005). A neurobehavioral model of affiliative bonding: Implications for conceptualizing a human trait of affiliation. *Behav Brain Sci* 28(3):313–350.
32. Fredrickson BL, Levenson RW (1998). Positive emotions speed recovery from cardiovascular sequelae of negative emotions. *Cognition and Emotion* 12:191–220.
33. Ekman P, Davidson R, Friesen WV (1996). The Duchenne smile: Emotional expression and brain physiology II. *J Personal Social Psychol* 58:342–353.
34. Provine R (2000). *Laughter: A Scientific Investigation*. New York: Viking.
35. Reviewed in Provine R (2000). *Laughter: A Scientific Investigation*. New York: Viking.

36. Osaka N, et al. (2003). An emotion-based facial expression activates laughter modules in the human brain: A functional magnetic resonance study. *Neurosci Lett* 340(2):127–130.

37. Fisher HE, Aron A, Brown LL (2006). Romantic love: A mammalian brain system for mate choice. *Philos Trans Royal Biol Sci* 361(1476):2173–2186.

38. Gizewski ER, Krause E, Wanke I, Forsting M, Senf W (2006). Gender-specific cerebral activation during cognitive tasks using functional MRI: Comparison of women in mid-luteal phase and men. *Neuroradiology* 48:14–20.

39. Coan JA, Schaefer HS, Davidson RJ (2006). Lending a hand: Social regulation of the neural response to threat. *Psychol Sci* 17:1032–1039.

40. Malarkey WB, Kiecolt-Glaser JK, Pearl D, Glaser R (1994). Hostile behavior during marital conflict alters pituitary and adrenal hormones. *Psychosom Med* 56:41–51.

41. Kiecolt-Glaser JK, Loving TJ, Stowell JR, et al (2005). Hostile marital interactions, proinflammatory cytokine production, and wound healing. *Arch Gen Psychiatry* 62:1377–1384.

Chapter 7

1. Spiegel K, Leproult R, Van Cauter E (1999). Impact of sleep debt on metabolic and endocrine function. *Lancet* 354(9188):1435–1439

2. Bliwise DL (1993). Sleep in normal aging and dementia. *Sleep* 16(1):40–81.

3. Ferrie JE, Kumari M, Salo P, Singh-Manoux A, Kivimäki M (2011). Sleep epidemiology—a rapidly growing field. *Int J Epidemiol* 40(6):1431–1437.

4. Yaffe K (2011) Sleep disordered breathing, hypoxia, and risk of mild cognitive impairment and dementia in older women. *JAMA* 306(6):613–619.

5. Spiegel K, Tasali E, Penev P, Van Cauter E (2004). Brief communication: Sleep curtailment in healthy young men is associated with decreased leptin levels, elevated ghrelin levels, and increased hunger and appetite. *Ann Intern Med* 141:846–850.

6. Frank MG, Issa NP, Stryker MP (2001). Sleep enhances plasticity in the developing visual cortex. *Neuron* 30(1):275–287.

7. Maquet P (2001). The role of sleep in learning and memory. *Science* 294:1048–1051.

8. Stickgold R, James L, Hobson JA (2000). Visual discrimination learning requires sleep after training. *Nat Neurosci* 3:1237–1238.

9. Guzman-Marin R, Suntsova N, Methippara M, Greiffenstein R, Szymusiak R, McGinty D (2005). Sleep deprivation suppresses neurogenesis in the adult hippocampus of rats. *Eur J Neurosci* 22:2111–1116.

10. Hauri P, Fischer J (1986). Persistent psychophysiologic (learned) insomnia. *Sleep* 9:38–53.

11. Kubitz KA, Landers DM, Petruzzello SJ, Han M (1996). The effects of acute and chronic exercise on sleep: A meta-analytic review. *Sports Med* 21:277–291.

Chapter 8

1. Sullivan RM, Gratton A (2002). Prefrontal cortical regulation of hypothalamic–pituitary–adrenal function in the rat and implications for psychopathology: Side matters. *Psychoneuroendocrinology* 27:99–114.

2. Cherkas LF, Aviv A, et al. (2006). The effects of social status on biological aging as measured by white-blood-cell telomere length. *Aging Cell* 5(5):361–365.

3. Epel ES, Blackburn EH, et al. (2004). Accelerated telomere shortening in response to life stress. *Proc Natl Acad Sci USA* 101(49):17312–17315.

4. Johnson JD, et al. (2002). Prior stressor exposure sensitizes LPS-induced cytokine production. *Brain Behav Immun* 16:461.

5. Pace TW, Mletzko TC, Alagbe O, Musselman DL, Nemeroff CB, Miller AH, Heim CM (2006). Increased stress-induced inflammatory responses in male patients with major depression and increased early life stress. *Am J Psychiatry* 163(9):1630–1633.

6. Glaser R, Robles T, Sheridan J, Malarkey WB, Kiecolt-Glaser JK (2003). Mild depressive symptoms are associated with amplified and prolonged inflammatory responses following influenza vaccination in older adults. *Arch Gen Psychiatry* 60:1009–1014.

Chapter 9

1. (Trafton, Gordon, and Mistra, 2011) Hawkley LC, Cacioppo JT (2005). Sleep quality as a function of psychosocial risk factors in a population-based sample of older adults: Loneliness as a proximal and distal predictor. Poster presented at the annual meeting of the American Psychosomatic Society, Vancouver, BC.

Index

Page numbers with *n* indicate note.

About the Author

Dr. John Arden is the director of mental health training for the Kaiser Permanente Medical Centers. He also practices part-time at Kaiser Permanente in Petaluma and San Rafael, and for several years he has been the Chief Psychologist at Kaiser Vallejo. He has written several other books, including the bestselling *Rewire Your Brain* as well as *Brain-Based Therapy for Adults*. For more information, visit drjohnarden.com.